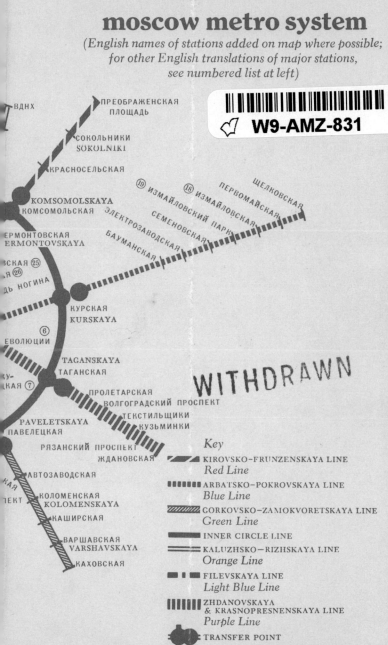

smith's moscow

smith's moscow

desmond smith

alfred a. knopf
new york
1974

THIS IS A BORZOI BOOK
PUBLISHED BY ALFRED A. KNOPF, INC.

Copyright © 1974 by Desmond Smith

All rights reserved under International
and Pan-American Copyright Conventions.
Published in the United States by
Alfred A. Knopf, Inc., New York, and
simultaneously in Canada by Random House
of Canada Limited, Toronto.
Distributed by Random House, Inc., New York.

Library of Congress Cataloging in Publication Data

Smith, Desmond. Smith's Moscow. (Date)

Bibliography: p.
1. Moscow—Description—Guide-books. I. Title.
DK597.S57   914.7'31   73-20770
ISBN 0-394-48515-7
ISBN 0-394-70692-7 (pbk.)

Manufactured in the United States of America

FIRST EDITION

For Charly

contents

acknowledgments

The idea of writing this book has been with me in one way or another ever since I first visited Moscow on behalf of ABC News in 1966. It therefore gives me particular pleasure to thank Tom Wolf and Bill Sheehan of ABC for sending me to Russia in the first place. I have had a great deal of help from a quite unlistable number of Soviet friends; to all of them I would like to offer my most grateful thanks. I know that none of them will feel hurt if I specially thank George Watson, former ABC News correspondent in Moscow, Ed and Nina Stevens, Leo Gruliow of the *Christian Science Monitor*, Hughes Rudd of CBS News, Dusko Doder of the Washington *Post*, David Halton of CBC News, and Helen Moed of CBS News.

I would like to express my appreciation to Mr. Sidney Reiner and Ms. Eugenie Klebanoff of Cosmos Travel, Inc., of New York, for sharing with me their expertise and experience in the field of Soviet travel.

I must thank my agent, David Obst, and my editors, Ed Victor and Judith Jones of Knopf, for their helpful comments and steadfast encouragement. Lindy Hess and Mel Rosenthal also earn my gratitude for the cheerful manner in which they attended to the endless amounts of checking involved in seeing the manuscript into print. Finally, my appreciation for all her help to Marjaleena Jappinen of Etela Suomen Sanomat.

D. S.

foreword

I wrote this book chiefly because I could have used something like it on my first visit to Moscow. Its central purpose is to help you get the most out of this compelling and remarkable city.

Of course, there are numerous guide-books on the general subject of Russia. There is Baedeker's superb *Russia*, published in 1914 and recently reprinted, which describes in the most engaging manner the sights of pre-revolutionary Moscow. There is also Nagel's admirable travel guide, *U.S.S.R.* But apart from these two books—and the official guide-books to the city, which do not have the needs of Western tourists in mind—I have found nothing amongst the voluminous literature dealing with the Soviet Union which attempts more than a sidelong glance at Moscow.

To many visitors Moscow appears a confusing kind of place. The questions abound: Where to enjoy a memorable dinner? What to do after midnight? What happens if a tooth is broken? Where are the city's more interesting shops? How to send a parcel, use a taxi, make a long-distance call? How to meet ordinary Russians, and where? Are there restrictions on individual travel inside the city? Where to visit a church or a synagogue? In this guide I have tried to provide answers to these questions and to show that this least known of European cities, Moscow, can be quite a rich experience for a visitor.

The book begins with the basic information needed to get you there (including a few tips that could save you money). It proceeds with your arrival in Moscow, where, like every other visitor to the USSR, you will be in the hands of Intourist, the state-run travel agency. Next, a help-yourself guide to services, facilities, and things to do in Moscow. Then follows a brief history of the city, coupled with walking tours that you can take on your own. We proceed to food and where to find it (the reputation for indifferent food is exaggerated, and standards have risen sharply in recent years). Next comes a look at what Moscow has to offer in the way of shops, with a word about prices and a "What's Where" guide to the most interesting stores. Finally, a chapter for businessmen who intend to visit Moscow not only to see the sights but also (hopefully) to negotiate a business deal. In conclusion, I have added some suggestions for reading. Conditions in the Soviet Union can change more rapidly than is sometimes imagined, and the "comprehensive" general work remains to be written. Nevertheless, the reading list is catholic in range and should add to the enjoyment of your visit.

Moscow is a secretive city, yes, but it is not a scary one. It can be as much fun to wander around alone in as London or Paris. This book will help you get around Moscow on your own when you want to do so. Its aim and hope is to provide both an alternative and a complement to the organized aspects of an Intourist-arranged visit.

smith's moscow

introduction to moscow

Moscow is the fourth-largest city in the world. Something like six and a half million people live there (including more than half a million college and university students). It lies at the same latitude as Hudson Bay, and on approximately the same longitude as Damascus. Its lowest point—the Metro—is 200 feet below ground, and its tallest building—the TV Centre in Ostankino —is 1,700 feet high.

Like crabgrass on a June lawn, the city has spread over a 342-square-mile area, and is still growing. Everywhere you look, you will see new apartment houses under construction. Nearly three million Muscovites— more than half the adult population—have moved into new flats in the past ten years. Some of the amenities that Westerners take for granted are sorely lacking: apartments are small and cramped, there are not enough telephones, and few homes have washing machines. On the other hand, there are no massive slums comparable to those of London or New York. Moscow's public transportation system is quick, efficient, and cheap. The Metro (Muscovites proudly call it "the world's most beautiful subway") carries more than four million passengers a day.

This place with the vivid double-syllable name— MOSKVA!—like a door being closed twice, is one of the world's most extraordinary cities. It is a delight as well as a mystery. The poet Pushkin says it best: "Moskva: those syllables can start/A tumult in the Russian heart." What you ought to keep in mind is that Moscow has a certain mystery and inscrutability—

partly it's the closedness of Soviet society, partly it's the fantastic buzz of Russian, partly it's all those red streamers with revolutionary slogans, those dour granite busts of Lenin and Marx. It makes the city strange, unreal. And then, the towers and spires and onion-shaped domes. Dreiser, when he saw them, called Moscow the most Oriental scene in Europe.

The city is peppered with spectacular monuments, grandiose avenues, and marble splash. You have to get used to the larger-than-life scale of central Moscow. The great cobblestoned squares that radiate fanlike from the Kremlin are designed for vast parades. This lavish use of space is in marked contrast to a city like London, with its neat row houses and small green squares.

It is on the surrounding streets and side streets where you get caught up in the great rip-tide of Moscow's daily life. The crowds, often five and six deep, ebb and flow like some vast river that has neither beginning nor end. Gorkovo, Moscow's chief thoroughfare, is no different from Lexington Avenue or Regent Street when it comes to shove and push. If you dawdle, you will almost certainly get a dig in the ribs from some impatient person in a hurry. Moscow, after all, is the mother city of Communism—and it is a going concern. This is a hard-working city. In restaurants, shops, factories, museums, and airports there are bright red banners with two kinds of messages. One reads: "Here works the Brigade fighting for the title of Brigade of Communist Labor"; the other: "Here works the Brigade of Communist Labor."

What does strike a visitor is that Moscow is a city that runs on woman-power, a place where women seem to do just about any job. They get up early, take their children to day-care centres, work long hours, and earn the same pay as men. Two-thirds of all the doctors in the Soviet Union are women, we are told. But what catches the visitor's eye are the large numbers of women doing heavy manual work. You can't help noticing at building sites that it is the women who seem to mix the cement and carry the bricks while the men operate the cranes. I don't ever recall seeing a man sweeping the streets with a whisk broom, although I have seen plenty driving street-cleaning equipment. The Communist doctrine is that woman bears equally the duty of labor—the child-rearing "kitchen wife" is scorned.

Moscow women are certainly an independent lot. The under-thirty generation doesn't remember the harsh Stalin years and knows of the war only from their parents' stories. When they aren't working, they get out a lot more than their mothers did. They dress more fashionably, and the beehive hair-style of the older generation has given way to a shorter, more practical cut. Make-up is no longer frowned upon as it was in the past, and a woman will think nothing of spending the equivalent of a full week's wages for a pair of imported English shoes. The young woman who stands waiting for a late night "route taxi" in Manege Square knows that she won't be sent to a labor camp if she's five minutes late for work the next morning. Having a good time is no longer a crime against the state.

To catch some of this mood, some of the atmosphere of modern-day Moscow, you might go one evening to some of the new restaurants on or near Kalinin Prospekt (see pp. 213 ff.). Here you can listen to Moscow-style jazz, drink wine or inexpensive Soviet *champanskoye*, and talk to your neighbors. In Moscow, many young people speak some English; and there is an insatiable appetite among them for Western fashions, Western films, Western pop music.

To be sure, the Soviet Union remains a rigid and authoritarian society. But there is no denying the highly visible pace of change. If you walk from Red Square down Razin Street and turn left, you will get a vivid sense of this change; for here is a courtyard that is like a page torn from Dostoevsky. Here Old Russia suddenly comes alive, and the old women in their shawls and colored kerchiefs seem to be doing exactly the same things they were doing a hundred years ago. But then—a few hundred yards away—a bulldozer has opened up another view, and towering over you is the glittering glass-walled Hotel Rossiya.

It is Russia. It is the USSR. It is that amazing goulash of the Victorian and post-Sputnik ages that is present-day Russia in transition.

The new skyline of the city is a matter of tremendous pride for most Muscovites. But you have to look behind the gloss and glitter and wander down the rambling, disjointed streets to find the soul of this city. One purpose of this guide is to help you seek them out. Here on Bread Street, and Fish-Stew Lane, and Crooked Back Alley, can be discovered the Moscow that enraptured Gogol and Pushkin.

Here, too, are the once-grand private homes, the cobblestoned courtyards, the churches with lovely green or gold or red-brown pineapply domes.

Moscow is an agglutination of districts that, like leaves in a book, have stuck together in the course of centuries; a city that is still as inward-turning as when it was walled and gated: acres of ruddy brick apartments built at the turn of the century, two-story wooden houses with fretted window frames, cheese-colored villas seen beyond the railed-in gardens. There is an unexpected sense of individuality here, something that reveals the warmth and cosiness of a city that has room for something beyond the grand gesture.

The thing about Moscow is that it is simply not like anyplace else. The strangeness of it all tends to inhibit even the most experienced traveller. If you walk down Gorkovo alone, it is a reasonable bet that pretty soon you will be wondering how far you are from your hotel, wishing you had your Intourist guide with you, and feeling vaguely worried that something untoward may happen. (Intourist staffers are familiar with this phenomenon, which they call "the salt mine factor.") Of course it is nonsense. But we have been talking, reading, and worrying about the formidable Soviet system for more than a generation. It is going to take quite a few more years before we feel completely relaxed inside the USSR. Consider what Norval Stephens, a New York advertising man and seasoned traveller, has written about *his* first morning in Moscow:

[*The lady from the Intourist Service Bureau*] *came up to me and said I should calm down and stop worrying. She said I was in no danger, that I would not be followed, that no one would go through my luggage and immediately inventoried all the intrusions which the popular novels and the journalists of yesterday have conveyed as the normal part of a visit to Russia.*

Mr. Stephens then goes on to say what a stimulating time he had in Moscow—and so will you.

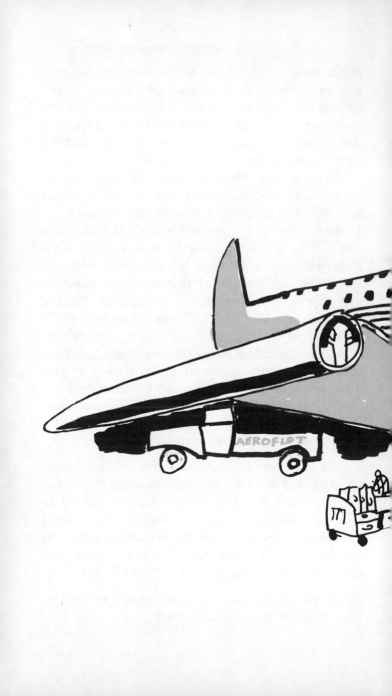

getting there

the first step

There is no free-lance travel to the USSR. You can't go up to an airline counter, buy a ticket, and take off. You must use a travel agent, and he, in turn, has to work with the state-run travel agency, Intourist. Moreover, you buy days, not mere travel, from Intourist: a complete package that includes meals (this ranges from breakfast only to full board), hotel accommodations, transportation inside the USSR, and all guided tours. You have little or no choice of hotel. If you decide to go "De Luxe" or "De Luxe Suite," you may request your preference. This, however, is far from a guarantee, and until you arrive in Moscow you will rarely receive a confirmation of location. A bed for sure, but just where will be a mystery until you arrive.

It is strongly recommended that you use a knowledgeable travel agent, someone who has had experience in sending visitors to the USSR. If in doubt, write to:

In the United States: The American Society of Travel Agents, Inc., 360 Lexington Avenue, New York, New York 10022
In Britain: Association of British Travel Agents, 10, Mayfair Place, London W.1

You can choose among four main classes of travel:

De Luxe

Covers a single room with bath at a centrally located hotel; breakfast or full board; private car up to three hours daily within city limits; entrance fees to museums;

services of a guide-interpreter up to six hours daily; transportation on arrival and departure by private car; porterage.

First Class

Comprises a single room with bath or shower; breakfast or full board; one city sightseeing tour in a group—up to three hours—by motorcoach or car, with a guide-interpreter; entrance fees to museums; transportation on arrival and departure; porterage.

Tourist Class

Includes a room with running water (bath or shower on the same floor); breakfast or full board within First Class price limit; one group sightseeing tour—up to three hours—by motorcoach or car, with a guide-interpreter; transportation on arrival and departure; porterage.

Businessman's Schedule

Includes private room with bath or shower in centrally located hotel; breakfast; one city sightseeing tour by private car (three hours with guide-interpreter); transportation on arrival and departure; porterage.

For the super-rich

Intourist has created a new super-class of tour known as De Luxe Suite. If you are prepared to pay *five times* the normal First Class rate, you can live rather grandly in Moscow. The price (rates on request from your travel agent) includes a three- or four-room suite at the Hotel Intourist, breakfast (dining room or room service, guest's option), a chauffeured car for travel within city limits from 8 a.m. to 12 midnight daily, the services of a guide-interpreter up to eight hours daily (for sight-seeing, two tours per day), and help in special arrangements, entrance fees to museums, and transportation by car on arrival and departure.

Some recommendations that will save you money

1. The best bargain of all is the Businessman's Schedule. Of course, you have to be a bona fide businessman to qualify, with business in the USSR. For the price, you get a top hotel, top service.
2. Before you opt for De Luxe travel, give the matter some thought. Aside from a slightly better room and a greater likelihood of getting a centrally located hotel, there is really no significant difference (except price) between De Luxe and First Class. The fact is that in Moscow First Class and De Luxe travellers share the same hotels, same dining rooms, and same guides.
3. No matter what class of travel you choose, do not take full board. All "full board" means is that before you leave home you get a thick book of meal coupons marked breakfast, lunch, tea, and dinner. In Moscow, this can be very confusing. The visitor never knows what he is entitled to in the way of a meal, and finds himself at the mercy of the waiter. Better to pay as you go.

visas & passports

Your travel agent takes care of all the details. Allow a month, you will need it. To enter the USSR, a visitor requires a valid national passport and a Soviet visa. You

must fill in and sign an application form and enclose three photographs of passport size; the travel agent sends these along to the Soviet Embassy, along with a voucher to the effect that you have prepaid the full cost of the tour. Here are a few points to note about Soviet regulations:

1. Your passport should not expire before the date of your departure from the USSR.

2. A Soviet tourist visa is valid for entry and exit from the USSR during the time period specified and is valid only for visiting the cities itemized in the visa. A visitor arrives in and leaves the USSR only through the border points indicated on the visa.

3. Should your plans change unexpectedly, your visa may be extended, the itinerary altered, and the border entry and exit points changed without additional formalities, provided Intourist is able to arrange accommodations and transportation to comply with the change.

4. Visitor's visas for visiting relatives in the USSR are granted through the usual channels.

5. Group visas may be issued to tourists on cruises and to large tourist groups travelling together.

medical regulations

Formerly, all travellers to the Soviet Union had to hold a current International Smallpox Vaccination Certificate; but this is no longer necessary. Travellers arriving from certain Asian countries, however, are still required to present valid cholera vaccination certificates.

weather & clothing

Moscow has Chicago-style winters, with blasts of sub-zero winds and heavy snowfalls. This may commence as early as September and continue until the end of April. September, October, and November are usually the rainy months, when the snow does not settle and the streets are slushy. March and April are the time of spring thaw. In July and August, you may experience 90-degree heat—a bit uncomfortable in a city with little air conditioning. In May, cold spells are often caused by Arctic gusts. June and July are the typical summer months, with warm days and warm nights. Russian weather experts describe Moscow in summertime as "a warm island in a sea of cold air."

In June, July, and August, lightweight clothing and a light raincoat should be packed. In winter, take along rubber overshoes and a heavy warm coat (you can buy a fur hat when you arrive).

your health

Moscow is a meticulously clean city. The air is virtually smog-free. One major reason: there are almost no factories near the city center. Aircraft are not allowed to overfly the city. Gas, piped in from Saratov (a city 650 miles away), is the chief fuel; oil heating is forbidden. Although road traffic is increasing, Moscow's traffic is sparse indeed by Western standards. One of the benefits is peace and quiet. Take notice of this extraordinary phenomenon; the streets are crowded with life, yet the silence is almost eeric.

More good news: you are unlikely to get dysentery from poor food handling. Kitchen regulations in the USSR are rigidly enforced. The true perils lie in overeating—the Russian cuisine is rich and takes a few days to become accustomed to.

Bathrooms in hotels are usually spotless. The same cannot be said for restrooms in restaurants and other public places. You have been warned.

(For medical emergencies, see pages 320–1.)

money

There is no limit to the amount of currency allowed into the country. You must make a complete and accurate declaration of your funds—cash and traveler's checks—on entering the Soviet Union, and keep that declaration until you leave. While in the country, you should make a point of retaining all sales slips: on your departure you may be asked for proof of purchase of the items you're taking home.

It is not permitted to take roubles into or out of the

Soviet Union. Not all traveler's checks are honored. North American visitors should use any of the following: First National City Bank, Chase Manhattan Bank, Bank of America, American Express Company, Thomas Cook & Son, Perera Express Company.

To exchange hard currency or traveler's checks is simple—though often time-consuming—in Moscow. Nearly every hotel has a branch of the State Bank, usually in the Intourist Service Bureau. There are also exchange facilities at the USSR State Bank (Neglinnaya No. 12—near the Hotel Metropole), which is open 10 a.m. to 3 p.m. daily except Sundays and holidays (Saturday 10 a.m. to 1 p.m.), as well as exchange bureaux open every day of the week in the following hotels:

	A.M.	P.M.
METROPOLE	8:30 —	11:30
ROSSIYA	9:00 —	8:30
NATIONAL	9:30 —	8:30
UKRAINE	9:00 —	8:30
LENINGRADSKAYA	8:30 —	8:30

You will be asked to present your passport for each such transaction, so be sure to have it with you. Roubles may be re-exchanged for foreign currency at a special window in the Customs Hall at the airport (see page 314). This can be a slow process, so allow yourself plenty of time before departure.

A useful hint

Do not convert all your cash into traveler's checks; it is extremely useful to have foreign currency inside Russia. The best method is to take small bills. The reason: Traveler's checks can only be converted into roubles. There are, however, many restaurants and bars that accept payment only in hard currency. The so-called "dollar bars" for late-night drinks, for example, take any form of hard currency but refuse roubles. It is almost impossible to change a traveler's check during an evening in a dollar bar. Even if you succeed, you will find your change coming in the form of other hard currency. It is not unusual to receive in return for, say, a $20 American traveler's check (or a large-denomination bill), a handful of French francs, some Italian lire, and a pocketful of Danish kroner. To avoid this unnecessary headache, take as many bills of small denomination as you think you will require. (See p. 262 for information on current exchange rates and the prices of various items.)

A *further note of warning*: There appear to be any number of Soviet citizens who will trade roubles for hard currency—and at a very favorable rate indeed. These individuals hang around the major tourist hotels, and will often approach you with very tempting offers. The trouble is that (1) draconian Soviet laws make it strictly illegal to exchange money except at the official exchange bureaux; (2) the KGB (Security Police) has been known to put its agents on the street to entrap foreigners who flout the law. Three roubles for one dollar can appear a great bargain, but not from behind the bars of a Moscow prison cell. Avoid all such offers to exchange money unless you are prepared to risk the consequences.

time & electric current

Moscow time is eight hours ahead of U.S. Eastern Standard Time in winter and seven hours ahead in summer, and two hours ahead of Greenwich Time. Electric current in the Soviet Union varies from city to city and even within the same city: 50-cycle a.c., 110, 127, and 220 volts, with two-prong European-type plugs and wall outlets.

mail

Mail can be forwarded to you in Moscow c/o *Poste Restante, K–600, 1, Gorkovo, Moscow USSR*. This is located in the Hotel National at the corner of Gorkovo and Manege Square. (It is none too reliable, however —even air mail takes seven to ten days to arrive.) Travellers' mail to other cities can be addressed: *c/o American Department, Intourist, name of city*.

photography & films

By all means take your camera along. There are some basic rules to follow, which can be found on page 81. There is no shortage of black-and-white film in the USSR; color film is also available, but not recommended. Soviet color film is suitable for the Agfa developing process, but not for Kodak processes. If you have a Polaroid camera bring it along (with film); it will be a great hit with your Russian friends.

travel routes

Most people take the plane, but you can also reach Russia by train, boat, bus, or car.

Dozens of international airlines operate direct air service to Moscow, including Aeroflot, the Soviet flag carrier, which is big, comfortable, and efficient. From New York it takes between nine and ten hours, four hours from London, two hours from Copenhagen, 1½ hours from Helsinki.

By Train

If you have plenty of time, rail travel is a far more interesting way to go. There is a through sleeper service to Moscow during the winter months on Tuesdays, Fridays, and Sundays from the Hook of Holland, and other days from Aachen. The summer service, via Berlin, Warsaw, Brest, Smolensk, runs daily from Ostend, and on Mondays, Wednesdays, Fridays, and

Sundays from the Hook. There is also the Chopin Express of Vienna, a 47-hour trip. Helsinki–Moscow is a 23-hour journey and passes through some startlingly lovely countryside.

Soviet sleeper-coaches are quite roomy, with one or two berths per compartment in first-class coaches and three berths in the second-class ones. Inside the Soviet Union, it is the custom to assign strangers—men and women—to the same compartment. On international routes, however, there are "ladies only" compartments available. Washrooms are shared between two compartments. Soviet trains are wired for Moscow Radio, though in private compartments you can pull out the plug—that is, if you can find it. Most trains have a restaurant car, but double-check before leaving; otherwise you are advised to bring your own food. A final point worth considering: rail travel is considerably cheaper than plane travel.

By Boat

If you have nothing but time on your hands, travel by sea is a fine way to reach the Soviet Union. There is regular passenger service from New York and Montreal to Leningrad. One of the most popular routes is by the comfortable ships of the Baltic State Steamship Line from London and Le Havre to Leningrad. The trip takes five days, with sightseeing stopovers (four to six hours) in Copenhagen, Stockholm, Helsinki, and Riga. All accommodations are outside cabins. Ships of the same class ply two Black Sea routes: Sochi–Yalta–Odessa to Beirut, with calls at Istanbul, Piraeus, Latakia, Alexandria, and Port Said; Sochi–Yalta–Odessa to Marseilles with calls at Constanta, Varna, Istanbul, Piraeus, and Naples.

Note: All steamers are one-class vessels, except on the North Atlantic run, which is a two-class line.

Motoring

You may enter the Soviet Union by car or bus from Finland, Poland, Czechoslovakia, Hungary, or Romania. If you are planning to drive to Moscow, consult Intourist before you leave (see pp. 70–3) for more details on car travel inside the USSR.

what to take

For all its unfamiliarity, Moscow is very much a big cosmopolitan city, a European capital. Pack the normal common-sense articles. Compared to London or Paris, it is a quite informal place. No one bothers to dress for dinner or for the theatre. You can wear an open-necked

shirt in any restaurant in town and no headwaiter will think the less of you.

What you will not find in Moscow is your favourite brand of toothpaste. Bring adequate supplies of personal cosmetics and toiletries. In hotels the soap tends to be the size of butter pats and is strongly carbolic, so you might want to include a few bars of your own soap. The towels are always adequate but are on the coarse side. Toilet paper ditto. You can buy most brands of American and British cigarettes, though mentholated ones are hard to find; if you are a pipe smoker, bring your own tobacco along. There are no U.S. or British magazines on sale, and few foreign-language newspapers (see page 275). If you enjoy reading, pack a few pocket books.

There are several books on the Soviet Union that you might care to read before leaving home. The single best introduction to the Russian people is Wright Miller's *Russians as People*, obtainable in paperback. For a highly readable account of the origins of the Soviet state, Alan Moorehead's *The Russian Revolution* is a good bet. John Reed's *Ten Days That Shook the World* is an American journalist's eyewitness account of the Revolution. Also highly readable and authoritative is J. H. Billington's *The Icon and the Axe*, an analytical history of Russian culture. (For a more detailed reading list, see page 330.)

Soviet customs officials are, on the whole, a lenient bunch. They wink a kindly eye at a suitcase with several bottles of liquor (provided they are for personal consumption). You can, of course, bring in your camera and all the film you feel you require. Binoculars are O.K., and so too is your portable radio.

You might want to pack a few gifts for Russian friends, for the chambermaid, and for your Intourist guide. Among hard-to-find items in the Soviet Union are blue jeans, bikinis, drip-dry shirts, sweaters, fashion accessories of the kind that are commonplace in British and American boutiques, panty hose, and men's ties (Russian ties are narrow, and generally dull as dishwater). LP records are especially appreciated, folk music and rock being among the most desired. Paperbacks are a good idea, especially those of present-day Western novelists. One Intourist guide, a friend of mine, did ask me to mention ball-point pens—Russia, she said, is rolling with every possible variation on the ball-point pen, so leave them at home if you don't mind!

There are a few things you should be rather careful about. *Never* carry sealed letters or parcels "for a friend." This is severely frowned upon by the authorities and could land you in a great deal of unnecessary trouble. A personal Bible is O.K., but not religious literature in bulk. And it is an obvious insanity to bring drugs (other than for medicinal purposes) into the USSR; you will be inside for a long time, and don't expect your embassy to bail you out. Finally, don't bring with you any Soviet currency—this is illegal, and in any case you don't need it for the first bus or taxi, since this is prepaid as part of the Intourist "package."

—arrival!

from the air

Below you are the green forests and lakes of Moscow's environs. Away to your right is Moscow itself, a yellow patch on the banking horizon. Sheremetyevo International Airport, located on land that once belonged to one of Imperial Russia's wealthiest families, is a stepladder airport. Your plane taxis to an apron and the ladder is wheeled up to planeside. A gray- or blue-suited Aeroflot girl escorts you to an airport bus at the foot of the ramp. Two minutes later you enter the main terminal. It is a good idea to carry as little hand-luggage as possible; the walk to Customs & Immigration can be tiring.

The first person to meet you will be a representative of Intourist. The representative checks your name against a master list and advises you what hotel you will be staying in. Other representatives take over after you pass through passport control.

customs & immigration

Next you are asked to join a line at one of several glass-enclosed booths. These are manned by green-hatted members of the border police. The line goes quickly. Your passport is stamped and returned. Now you are in the Customs Hall. While waiting for your baggage, go over to one of the counters and pick up a Customs Declaration form. THIS SLIP OF PAPER MUST BE RETURNED WHEN YOU LEAVE MOSCOW. Always make sure that every currency exchange transaction is marked down and stamped on the back of this

CUSTOMS DECLARATION

(name in full)

a citizen of _____ am proceeding to _____
and hereby declare that I have with me _____ articles of
hand luggage; _____ articles of luggage have been forwarded
by passenger express and _____ articles by goods express.
    I have on my person and in the above-listed luggage the following:
    1. Currency and currency equivalent:
    (a) U.S.S.R. currency, U.S.S.R. State Loan Bonds and Soviet
lottery tickets _____

_____

    (b) currency of other countries (including cheques and letters
of credit) _____

_____

_____

    (c) gold, silver, platinum and metals of the platinum group
contained in jewelry, coins, ingots, scrap and crude metal; precious
stones, pearls and jewelry containing them _____

_____

_____

    2. All types of fire-arms and ammunition _____

_____

_____

I Am Aware that Under the Laws of the U.S.S.R.

    (a) I must give exact information on the articles listed in the
Customs Declaration, currency and valuables, and indicate their
quantity or value;

    (b) in addition to the articles listed in the Customs Declarations,
I must submit for inspection all articles intended for delivery to third
persons as well as all antiquities, *objets d'art*, printed publications,
manuscripts, cinema films, all postage stamps, all miniature engravings (labels, etc.), plants, fruits, seeds, live animals and birds, raw
produce of animal origin and dead game birds;

    (c) the exchange of foreign currency brought into the U.S.S.R.
for Soviet currency is effected only through the branches of the State
Bank of the U.S.S.R. or the Foreign Trade Bank of the U.S.S.R.;

    (d) currency, valuables, all fire-arms and ammunition that I have
not listed in the Customs Declaration as well as any other articles
secreted from the customs authorities are liable to confiscation as
contraband.

Owner of the luggage _____
(signature)

Customs Officer _____
(signature)

" _____ " _____ 197

document. There is no limit to the quantity of fur pieces, precious metals, pearls and other precious stones, and jewellery that may be brought into the USSR. However, all such items must be listed on the Customs Declaration form.

Next, count your currency. Itemize all of it separately —so much cash, so much in traveler's checks. All of this form-filling takes only a few minutes. Don't worry about itemizing such things as cameras, a portable typewriter, alcohol, or cigarettes. When you have completed the form, you collect your luggage (there are porters handy to help you) and go over to a customs official. Most of the time you will pass through without your luggage being opened. It is one of the most efficient customs procedures in the world. But remember to keep that Customs Declaration form in a safe place, and to have it with you, along with your passport, whenever you want to exchange currency. If you should happen to misplace it, advise the Service Bureau at once. It will be needed on your departure from the Soviet Union.

on the way to the city

Russian airports are no different from other airports: noisy places . . . confusion . . . the Intourist agents are busy. Don't be alarmed. In a matter of minutes they will have you on the way to Moscow, either by private car or by autobus. You have already prepaid for this service, and also for porterage; no cash is required.

You are an hour away from the city centre so relax and enjoy the 32-kilometre ride. As soon as you leave

Sheremetyevo, you are deep in the countryside. Occasionally you may catch a glimpse of the fast-disappearing traditional log cabins called *izby*. A few minutes later, and your car turns onto the Leningrad Highway, which runs from Moscow to Leningrad and on to the Finnish border. Another few minutes, and on your right appears a monument in honor of the defenders of Moscow. It is a gigantic work of sculpture in the shape of the anti-tank barriers that once surrounded the city. It is placed on the exact spot where Hitler's armies were stopped in 1941.

The highway is associated with aviation and sports. You will quickly see why as you travel in towards the city. Next on your right are the twin glass buildings of the Hotel Aeroflot and the Ministry of Civil Aviation. Behind them, the Moscow Air Terminal. Located here is a heliport that provides service to and from Moscow's four main air terminals—Sheremetyevo International Airport, and the three domestic airports, Domodedovo, Vnukovo, and Bykovo.

On your left, the Petrovsky Palace, built in 1775. Today it is the Soviet Air Force College of Engineering. In 1812, Napoleon spent several days here after he was forced to abandon the burning Kremlin.

Almost immediately after the Petrovsky Palace you will see, again on your left, the giant Dynamo Stadium, a sports complex that houses one of the world's great soccer teams—the Moscow Dynamos.

The Leningrad Highway at this point is 328 feet wide. Lined with apartment houses and landscaped with trees, flowers, and grass, it is fondly described by Muscovites as their "Champs-Élysées."

Now the traffic thickens and you are entering central

Moscow. Leningrad Highway turns into Gorkovo* and leads into Manege Square (see map, page 109). Ahead of you is the Kremlin. You have arrived.

moscow hotels

In the 1890's Moscow, according to Baedeker, was served by a couple of dozen hotels—the leading ones being the National and the Metropole.

In the 1970's, according to Intourist, Moscow is served by a couple of dozen hotels—the leading ones being the National and the Metropole.

Five-Year Plans have come and gone since the great October Revolution, but hotel space has scarcely figured in any of them. As a result, there is a chronic shortage of hotel rooms in the city. And, in contrast to London or Paris, there are no boardinghouses or bed-and-breakfast places to be found anywhere. Not surprisingly, then, Intourist finds its resources stretched to their outermost limits in June, July, and August, when the flow of visitors swells into a full-scale flood. To be sure, the awful space squeeze has been somewhat eased by the addition of the 1,000-room Hotel Intourist and the opening of Europe's biggest hotel, the 6,000-bed Rossiya. Still, this is one city where you have to consider yourself lucky to have a room to yourself in the peak season.

* Gorkovo literally means "(street) of Gorki," being named after the famous Soviet writer. You will also find it referred to as Gorki Street, which is simply the English translation.

Where are you staying?

Unless you have paid a healthy premium before leaving for Russia (even this entitles you only to priority consideration—see page 12), you have no choice at all as to where you will stay. Intourist puts your name into a computer and you are assigned hotel space. The first word on where you will be staying is given to you on arrival at Sheremetyevo Airport. What follows are thumbnail sketches of some of the likely places where you may be lodged.

Among the newest hotels are the Rossiya, just off Red Square, and the Intourist on Gorkovo. The **Rossiya**, dubbed the "Moscow Hilton" by the locals, is designed in the Park Avenue Transitional style of international architecture—all glass curtain walls and marble floors. Much of the furniture comes from Finland. The main dining room is somewhat like a cross between the dining salon of the *Queen Mary* and an airplane hangar. It is vast. A 25-piece orchestra attired in gold lamé seems almost lost among the 2,000 diners. Service is good. The cocktail bar can be found up a marble staircase located in the foyer. Here you can sample Russia's answer to the Manhattan: a powerful concoction made up of brandy, old vodka, and a smash of chartreuse, known as a "battering-ram."

The **Intourist** is also an American-style hotel. The facilities include three restaurants, a late-night "dollar bar" known as the Labyrinth, and a snack bar on the main floor. If you are on a business trip, chances are you will be assigned to this hotel.

Next door to the Intourist is the *grande dame* of all Moscow hotels, the **National**. This is a very Russian hotel which has become a favorite spot for Western businessmen. It is quite the best hotel in Moscow, the service is excellent.

"Everybody" has stayed here at one time or another. During the early years of the Revolution Lenin lived here (room 107). The late impresario Sol Hurok always stayed here, in the hotel's biggest suite (115). John Gunther, Dmitri Tiomkin, Arthur Watson of IBM, have all lodged here during their Moscow visits. If you are lucky enough to find yourself at the National, remember that all odd-numbered rooms face outward (and are more desirable); all even-numbered rooms face inward on stairways and the kitchen, and these tend to be noise-polluted. At the National you can get breakfast in your room, a service not always available at other hotels. The chambermaids wear black dresses and white aprons and have been here forever. The furnishings are in the style of Grand Rapids at the turn of the century, but charming all the same. If you are extremely lucky and have a room overlooking Manege Square, you can open your French windows and enjoy a magnificent view of the Kremlin. Unlike in American hotels, the TV set is in the hall, not the bedroom. A new wing was added to the National some years ago, but it is decidedly inferior in design to the older rooms.

Further north on Gorkovo are the **Tsentralnaya** (Central) and the **Minsk.** The former is another turn-of-the-century hotel, with a fine restaurant. The Minsk, built in the Stalin years, is a bit YMCA-ish in atmosphere.

About a 15-minute walk from downtown, but only

6 minutes away from the new shopping area of Kalinin Prospekt, is the **Ukraine**. This is a gigantic skyscraper hotel built in "Stalin Gothic" style. Winston Churchill's son, Randolph, is reputed to have stormed out of this hotel, growling—perhaps unfairly—that "It may be good enough for Ukrainians, but it isn't fit for a Churchill." It is a vast place, and may remind you of Grand Central Station without the trains. Although completed as recently as 1954, the hotel has a markedly Victorian ambiance.

The **Metropole**, smack in the middle of Moscow, is a first-rate hotel which dates from the pre-Revolutionary era. Service is only fair, but long-time Moscow hands rate it overall as on a par with the National.

The **Sovietskaya** and the **Moskva** are usually reserved for important guests, Soviet or foreign. Both hotels, built in the 1930's, would be in the class known as "moderate" in Western Europe. Many delegations stay in these hotels.

The **Varshava** (Warsaw), **Bucharest**, and **Budapest** are all a bit on the seedy side. It is in these hotels that tourists who are doing Russia on the cheap are usually billeted. Accommodations are considered adequate. Actually, the Varshava has one of the liveliest restaurants in town (see page 223). For young people it might be more fun to stay here than at the mausoleum-like Ukraine.

German tourists often find themselves in the **Berlin** on Zhdanova Street. This is another leftover from pre-1914. The **Yunost**, as its name ("Youth") implies, is mainly for young people, and is located in the Lenin Hills.

Registration

This is the one single part of your trip where you may mutter aloud, "Is it worth it?" Please be patient; you are not at home, you are in a country where people have a different way of looking at things. The appearance of confusion is permanent. Intourist knows it, and numerous critical articles have appeared in such journals as *Pravda* on the subject of hotel receptionists. They all appear to have suffered from harrowing love affairs. When one of them finally locates your name and awards you a room, be grateful and quietly hand over your passport—outside there are others who may not be so fortunate.

If you do not like your room, go to the Service Bureau and see if they can help. Occasionally they will be able to change the room for you.

Room with a view

Is your room "bugged"?

This is a question all Western tourists ask. The short answer has to be "It depends." If you are a high-ranking diplomat, a top military officer, or an important industrialist, the Russians are apt to have as much interest in you as your Soviet counterpart arouses in London or Washington. But if you are an ordinary visitor, the answer is almost certainly no, you are not bugged—if for no other reason than that, with more than two million visitors a year in the Soviet capital, the sheer effort involved would clearly drain the KGB's resources dry. Besides, can you imagine the insanity of recording the average tourist conversation? It is, however, generally believed that telephone calls are monitored. There is no accurate information on this subject, but Russians themselves prudently avoid discussing sensitive or intimately personal matters on the phone.

About beds

Russian beds don't have inner-spring mattresses. Like fresh-baked loaves, they tend to rise in the middle. Unpromising though this may sound, once you're in the center a good night's sleep usually follows.

The top sheet enshrouds the blanket and isn't tucked in a folded-over blanket, as in the West. What you have, in effect, is a double top sheet with a diamond-shaped opening through which the maid stuffs the blanket each morning.

About windows

Windows in Russia are double-glazed to keep out the winter cold. If you feel the need for fresh air during the night, be warned that keeping both windows open can be perilous: a sudden gust of wind can cause the first window to smash the second. Do what the Russians do—open the tiny trap window, called the *fortochka*.

About room service

Some hotels have it, some don't. The best way to find out is to ask your *dezhurnaya*, or floor-lady (see below). The *only* way you get it is to make a simple list of your demands on a scrap of paper and give them to her. If possible, show her the basic Russian words in the useful-phrases list (pp. 53–4). By the way, it does not matter what rate you are paying. Room service is entirely a question of hotel tradition.

The dezhurnaya *(floor-lady)*

"Old ladies don't retire in Russia," someone has remarked, "they become floor-ladies." Vigilant, alert a *dezhurnaya* almost invariably is, with a sharp eye for any form of hanky-panky. (She will not, for instance, allow you to bring to your room any member of the opposite sex during the evening hours—something that is decidedly *interdit* everywhere in the USSR.) This kindly Cerberus is on duty for 24 hours at a stretch. She dozes next to the room keys (kept in an open box on her desk by the stairs) after midnight—by then all the hotel's outer doors are locked. In case of trouble, she has a system of secret buzzers that can bring up reinforcements. The *dezhurnaya* is as much a part of the Soviet hotel system as Muzak is of other countries' hotel life. As the absolute mistress of your floor, she will take care of your laundry, arrange for a wake-up call, get your shoes shined, and take your order for room service. One language she rarely speaks is English, so (as noted above) you should avail yourself of the useful-phrases list. If you have enjoyed good service, one of the nicest things you can do is to buy her a bunch of flowers. In return, when you depart she might ask you to sign the guest book. This is a signal honor. In her eyes you have been a "dear guest."

the service bureau

There is a Service Bureau in almost every hotel in Moscow. They are all owned and operated by Intourist. Some are efficiently run, others are an absolute nightmare. Any visitor to Moscow quickly discovers that his day is either brightened or made miserable by the Service Bureau. It is the Soviet equivalent of the hotel concierge.

Every Service Bureau is open from 8 a.m. to 10 p.m. on weekdays, from 8 a.m. to 8 p.m. on Saturdays and Sundays. It is here that you rent a car, arrange for an overseas telephone call, buy theatre or movie tickets (except on Sundays), make travel arrangements in or out of the USSR, book a tour of the city, and so forth.

You can change money here. They will also call a taxi for you. If you want to know what is playing in the major theatres and cinemas, the Service Bureau has a list of attractions for the ensuing ten days. If you wish to have a guide-interpreter to go shopping, this can be arranged with the Service Bureau (sometimes they charge, sometimes not).

In the summer months the workload on the staff is extremely heavy. As a result the atmosphere appears to be one of total confusion. Do not despair, it is important to exercise patience. Each individual in the Service Bureau has a specific job. Check carefully the sign (in English and Russian) in front of the given individual—no use waiting on line in front of THEATRE TICKETS when you want TOURS. *One final word:* when you checked into the hotel, the desk took away your passport (a normal custom in many European countries). You will usually get it back within a day or so from the PASSPORT desk in the Service Bureau.

language

You will be well provided with interpreters in Moscow, and in most of the larger hotels menus are translated into English, French, and German. (You will find a sample menu on pp. 202 ff.). The first time you enter a restaurant it is a good idea to ask if you can keep the menu; beyond the big hotels most menus are in Russian only.

There is no denying that to speak and read Russian fluently is a matter of several years of arduous study. Nevertheless, there is altogether too much nonsense spoken about the "complexity" of the Russian language. The chief difficulty arises from accent, but the syntax is relatively simple.

Given only a minimal effort on your part, you can quickly learn the Russian for "please," "thank you," "how much," "good night," and scores of other expressions that are no trouble at all to pronounce.

Begin with the alphabet. A few days of quiet study will put it in your grasp. Some letters are actually the same as English. Others, of course, will be completely strange to you. Common to both Russian and English are: A, E, K, M, O, T. The following letters appear to be similar but have a different pronunciation:

B   pronounced as English V
H   "   "   "   N
P   "   "   "   R

C   "   "   "   S only (not as K)

Y   "   "   "   OO

X   "   " in the word "loch"

What looks like a backwards R (Я) is pronounced *Ya*.

The Alphabet (The third letter is the italic letter where it differs from the normal)

          Pron.

А а *а*   a (Continental pron.)

Б б   b

В в *в*   v

Г г *г*   g

Д д *д*   d

Е е   ye (as in "yes")

Ё ё   yo (as in "York")

Ж ж   French j, or the middle sound in "pleasure"

З з   z

И и *и*   i (as in "machine")

Й й *й*   y (consonant)

К к   k

Л л   l

М м   m

Н н   n

О о   o (as in "soft" in accented syllables)

П п   p

Р р   r

С с   s

Т т *m*   t

У у   u (as in "true")

Ф ф	f
Х х	kh (as in "loch")
Ц ц	ts
Ч ч	ch (as in "each")
Ш ш	sh
Щ щ	shch
Ъ ъ	"hard sign"—may be ignored
Ы ы	i (as in "it", roughly)
Ь ь	"soft sign"—y (consonant) or may be ignored
Э э	e (as in "eh")
Ю ю	you
Я я	ya

Once you've mastered the alphabet, you will find out for yourself what many words mean. Cafe (КАФЕ) is one such word. Restaurant (РЕСТОРАН) is another. Theatre (ТЕАТР) is simple enough. You can't mistake America (АМЕРИКА) or Coffee (КОФЕ) or Cognac (КОНЬЯК).

It is also helpful to familiarize yourself with such obviously useful words as these:

АЭРОПОРТ	AIRPORT
УЛИЦА	STREET
ПРОСПЕКТ	AVENUE
ДОРОГА	LANE
ПЛОЩАДЬ	SQUARE
ГОСТИНИЦА or ОТЕЛЬ	HOTEL
ВХОД	ENTRANCE
ВЫХОД	EXIT
ЭТАЖ	FLOOR, STORY

ВНИМАНИЕ, ОСТОРОЖНО	TAKE CARE!
ЗАКРЫТО	CLOSED
КУРИТЬ РАЗРЕШЕНО	SMOKING
НЕ КУРИТЬ	NO SMOKING
БУФЕТ	BUFFET
ТУАЛЕТ (М) (Ж)	LAVATORY (M) (F)
КАССА	CASHIER'S DESK

If you are going to spend a great deal of time in the Soviet Union, or you simply wish to become more familiar with the language, there are two rapid-study methods available. The *Assimil* system uses LP records combined with a series of paperback texts. For those who learn better by ear, the *Berlitz* system offers a fine short cut to conversational Russian. Highly recommended is the handy Berlitz Russian phrase book, which manages to crowd more than 2,000 useful words and phrases into a pocket-sized edition.

Below is a basic vocabulary of less than 150 words and phrases. It is a good idea to ask a Russian friend (your interpreter, for example) to go over a few of these expressions with you. The phonetic renderings will then become quite readily understandable. The pronunciation is approximate: *a* is to be pronounced short, *o* as in "soft" in accented syllables and like short *a* in unaccented syllables, *kh* represents the sound of *ch* as in "loch," and *zh* the French *j* or the sound of *s* in "leisure."

Remember that, in Russian, a great deal can be said with a single word if you use an interrogative tone.

Greetings and introductions

ЗДРАВСТВУЙТЕ	Hello or How do you do	ZDRAHST-vwy-tye
ДОБРОЕ УТРО	Good morning	DOB-ra-ye oo-tra
ДОБРЫЙ ВЕЧЕР	Good evening	DOB-ry VYECH-er
СПОКОЙНОЙ НОЧИ	Good night	spah-KOY-ncy NOCH-ee
ДО СВИДАНИЯ	Goodbye	da-svee-DAHN-ya
ОЧЕНЬ ПРИЯТНО	Happy to meet you	oh-chen pree-YAHT-nah
МЕНЯ ЗОВУТ	My name is	mehn-YAH za-VOOT
ЭТО МОЯ ЖЕНА	This is my wife	EH-tah ma-YAH zhe-NAH
« МОЙ МУЖ	" " my husband	moy MOOZH
« МОЯ ДОЧЬ	" " my daughter	ma-YAH DOCH
« МОЙ СЫН	" " my son	moy SYN
ЭТО МОЙ ПРИЯТЕЛЬ	" " my friend	moy pree-YAH-tyel
КАК ВАШЕ ИМЯ?	What is your name?	kak VAH-sheh EEM-yah?
МОЖНО?	Can I? Is it possible?	MOZH-na?

At the hotel

МОЙ КЛЮЧ, ПОЖАЛУЙСТА	My key, please	moy KLYOOCH pa-ZHAHL-sta
ЗАВТРАК, ПОЖАЛУЙСТА	I would like to have breakfast	ZAHV-trak pa-ZHAHL-sta
ВОЙДИТЕ	Come in! Enter!	vah-ee-DEE-tye

48)

ПОДОЖДИТЕ	Wait!	pa-dazh-DEE-tye
КОМНАТА	Room	KOM-na-ta
ЭТО В СТИРКУ	This is to be washed	EH-ta eff STEER-koo
ТУТ ОЧЕНЬ ЖАРКО	It is very hot here	toot oh-chen ZHAHR-ka
ТУТ ОЧЕНЬ ХОЛОДНО	It is very cold here	toot oh-chen kHO-lahd-na

In the restaurant

ЗАНЯТО?	Occupied?	ZAHN-ya-ta?
СВОБОДНО?	Free?	sva-BOD-na?
МЕНЮ ПОЖАЛУЙСТА	The menu, please	meh-NEW pa-ZHAHL-sta
ПРИНЕСИТЕ ОДНУ ПОРЦИЮ	One of this	pree-nyeh-SEE-tyeh ah-DNOO POHR-tsee
ПИВО	Beer	PEE-va
ВОДА, МИНЕРАЛЬНАЯ ВОДА	Water, mineral water	va-DAH, meen-er-AHL-na-ya va-DAH
ВОДКА	Vodka	VOT-ka
КОНЬЯК	Brandy, cognac	kohn-YAK
ЛЁД	Ice	LYODD
КРАСНОЕ, БЕЛОЕ ВИНО	Red, white wine	KRAHS-na-ye, BYEHL-a-ye vee-NO
ВИСКИ	Whisky	VEES-kee
ШАМПАНСКОЕ	Champagne	sham-PAHN-ska-ye

ВЕТЧИНА	Ham	vait-chee-NEE
БАЛЫК	Smoked fish	ba-LEEK
ЗАКУСКИ	Appetizers	zah-koos-kee
СЁМГА	Salmon	SYOHM-ga
ИКРА	Caviar	ee-KRAH
ОМЛЕТ	Omelet	ahm-LET
ЯЙЦА В СМЯТКУ	Eggs, soft	yah-ee-TSO f'SMYAT-koo
ЯЙЦА В КРУТУЮ	Eggs, hard	yah-ee-TSO f'kroo-TOO-yoo
ЯИЧНИЦА	Eggs, fried	yah-EECH-ni-tsa
ХЛЕБ	Bread	KHLYEB
ЧЁРНЫЙ, БЕЛЫЙ	Black, white	CHOR-пу, BYEHL-у
КОФЕ	Coffee	кон-fay
ЧАЙ	Tea	CHIGH
ЧАЙ С ЛИМОНОМ	Tea with lemon	CHIGH slee-MOHN-am
САХАР	Sugar	sa-KHAR
СОЛЬ	Salt	SOL
ПЕРЕЦ	Pepper	PEH-rets
МАСЛО	Butter	MAHZ-la
БЛИНЫ	Pancakes	blee-NEE
ТОРТ	Cake	TORT

| МОРОЖЕНОЕ | Ice cream | mah-ro-zheh-na |
| СЧЁТ, ПОЖАЛУЙСТА | Please bring the check | s'CHOT, pa-ZHAHL-sta |

In the street, or shopping

ГДЕ КРАСНАЯ ПЛОЩАДЬ?	Where is Red Square?	GD'YEN KRAHS-na-ya PLOSH-shat?
НАЛЕВО	To the left	nah-LYEH-va
НАПРАВО	To the right	nah-PRAH-va
ПРЯМО	Straight ahead!	pree-YAH-mah!
СКОЛЬКО ЭТО СТОИТ?	How much is it?	SKOHL-ka EH-ta STOH-eet?
ДАЙТЕ МНЕ ЭТО	Give me this	DAH-ee-te mnyeh EH-ta
КАК ЭТО	Like this one	kak EH-ta
БЕЛЫЙ	White	BYEHL-y
КРАСНЫЙ	Red	KRAHS-ny
ЧЁРНЫЙ	Black	CHOR-ny
СИНИЙ	Blue	SEE-nee
КОРИЧНЕВЫЙ	Brown	ka-REECH-nyeh-vy
СПИЧКИ	Matches	SPEECH-kee
СИГАРЕТЫ	Cigarettes	si-ga-RYET-y
БОЛЬШОЙ	Big	BOIL-sheh
МАЛЕНЬКИЙ, МАЛЫЙ	Little	MAH-lyen-kee, MAH-lee

Basic words

ДА	Yes	DAH
НЕТ	No	NYET
МОЖЕТ БЫТЬ	Perhaps	MOZH-et BWYT
ПОЖАЛУЙСТА	Please	pa-ZHAHL-sta
СПАСИБО БОЛЬШОЕ	Thanks a lot	spa-SEE-ba bal-SHOY-e
ХОРОШО	Good! Fine!	kha-ra-SHO!
ТОЛЬКО	Only	TOIL-ka
БОЛЬШЕ	More	BOIL-sheh
МЕНЬШЕ	Less	myen-SHEH
СЕЙЧАС	At once!	see-CHAHS!
ГДЕ	Where?	GD'YEH?
ЗДЕСЬ	Here	ZD'YES
ТАМ	There (for place)	TAM
ТУДА	There (for direction)	too-DAH
КОГДА	When	kahg-DAH
ВРЕМЯ	Time	VREHM-ya
Я	I	YAH
ВЫ	You	VWY
МОЙ БАГАЖ	My luggage	moy ba-GAZH

МОЙ ПАСПОРТ	My passport	moy PAHS-port
МОЙ БИЛЕТ	My ticket	moy beel-YET
ПОЕЗД	Train	POY-ezd
САМОЛЁТ	Plane	sa-mah-LYOT
АЭРОПОРТ	Airport	ah-er-ah-PORT
ВОКЗАЛ	Railway Station	vahk-ZAHL
МАШИНА	Car	ma-SHEE-na
ТАКСИ	Taxi	tak-SEE
ДО or В	To	DOH, VEH
ИЗ	From	EEZ
ОТЕЛЬ or ГОСТИНИЦА	Hotel	oh-TEL, gas-TEEN-it-sa
МЕСТО	Seat	MYES-ta
ЗАНЯТО	Occupied	ZAHN-ya-ta
СВОБОДНО	Free	sva-BOHD-na
ОТКРЫТО	Open	at-KRYT-a
ЗАКРЫТО	Shut	za-KRYT-nya
СЕГОДНЯ ВЕЧЕРОМ	Tonight	zi-VOD-nya VYECH-er-am
СЕГОДНЯ	Today	zi-VOD-nya
ЗАВТРА	Tomorrow	ZAV-tra

Basic commercial and institutional signs

ГОСТИНИЦА	HOTEL
РЕСТОРАН	RESTAURANT
КАФЕ	CAFE
ПОЧТА	POST OFFICE
ПАРИК МАХЕРСКАЯ	BARBERSHOP, HAIRDRESSER'S
АПТЕКА	DRUG STORE, PHARMACY
МАГАЗИН	STORE, SHOP
ПРОДОВОЛЬСТВЕННЫЙ МАГАЗИН	GROCERY STORE
ГАСТРОНОМ	GROCERY STORE, DELICACIES
КНИГИ	BOOKS
МЕТРО	METRO, SUBWAY
СТОЯНКА ТАКСИ	TAXI STAND
ОСТАНОВКА ТРОЛЛЕЙБУСА	TROLLEY BUS STOP
ОСТАНОВКА АВТОБУСА	MOTORBUS STOP
ТУАЛЕТ (Ж), (М)	PUBLIC LAVATORY (L), (M)
СПРАВОЧНОЕ БЮРО	INFORMATION OFFICE
СОЮЗПЕЧАТЬ	NEWS-STAND
ТЕЛЕФОН-АВТОМАТ	PUBLIC TELEPHONE
ПЕРЕХОД	STREET CROSSING
ТЕАТР	THEATRE
КИНО-ТЕАТР	MOVIE THEATER
МУЗЕЙ	MUSEUM

Basic breakfast order

Do not try to pronounce the words here; simply copy out a list of the items desired from the column below and show it to the *dezhurnaya* in your hotel. (If you are reading this before your departure, it might be a good idea to Xerox or photocopy this list.) This can be a regular order. It will save you the time you would otherwise spend waiting in the restaurant. Not all hotels have room service, but many do. You pay on delivery of the order.

Tell the floor-lady *before* retiring, and indicate what time you wish breakfast. This method, although not fool-proof, has been well tested and usually works fine.

ПОДЖАРЕННЫЙ ХЛЕБ	TOAST
СЛИВОЧНОЕ МАСЛО	BUTTER
ЯИЦА В МЕШОЧКЕ	SOFT-BOILED EGGS
КРУТЫЕ ЯИЦА	HARD-BOILED EGGS
ЯИЧНИЦА ГЛАЗУНЬЯ (И БЕКОН)	FRIED EGGS (AND BACON)
ВЕТЧИНА	HAM
СЫР	CHEESE
АПЕЛЬСИНОВЫЙ СОК	ORANGE JUICE
ФРУКТОВЫЙ СОК	FRUIT JUICE
МИНЕРАЛЬНАЯ ВОДА	MINERAL WATER
ВОДА СО ЛЬДОМ	ICE WATER
ЧЁРНОЕ КОФЕ	BLACK COFFEE
КОФЕ СО СЛИВКАМИ	COFFEE WITH CREAM
ЧАЙ С ЛИМОНОМ	TEA WITH LEMON
ЧАЙ С МОЛОКОМ	TEA WITH MILK
МОЛОКО	MILK
КЕФИР	YOGHURT
ХЛЕБ—БЕЛЫЙ, ЧЁРНЫЙ	BREAD—WHITE, BLACK

Basic picnic order

Same method applies. On the list below, point out to the shop assistant what you desire and let her gather the items.

МИНЕРАЛЬНАЯ ВОДА	MINERAL WATER
КРАСНОЕ ВИНО	RED WINE
БЕЛОЕ ВИНО	WHITE WINE
ПИВО	BEER
ФРУКТОВЫЙ НАПИТОК	FRUIT DRINK
ИКРА	CAVIAR
КОПЧЁНАЯ ОСЕТРИНА	SMOKED STURGEON
КОПЧЁНАЯ СЁМГА	SMOKED SALMON
КОПЧЁНАЯ РЫБА	SMOKED FISH
СЛИВОЧНОЕ МАСЛО	BUTTER
ХЛЕБ—БЕЛЫЙ, ЧЁРНЫЙ	BREAD—WHITE, BLACK
БАЛТИЙСКИЕ ШПРОТЫ	BALTIC SPRATS
СЫР	CHEESE
СЕЛЬДЬ	HERRING
КОПЧЁНАЯ КОЛБАСА	SMOKED SAUSAGE
ВАРЁНЫЕ ГОВЯЖЬИ СОСИСКИ	BOILED BEEF SAUSAGE
КОПЧЁНЫЙ ОКОРОК	SMOKED HAM
ПИРОЖКИ	MEAT PIE
ПОМИДОРЫ	TOMATOES
САЛАТ	LETTUCE
ОГУРЦЫ	CUCUMBERS
СОЛЁНЫЕ ОГУРЦЫ	PICKLES
ЛУК	ONIONS
МАСЛО (РАСТИТЕЛЬНОЕ)	OIL
УКСУС	VINEGAR
СОЛЬ	SALT
ПЕРЕЦ	PEPPER

See page 274 for the best place in Moscow to shop for this order.

Streets, squares, lanes, and malls

A square or plaza is known as a *ploshchad* (pronounced PLOSH-shat). Red Square, for instance, is pronounced KRAHS-na-ya PLOSH-shat. A street is known as an *ulitsa* (OO-lee-tsah), a lane or side street is a *pereulok* (peh-ROO-lok), a broad avenue or mall is called a *prospekt* (pro-SPEKT), and *proyezd* (pra-YEZD) or *bulvar* (bool-VAR) is a boulevard.

russian forms of address

The formal way to address a person in Russian is to call him or her *Tovarich* (Comrade). As a visitor, you may well find yourself addressed (especially in the hotel) as *Gospodin* or *Gospozha* (Sir or Madam), but Russians rarely, if ever, use this form of address among themselves. They prefer the homelier *Tovarich*, which has a nice friendly ring about it. You can use it to address a member of the Presidium of the USSR or your taxi driver.

After a first meeting or in a social group, the customary mode of address is to use the first name and the patronymic. For example, if a man's name is Ivan and his father is also named Ivan, he will be addressed as "Ivan Ivanovich." (The patronymic is frequently contracted, however, usually by omission of the "ov"; "Ivanovich" thus becomes "Ivanich.")

It is simple enough to understand how Russians are named. Here is an example: Edward and Dorothy Watson are an English brother and sister whose father was also called Edward. Translated into Russian, their names would read: Edward Edwardovich (or Edwardich) Watson and Dorothy Edwardovna Watsona (the final "a" being the feminine ending).

Russians do far more tinkering with names than English-speaking people. This makes reading a Russian novel quite a challenge as regards keeping track of who is who. Alyosha, or Alexei Feodorovich, and Karamazov, for example, all refer to the same person in Dostoevsky's great novel. This brings up yet another variation that occurs frequently. On becoming close friends (as in many other languages, the state of intimacy in which people address each other in the second person singular, "thou," instead of in the polite second person plural), Russians drop the full Christian name and patronymic and use nicknames or short forms: Vanya in place of Ivan, Alyosha for Alexei, Nadia for Natasha, Volodny for Vladimir, and so forth.

The common form of greeting in Russia, the equivalent of the English "hello" or "how do you do," is ЗДРАВСТВУЙТЕ, zDRAHST-vwy-tye, often abbreviated as zDRAHSS! To this you can respond with ОЧЕНЬ ПРИЯТНО, oн-chen pree-ΥΑΗΤ-na—"Happy to meet you." Goodbyes are simple. Everyone knows ДО СВИДОНИЯ, da-svee-DAHN-ya.

you're welcome

introducing yourself to moscow

The best way to get over that strange lost feeling is to get out of your room and go and meet people. If you arrive and settle in during daylight hours, your first stroll might be along Gorkovo (see page 109), walking up from Manege Square, keeping to the right-hand side, until you reach Pushkin Square. Alternatively, you might head for Gorki Park (see page 172). The fastest way to get there is to grab a taxi, which you can recognize by its distinctive checkered bands (see page 184). In and around the park you will see plenty of outdoor cafes. Enter one of them and order a bottle of wine. If your Russian neighbors are curious, you can invite them to join your table. Russians are shy as mice, yet direct and warm. Raise a glass and say *Mir i Druzhba!* (MEER ee droozh-BA!)—"Peace and Friendship."

In many Russian restaurants and cafes there is a dance orchestra. If you're a woman, it is perfectly correct to ask a man to dance—don't be shy. If you're a man, don't get the wrong impression just because Natasha or Olga asks you to foxtrot: she may simply enjoy dancing. It is equally proper, of course, for you to invite her to dance.

If you have arrived at night, there are always the dollar bars (see page 226) for a drink and a bit of conversation. There are few Russians to be found in these places, however. For one thing they don't have the hard currency, and for another it is considered *nekulturny* (unrefined) for a Soviet citizen to frequent

these spots. Instead, you will meet wheat dealers from the Midwest, British businessmen from London, *Wirtschaftswunder* types from Düsseldorf, and furniture salesmen from Helsinki.

Though these places are heavily male-dominated, women are welcome. In fact, Moscow is in general a great place for a single woman to visit. In dollar bars, men will fall over each other to buy her drinks.

The atmosphere tends to be on the raucous side—a mixture of cigarette smoke, the clink of whisky glasses, the rasp and hum of polyglot conviviality, the noise of the Polish juke-box. With it all, you will savour the peculiar what-the-hell ambiance of late-night Moscow.

If you want to meet Russians, you can visit the downstairs cafe in the Hotel National or the bar-restaurants on Kalinin Prospekt (see page 229). Unlike the dollar bars, which stay open until 2 a.m., Russian restaurants are invariably closed by 11 p.m. This is an early-to-bed town. By 11 the city is slowing down, going home. By midnight most Muscovites are safely tucked away in bed.

first morning

The first morning you wake up to find yourself in Russia is always a bit unsettling. No matter how rational you try to be, you're apt to experience at least a touch of infection by the "salt mine factor"—that uneasy feeling that something dreadful may be about to happen. All we can do here is repeat the same simple advice given earlier: Please stop worrying and start enjoying Moscow.

When you leave your room, turn your key in to the *dezhurnaya*. If you have laundry, bundle it together and hand that over at the same time—it will usually be returned the same day. Don't wait for the elevator unless you are in a very new hotel; it is the custom in Russia to walk down. When you reach the restaurant, don't wait outside for a maître d' to seat you, just walk in and take any available table. After a probationary waiting period (this can last up to twenty minutes) a standard breakfast will be set before you, usually consisting of yoghurt, a soft-boiled egg, and tea or coffee. You pay in either food coupons or roubles. If you want something nonstandard, ask for the menu (see page 49 for a sample menu). Breakfast is usually served in the major Moscow hotels between 8 and 11 a.m.

If you are up early, you may want to consider a brisk walk. Moscow wakes up early, and there is plenty to see on the streets after 6 a.m. It's also a good idea to get down to the Service Bureau early (open 8 a.m.) to check on your arrangements for the day, to order theatre or movie tickets, or to confirm a visit to the museums or a guided tour. Most big hotels have a hairdresser, and beauty salons open at 8 a.m.

a word about manners

In general, Soviet citizens tend to be more formal than Britons or Americans (though less so than Germans or Swedes). There is more bowing and hand-shaking than in London or New York.

When it comes to conversation, friendliness and frankness are normal. But it is worth remembering that Russians take a genuine pride in their country's achievements. If you feel inclined to argue, be prepared with plenty of hard facts about conditions at home. If you talk about consumer goods, for instance, you may well be challenged to discuss health care or the treatment of minorities in your own country. It is also wise to recall that much of World War II was fought on Russian soil, that there is scarcely a family in the Soviet Union that did not lose someone during the Nazi invasion, and that the country suffered incredible material destruction; this is an understandably emotional subject in the USSR.

Very few Russians will deliberately seek out political discussions. Talk on religious subjects is perfectly all right, but a Soviet citizen is not accustomed to having his institutions or basic views attacked. The main point is to keep all such exchanges within the bounds of friendly conversation.

Though open and frank discussion may at times be welcomed, anything that may be construed as anti-Soviet activity is definitely not appreciated. There are stiff legal penalties for people who engage in deliberate propaganda against the Soviet state. Carrying signs, picketing, distributing leaflets of any kind are forbidden.

All of this is, of course, common-sense stuff. Few Russians seem really to enjoy the give-and-take of a good debate, and you are more likely to enjoy yourself and your new-found Russian friends if you stay clear of controversial and provocative subjects.

nichevo—a useful word

In any event, it is not ideological disagreements but differences in temperament and outlook that are likely to pose the main threat to your enjoyment—that is, if you let them. Advice to the point: don't get exasperated when things don't go according to plan. In Russia things rarely do, even though this is a country that is supposed to live by plans.

It only takes one glance at the Soviet press to realize that everybody is in the same situation. It is not uncommon to arrive in Moscow only to discover that Intourist claims to know nothing about you. But then it is not uncommon for a new apartment house to be sent the wrong set of elevators. The Russians are used to this sort of thing, and they even have a marvellous shopping-bag expression for all such occasions. *Nichevo*, according to the dictionary, means "never mind," but it

stuffs all the implications and overtones of *C'est la vie,*
mañana, and *dolce far niente* into just three tripping
syllables—nee-chee-vo.

Nichevo if there is a TV set in your room without a
plug.
Nichevo if the Service Bureau does not respond to
your telephone call.
Nichevo if the slow-motion service in the restaurant
turns lunch or dinner into a two- to three-hour affair.
Nichevo if you try dialing another room and only get
static on the end of the line.
Nichevo if you press the button for the elevator and
it does not arrive.

The Russians are a well-disciplined people, and they
get lots of practice in saying *nichevo.* So when things
seem to be going wrong for you, it might help (at least
a bit) to follow their example.

how to get to the city centre
from your hotel

**The Metropole, National, Intourist, Rossiya, Moskva,
Tsentralnaya, Budapest, Armenia, Oktyabrskaya, Ural,
and Varshava** are situated in the city centre.

Sovietskaya: Dynamo or Byelorusskaya Metro stations:
trolley buses 1, 12, 20.
Pekin: Mayakovskaya Metro Station; trolley buses
1, 10, 12, 20, 29, B.
Ukraine: Kievskaya Metro Station; motorbuses 69, 70,
89, 107, 116, 139; trolley bus 2.
Leningradskaya: Komsomolskaya Metro Station; trolley buses 14, 22, 41; motorbuses 19, 40, 85, 152.

Bucharest and *Balchug:* Novokuznetskaya Metro station; motorbuses 6, 25, 28, 115; trolley bus 25.

Ostankino: VDNKh (National Economic Achievements Exhibition) Metro Station; trolley buses 9, 36; motorbuses 24, 76, 85; streetcars 7, 10.

city transit

(For the full story, see page 175.)

Metro: Traffic begins on all lines at 6 a.m. and ceases at 12:30 a.m. The fare is 5 kopecks and covers all transfers.

Trolley Bus: Traffic begins at 6 a.m. and ends at 12:30 a.m. The fare one way, regardless of distance, is 5 kopecks.

Streetcar: Traffic begins at 5:30 a.m. and ends at 12:30 a.m. The fare one way, regardless of distance, is 4 kopecks.

Motorbus: Traffic begins at 6 a.m. and ends at 12:30 a.m. The fare, one way, regardless of distance, is 5 kopecks.

Note: Many trolley buses, motorbuses, and streetcars operate without fare collectors. You drop your fare into a cash box by the entrance and tear off a ticket. You should carry small change for this purpose, since the machine does not make change.

Taxis: The municipal taxi system, with some 7,500 cabs, is a 24-hour-a-day operation. You can call a cab by phone from your hotel—the number is 25-00-00—but the most convenient way is to have the Service Bureau do it for you. Your fare is registered on the meter. Rates are low: 10 kopecks a kilometre plus a 10 kopeck service charge. Any waiting time is paid for at the rate of one rouble per hour.

For more details on how to cope with Moscow taxis, turn to page 184.

postal services

Same procedures as other countries. A letter or postcard may be mailed from Moscow to any part of the world. There is a post office in every hotel (stamps can also be bought at the souvenir counter).

POSTAGE TO FOREIGN COUNTRIES (*in kopecks*)

	Letter	Postcard
First-class mail	6	4
Airmail	16	14
Registered first-class	18	18
Registered airmail	26	26

On the ground floor of the Hotel National, at 1, Gorkovo, is the K-600 Branch of the General Post Office, which has been opened especially to service foreign visitors. As mentioned previously, you can have your mail addressed to you here: John Doe, Moscow, K-600, USSR. The K-600 Branch is open daily from 9 a.m. to 8 p.m. You can also mail parcels from this address.

telephone & telegraph services

The Soviet Union is many things, but most assuredly it is not Switzerland when it comes to the communications business. The one bright spot is that telephone calls to anywhere *outside* the Soviet Union are usually handled with dispatch. It will cost you about the same to telephone New York or London as it would if you were calling Moscow from those cities. Best idea if you are making an overseas call is to write down the telephone number you want and leave it with the Service Bureau in your hotel. You must state when you want the call placed, and experience suggests that you specify a time or you may have a long wait for the connection. You can, of course, go to the Central Telegraph Office to make your call. This is located at Gorkovo No. 7. Open around the clock.

Public telephones

These are available in streets, squares, Metro stations, post offices, theatres, shops, and elsewhere. The call charge is 2 kopecks. Place a 2 kopeck coin into the slot *before* picking up the receiver. Wait for a dial tone, then dial your number. Short buzzes indicate that the number is occupied; put down the receiver and take back your money. If the buzzes are long, wait for a connection. If no answer, put back the receiver and retrieve your money. Local telephone calls made from hotel rooms in Moscow are free of charge.

Telegraph rates

Telegrams and express telegrams may be sent to any city in the world. Express telegrams are charged at twice the regular rates.

CHARGE PER WORD FOR TELEGRAMS (*in kopecks*)

Austria	14	Iraq	54
Belgium	16	Italy	16
China	18	Netherlands	15
Denmark	12	Norway	14
Finland	11	Poland	9
France	15	Sweden	13
West Germany	13	USA (New York)	23
Britain	16	USA (elsewhere)	30

Telephone rates

Telephone calls may be put through to most European cities and anywhere in the United States. You can also telephone Australia and several countries in Asia and Africa. You may make the call from your hotel room or from the Central Telegraph Office.

LONG-DISTANCE TELEPHONE RATES (*charge for a three-minute conversation in roubles and kopecks*)

Austria	3.00	Iraq	7.50
Belgium	3.29	Italy	3.79
China	7.23	Israel	9.26
Denmark	2.88	Japan	10.58
Finland	1.23	Netherlands	2.46
France	4.35	Norway	3.44
West Germany	3.32	Poland	1.94
Britain	4.28	Sweden	2.41
Iceland	7.08	Switzerland	2.94
India	7.50	USA	10.80
Iran	3.53		

There are special rates for the following countries during the time periods specified:

Czechoslovakia, from 7 p.m. to 8 a.m.	1.21
Poland from 7 p.m. to 8 a.m.	0.97
USA, Sundays	8.10

autos & driving

Moscow is a city that believes in public transportation and not at all in the private automobile. There are less than 100,000 privately owned cars in the city. In Moscow there are no parking meters (no need for them), no used car lots, and only a single automobile showroom. If you bring your own car to the Soviet Union, you will soon become aware of the need to carry a spare five-gallon container, because service stations are few and far between. Moscow has better facilities for motorists than most Soviet cities—but not by much. Here is a list of service stations for car drivers. The number after the letter A denotes octane rating.

FILLING STATION	At 17th km. of Minsk Highway at Moscow Ring	A-72 gas	24 hr. *Motel & Rest.*
REPAIR AND FILLING STATION	At 21st km. of Moscow-Kharkov Highway at crossing with Moscow Ring	A-72 gas 24 hr.	Repairs 9 a.m.–5 p.m. *Motel & Rest.*

REPAIR STATION	6, Vtoroi Selskokhoz-yaistvenny Proyezd, off Prospekt Mira	Service Only	Repairs 9 a.m.–5 p.m. Sundays 9 a.m.–2 p.m.
FILLING STATION	Sverdlov Sq. (nr. Hotel Metropole)	A-76 & A-74 gas	24 hr
FILLING STATION	4, Vtoroi Selskokhoz-yaistvenny Proyezd, off Prospekt Mira	A-98 & A-72 & A-66 gas	8 a.m.–8 p.m.
FILLING STATION	Danilovskaya Sq.	A-76 A-72 A-66 gas	24 hr.
FILLING STATION	6, Krasin St. (nr. Hotel Pekin)	A-72 gas	24 hr.
FILLING STATION	Yefremov St. (nr. Frunzenskaya Metro)	A-72 gas	24 hr.
FILLING STATION	At 17th km. Yaroslavsky Highway at crossing with Moscow Ring	A-72 A-76 A-66 gas	24 hr.

72)

Driving in Moscow—Rules of the Road

1. Traffic moves along the right side of the street.

2. The speed limit in town is 60 kilometers an hour (35 mph).

3. Horn-blowing is forbidden within city limits, except in an emergency.

4. Fire engines, ambulances, police cars have right of way. Heed the sirens.

5. Traffic lights with four lights allow a left turn or a complete U-turn when the two green lights go on, a signal that should be awaited at the STOP (СТОП) line.

6. Never cross a solid white line running down the center of the road; you may turn left or make a complete U-turn only where there is a broken line or a sign indicating that it is permitted.

7. At a crossing where there are stripes marked on the road and no traffic lights, the pedestrian has the right of way.

8. In case of an accident, do not leave the area.

Note: If you forgot to insure your car at the border, you can do so in Moscow at the office of the Foreign Insurance Company (Ingosstrakh). This organization handles all accident insurance, both collision and liability.

Insurance premiums are accepted in any currency; all claims will be paid in that same currency. Ingosstrakh is located at 11/10 Kuibyshev Street. Arrangements can be made through the Service Bureau.

Car Rentals

It is best to make these arrangements before you arrive in Moscow. You can rent from Intourist, or else from Hertz International or the Avis Rent a Car system.

RENTAL WITHOUT DRIVER (*per day in dollars*)

Rental Period	Volga (5 seats)	Zhiguli or Moskvich (4)
1–10 days	7.00	5.00
11–20 days	6.50	4.50
21 and over	6.00	4.00
Charge per km.	0.06	0.05

If you rent by the week, you can make a saving by having the mileage charge included at the following rates:

	For 7 days	Extra charge per day over 7 days
Volga	74.90	10.70
Moskvich	48.35	6.90
Zhiguli	48.35	6.90

The rental rates include: insurance of the driver for third-party liability; insurance of the car; technical servicing of the car; a map of car routes. Gas coupons can be purchased from the Service Bureau either for cash or in exchange for vouchers.

RENTAL WITH DRIVER (*per day in dollars*)

	Chaika (6 seats)	*Volga* (4)	*Moskvich* (3)
Up to 240 km.	55.00	35.00	24.35
Extra Charge per each km. over 240 km.	0.22	0.14	0.09

Rates include: daily ten-hour use of car with driver; technical servicing; gasoline; washing of car, etc. If you need the driver's services beyond the ten-hour limit, the charges will be:

Chaika	$5.00 per hour
Volga	$3.20 per hour
Moskvich	$2.25 per hour

walking about moscow: a few useful tips

1. Traffic in the city proceeds on the right, though some thoroughfares have one-way traffic.
2. In midtown Moscow it is against the law to cross the street at random. Look for the underground walkways at street corners and use them. If you don't see one, look for the zebra stripes or arrows. Jaywalking may subject you to an instant fine by a policeman.

3. There are a lot of new drivers on Moscow's streets, and since it is against the law for them to use their horns except in an emergency, be extra cautious before stepping off the kerb.

newspapers & periodicals

There is practically no distribution of non-Communist foreign newspapers in Moscow. If you want *The Times* of London or the *International Herald Tribune*, you might try the newsstand in your hotel; occasionally they will have a copy beneath the counter. One local English-language publication that should prove useful is the *Moscow News*, which carries no news but lists all the current attractions in the city: films, theatre, concerts, art exhibitions, etc.

religious services

It is quite possible to attend religious services in Moscow, and many people do so. Of course, the choice is limited. There were four hundred churches in Moscow before the Revolution, serving a population of a little over a million. Today, in a city of six and a half million, the numbers have dwindled to less than fifty "working" churches. The great wealth of the Russian Orthodox Church has long since vanished. Their congregations are the sole support of the "working" churches, which must pay their share of taxes. By a law of 1921, public religious instruction is forbidden; in every Soviet school the wall newspapers revile religious worship, which is described as an "outmoded and superstitious practice." In spite of everything, however, the few remaining churches are usually packed—though to be sure, the average age of the congregation is above fifty. It is a thrilling experience to visit a Russian church during a service. But because they are generally so crowded, you should be prepared for sardine-can-like conditions.

The Baptists meet in a single hall (President Nixon worshipped there during his Moscow visit). There is only one Roman Catholic church in the city (although Catholic services are held at several foreign Embassies). The Moslem community has its own mosque; Moscow's 600,000 Jews have a single synagogue and two small apartment rooms converted for prayer.

The following churches are easily found within walking distance of the main hotels.

Russian Orthodox Church

Church of All Sorrows (Vsekh Skorbishchikh) From the Hotel Bucharest, turn left, down the Ordnaya Bolshaya, and the church is on your right. The Liturgy or Mass is celebrated on Sundays at 7 a.m. and 10 a.m., and Vespers at 6 p.m.

St. Nicholas' Church From the Hotels National, Intourist, or Metropole, proceed up Gorkovo and take the third turn on your left, after the Central Telegraph Office. The church can be seen from Gorkovo.

Our Lady of Tikhvin (Tikhvinskaya) From the Hotel Ostankino, take the bus to Metro Station VDNKh (Exhibition). A little south on the left side are the remains of the village of Alexeev. The church is here.

Znameny Church From the same hotel, turn left down Prospekt Mira. The church is directly opposite the Rizhsky Railway Station.

St. John "Na Presna" From the Hotel Ukraine, cross the bridge over the Moscow River. The church can be seen from the bridge on the hill on the left. Bear left after the bridge and through the park.

The Patriarchal Church (Yelokhovsky Sobor) This handsome church is on Spartakovskaya Street, just by the Baumanskaya Metro Station.

Services are also held in the Refectory church inside the walls of the Novo-Devichy Convent (see page 156). The Liturgy is celebrated in most churches daily at 8 or 9 a.m. and on Sundays at 7 a.m. and 10 a.m.

Roman Catholic Church

A five-minute walk from the Hotel Metropole. Bus or Metro to Dzerzhinsky Square (see map, page 128). You will find the church on the north side of the square, behind the Lubyanka prison. Here there is a little street called Malaya Lubyanka. The church is on your right.

Daily Mass 8:30 and 10:30 a.m.

Services are also held for diplomats and visitors, in English and French, on Sunday at 9 a.m. and 12:15 p.m. in the Community Room, U.S. Embassy; and at 6 p.m. at the Chapel of Our Lady of Hope, 12/24, Sadovo-Samotechnaya, Apartment 23.

Baptists and Seventh Day Adventists

The meetinghouse of two evangelical denominations is at 3, Maly Vuzovsky Pereulok. This is a narrow lane on the west side of Pokrovsky Boulevard (on the east side of the Boulevard ring road). Baptist services are held on Sunday at 10 a.m. and 6 p. m., and on Tuesday, Thursday, and Saturday at 6 p.m. On Wednesday and Friday, Seventh Day Adventist services begin at 7 p.m.

Armenian Church
The Armenian Church is located at 27, Malaya Dekabrskaya Street.

Anglican Services
Alternate Sundays in the British and U.S. embassies at 10:30 a.m. (for telephone numbers, check page 321). Sunday school is conducted at the U.S. Embassy at 10:30 a.m.

Jewish Synagogue
Located at 8, Arkhipova Street. Services are held daily at 10 a.m. and one hour before sundown.

Mosque
7, Vyolzov Pereulok near Kommuny Square. The Hamaz is recited five times daily; on Fridays at 1 p.m.

soviet holidays
Compared to that of most Western countries, the Soviet calendar is rather bare when it comes to public holidays. Here they are:

New Year's Day
The traditional family get-together the night before is followed by a day completely given over to the

children. There are trips to the circus; in Moscow, the Kremlin grounds are thrown open to the youngsters. Parents take their children to the ballet, movies, or puppet theatre. There is a visit from Ded Moroz (Grandfather Frost), who distributes presents and spicy gingerbread men.

International Women's Day *(March 8)*

The State gives women time off, husbands bring home bunches of flowers wrapped in crispy cellophane, children do the dishes, and the women are lauded in a day-long celebration in their honor.

Labor Day *(May 1–2)*

A marvellous occasion to be in Moscow! Parades, fireworks at night, streets festooned with lights, and a good time all round.

photography in the city

You can photograph everything and everywhere, save subjects and locations related to the nation's defence. These include all types of military technology, seaports, railway junctions, tunnels, railway bridges, certain kinds of industrial enterprises, and the like. All aerial photography is forbidden. Ask for permission of the administration before you use your camera inside factories, research institutes, and the like. It is only good manners to ask before you take photographs of individuals. (For where to buy film and for information on processing, see pages 21 and 285.)

getting about moscow

sightseeing with intourist

The Service Bureau is bedlam. You don't know what tour you are supposed to be on. You do know what tour you've been booked on, but you don't like the choice. There are eighteen ladies from Hadassah who want to visit the Central Synagogue and you have somehow been assigned to their party—and you're Catholic.

O.K., calm down. During the hectic May–September tourist season everything gets "out of synch" in Moscow. But one thing you ought to know is that you *can* change your sightseeing itinerary. Just go down to the TOUR desk in the Service Bureau and explain what you want. It is important to do this as much in advance as you can manage.

Depending on the class of travel you are in (see page 12), you are *entitled* to a certain amount of official sightseeing along with your food, accommodations, and travel arrangements. To help you sort out the various Moscow city tours, here is a list of favourite Intourist visits with appropriate comments.

Lenin Mausoleum (30 *minutes*)

The Russians themselves queue up for Lenin's tomb outside the Kremlin in a snaking line that stretches halfway across Red Square. At first glance the waiting time seems hopeless. But Intourist slips foreign visitors in near the front (there are no complaints) and waiting time is usually about 15 minutes. Due decorum is required: If you have a camera with you, you must put

it away when you enter the Mausoleum. Hands are expected to be removed from pockets.

A visit here is a remarkable experience, at once solemn and immensely moving. From the entrance you walk, single file, down a series of steps within the crypt. The temperature is chilly; every three yards in the half-darkness, soldiers face the bare-headed column of visitors. There is no pausing, no talking.

A pinkish light illumines the crystal sarcophagus containing the body of Vladimir Ilyich Lenin. The face and hands are the only visible parts, and seem perfectly preserved.

Coming out into the daylight, you will find yourself in a tree-shaded walk at the base of the Kremlin Wall. Here are buried a pantheon of Communist heroes and public figures. To the left of the Mausoleum is Joseph Stalin's simple grave. Then along the wall, Sverdlov, the first chairman of the Central Committee; Dzerzhinsky, head of the Cheka (the original Soviet secret police organization); Irene Armand, a Frenchwoman who was a close collaborator of Lenin's; Vladimir Komarov, the Soviet cosmonaut; John Reed, the American

Communist who wrote *Ten Days That Shook the World*; Lenin's wife, Nadezhda Krupskaya; the writer Maxim Gorki; and many others.

The Lenin Mausoleum is open five days a week, winter and summer. Closed Mondays and Fridays. 10 a.m. to 2 p.m. weekdays; 10 a.m. to 6 p.m. on Sundays.

The Kremlin (*3 hours*)

It is perfectly possible to tour the Kremlin without the help of Intourist, and the way to do so can be found on page 137. It is highly recommended, however, that you avail yourself of Intourist's guided tour the first time around. There is always a queue to enter the Armoury Museum, for one thing, and Intourist arranges preferential treatment for foreign visitors. A small point: Kremlin officials are fussy about their floors, and inside the Armoury you are required to put on canvas overshoes (supplied by the management). So don't wear high-heeled shoes on this visit. The morning tour ends at lunch-time; the afternoon tours finish in plenty of time for shopping and getting ready for the theatre.

The Tretyakov Gallery (2 hours)

This is described in more detail on page 168. You have to make a decision here. If you are not usually the type of person who spends weekends visiting art galleries or your local museum, skip this tour. The Tretyakov, although it possesses a stunning collection of ancient icons, is overall a dull place that smells of beeswax. It is almost always crowded with schoolchildren on a similar tour. There are masterworks by such classic Russian painters as Repin, Shishkin, and Surikov, to be sure; but if you are pressed for time, think carefully about this tour.

The USSR Exhibition of Economic Achievements (3–4 hours)

Actually you can spend two full days here and not see all the exhibits. This is the country's biggest "museum"—a permanent state fair that covers an area of 550 acres. There are more than 300 structures and 78 pavilions set in this vast parkland. Harrison Salisbury of *The New York Times* has aptly described the Exhibition of Economic Achievements as "a short course in Soviet plans and intentions." Quite apart from the dazzling display of technology (from ice-breakers to isotopes) and space achievements (there are special halls devoted to the flights of such Soviet cosmonauts as Yuri Gagarin and Valentina Tereshkova), there are a dozen different restaurants. After the tour you can enjoy the food and atmosphere in the pavilions of such nationalities as the Uzbeks, the Ukrainians, the Georgians, and the Kazakhs. The Soviet Union is a big country, and nowhere in Moscow will you get such a sense of its size, diversity, and aspirations as here.

Cruise on the Moscow River (*3 hours*)

This is one of the pleasantest excursions you can take during the summer months. You can do it on your own, of course (see page 126), but Intourist offers an easy way to enjoy the experience. There is plenty to see from the boat, and quite often there is someone with a piano-accordion on board. In contrast to a river like the Thames, this is more a canal, austere and well regulated. Gone the straggle of untidy villages that lined the river for centuries. Today you will see new apartment houses, pumping stations, reinforced concrete locks. Look around you at the pie-consuming, lemonade-drinking, smiling Muscovites hugely enjoying their day off. You'll have fun, too.

getting to know natasha

If you are a De Luxe-class visitor (or a member of a group), you will have your own guide for at least six hours a day. If you are a First Class visitor, you will spend three hours each day with your own guide. No matter what category of visitor you are, in fact, you will sooner or later spend some time sightseeing with an Intourist guide.

The guides are mostly attractive, intelligent, well-trained girls in their twenties. Many are either students or recent graduates of Moscow's Foreign Language Institute. They will tell you a good deal about the advantages and benefits of life in the USSR, and very little about the negative aspects—though they will certainly expect you to ask questions about the standard of living, social problems, and daily life in Moscow. You should keep in mind, however, that Soviet citizens measure progress in terms of the advances made in recent years, as well as by the ideal standards that their system is trying to achieve.

Intourist guides are courteous in the extreme. If you have any special wishes, they usually try to accommodate you. Tipping is officially disallowed. Nevertheless, if you have received good service and want to say thank you in some extra way, a small gift—perhaps from the group if you are travelling with one—is usually appreciated. (See page 273 or pages 289–90.)

how your guide sees *you*

They are impressed with your personal appearance and friendliness. You spend too much time worrying over diets (if you are a woman) and too little time on cultural interests (if you are a man). You are polite and complimentary about the things you see, but you really know very little about the Soviet Union.

You bring too many suitcases with you, especially American ladies, who seem to possess suitcases for everything (make-up, hair-dryer, etc.). The guides think a simple, unadorned dress is better at the Bolshoi than a glittering sequinned gown.

You complain a little too much in restaurants about slow service, forgetting that a meal should not be rushed. Businessmen—except from the East European bloc—are the most impatient men in the world.

The guides wish you could see more of Moscow, the "ordinary places" as well as the tourist sights, and not go to restaurants in bus-loads. You make guides quite angry when you suspect them of being police spies, or when you expect them to debate the question of political freedom.

You make them pleased when you recognize that their primary job is to help you enjoy Moscow, and when you understand that they, too, have to cope with Soviet bureaucracy. When you return home they rather hope you will write them a letter with your impressions. And if you have been well looked after by your guide, a letter saying so, addressed to Intourist Moscow, Main Office, 16, Karl Marx Prospekt, Moscow USSR, is a nice reward.

keep your eyes open

Personal memories are always the most highly prized part of any visit abroad. Here are some aspects of the Moscow scene that crowd into *my* memory:

1. Moscow is a remarkably *quiet* city. In contrast to New York or London, no aircraft traffic is allowed over the city. Automobile horns are forbidden. Police cars do not use klaxons.

2. Red Square after midnight when it is being watered down. Squadrons of old ladies in white aprons and black boots with twig brooms sweep across the square. They also empty all the ash-trays which are implanted in the sidewalks.

3. Plenty of advertising. Slogans a bit on the primitive

side. A blue-white neon sign in Pushkin Square reads: FLY PLANES. Another: USE TAXIS, THE MOST CONVENIENT FORM OF TRANSPORT. Across the street from Detsky Mir (Children's World) Department Store, a red neon sign reads: DIAL 01 IN CASE OF FIRE.

4. Few pets to be seen in the street. Dogs and cats, though not forbidden, are a rarity in Moscow.

5. Russian men rarely wear wedding bands, and women wear wedding rings on the fourth finger of the right hand. The most popular engagement ring is a modest-sized ruby in a plain gold setting.

6. The many hundreds of street vendors in Moscow. A great many of them can be found in the underground walkways. A man opens a suitcase and a crowd quickly gathers. He is selling cucumbers. Another vendor has a stack of books and a small card table. A queue quickly forms up. "What are they selling, comrade?" a woman asks. "Encyclopedias," she is told. It is Volume No. 3 that is on sale. No one has a clue about the rest of the series. In fifteen minutes the vendor's stock is sold out.

7. The glorious choral music, rich legacy of Russia, heard any Sunday morning in Zagorsk Cathedral.

8. A Russian writer telling me that in modern Russia, religion had been replaced by the Soviet space program. Any visitor will certainly be struck by how space-minded the Soviets are: Space stamps, space ashtrays, space desk ornaments abound. Magazines are full of space exploration stories. Restaurants, beauty parlors, even grocery stores, have names like Sputnik, Cosmos, Rocket.

9. A Russian girl who told me her biggest budget item was stockings that cost from three to five roubles a

pair—out of an average monthly salary of 100 roubles.
10. A sign in the maid's room at the Hotel National:
"Always study, know everything. The more you know,
the stronger you become." —Maxim Gorki.

getting your bearings

The secret of Moscow is that, like Russia itself, it has
never quite been able to make up its mind whether it
wants to be part of Europe or of Asia.

Today, of course it is very much part of Europe,
with its high-rise buildings and its superhighways. But
for hundreds of years the rulers of Moscow looked east
rather than west.

All this is reflected in the architecture around you.
The Muscovites of old expected every building, like
every painting, to tell a story. Russian architects re-
sponded to this demand with a will, borrowing themes
from the Arabian Nights and styles from every period:
Moorish and Venetian, Gothic and Greek, Renaissance
and Hindu, the styles of East and West in all their
panoply of texture and color.

To begin with, Moscow is not—comparatively speaking, at least—a particularly old city. The first mention
of Moscow is in an old chronicle dated 1147. By
history's measure this is only yesterday. Paris and London, for example, were both a thousand years old or
more when the first log cabins were built on Prince
Yuri Dolgoruky's estate. (In fact, Moscow is a young-
ster even by Russian standards: Kiev, Russia's ancient
capital, "the mother of Russian cities," is at least three
thousand years old.) Dolgoruky is generally considered
the founder of Moscow.

some historical background

The beginnings

When you walk around the Kremlin, observe that you are actually on top of a hill that slopes gently down to the Moscow River. This is where the city began. The first buildings were made of wood. But under the first two Ivans, white stone walls were put around these buildings as a defense measure. So from the 14th century on, the town was referred to as "Holy Mother Moscow with the White Walls." At one time all of Moscow was contained within the Kremlin walls. (The word "Kremlin"—*Kreml* in Russian—is derived from *krim* or *krem,* the old Greek word for "fortress.")

Growth

As Moscow expanded, the newcomers began to build their own settlements. Each, in turn, was surrounded by a circle of wall with watchtowers. Moscow is thus built outward from the Kremlin, the heart of the city. It has grown rather like a series of overlapping ink-blots. Once this historical pattern is understood, the plan of Moscow is simple to grasp. On the map in the front you can easily see the series of concentric circles —circular grand boulevards, or "rings"—radiating out from the Kremlin, to form what looks very much like a spider's web. Encircling historic Moscow (as the map shows) is the great Sadovoye Ring, an almost perfect circle, whose exact centre is the Bell Tower of Ivan the Great in the Kremlin.

As Moscow grew, the architectural emphasis came to be on the unusual, the original, or the fantastic, rather than on the elegant or refined.

Then, in 1712, Peter the Great shifted the capital from Moscow to St. Petersburg (now Leningrad). But Moscow refused to stop growing. And, in the course of time, churches and monasteries created a new focus of interest attracting population like iron filings to a magnet.

Amongst the most prominent of these is the Novo-Devichy (New Maiden) Convent, whose golden domes and buildings are second in splendor only to the Kremlin itself.

Tolstoy's Moscow

Moscow in the early nineteenth century was prosperous and booming. Then, virtually overnight, it was reduced to ashes as a consequence of Napoleon's invasion in 1812. Everyone who has ever read *War and Peace* is familiar with the story: The city burned for three days, the Kremlin was badly damaged, and three-quarters of the city was razed—not by the invaders, but by the defenders. "Who would have thought that a nation would destroy its own capital!" exclaimed Napoleon when he learned that one man had been left behind for each building to burn it to the ground.

Napoleon withdrew. What followed was the rebuilding of Moscow, with the great squares, today known as Manege, Sverdlov, Revolution, radiating fanlike from west to east. Then, to the north, beyond what is now Karl Marx Prospekt—Dzerzhinsky Square, the New and Old Squares, and Nogina Square.

One thoroughfare, Tverskaya (now Gorkovo), was the great trading road to Tver on the Volga. After 1812, it became the chief high road of the Russian Empire, lined with shops and elegant private residences.

By the close of the nineteenth century, Mr. Baedeker was observing in his guide to Russia that "Moscow is rapidly becoming modernized of late years." Textile mills, foundries, and machine works brought new clamor to the city.

By 1917, Moscow's population had reached two million—an eightfold increase in less than a hundred years—and it had become the commercial center of Eastern Europe.

New Moscow

Since the Revolution, the skyline of the city has changed dramatically. In the thirties, slums were razed, and entire quarters of crumbling dwellings were destroyed, to make way for the Metro and government offices.

Today Kalinin Prospekt, one of the radial streets leading away from the Kremlin, is what Moscow's city planners like to think of as representing the future.

A great deal is happening, as you will see for yourself walking around. Many of the ancient churches—the city has more than 400—are being spruced up. The city itself has been divided into eight zones. Each zone is to have a total population of around one million, and each will be self-contained so that no one will have to leave his zone to travel to work.

Around the city the forest and park belt will be extended and, if the planners have their way, Moscow will not expand through this "green zone."

exploring the city on your own

Let Intourist show you the main sights. But when the official sightseeing is over, take to the streets and explore the city on your own. You can walk the length and breadth of Moscow, and no one will stop you. This is a law-abiding metropolis, and safe streets are the rule, not the exception. A good tip to remember: try walking late at night if you find it too crowded by day. As I have noted, Moscow is an early-to-bed town, and the centre of the city is virtually empty by midnight.

The best way to explore without getting hopelessly lost is to have a definite starting and end point. So always begin at and return to Red Square. From here you can set out on walks that will show you all the major and many of the minor sights of historic Moscow. Let us proceed.

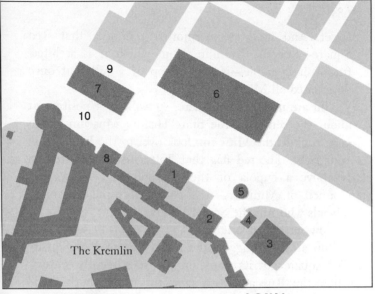

1 Lenin Mausoleum
2 Saviour's Gate
3 St. Basil's Cathedral
4 Minin and Pozharsky Monument
5 Lobnoye Mesto
   (Place of the Skull)

6 G.U.M.
7 History Museum
8 St. Nicholas Gate
   (closed)
9 Gorki Street extension
10 Unnamed street

Walk One: Red Square
(Time: 1 hour)

Enter from Revolution Square and go up the cobbled street that is, in fact, an extension of Gorkovo. On your right will be the great architectural hulk of the **State History Museum**, all red bricks, turrets, and gew-gaws.

As you walk, look to your left at a group of eighteenth- and early-nineteenth-century houses. The first building once housed a "pit," or debtor's jail. Here, Radishchev, an early revolutionary, was held in 1790 on his way to Siberia.

No traffic is allowed in Red Square, so like everyone else you have probably walked up the middle of the street. And it is steep, another reminder that Red Square—like the Kremlin, from which it is architecturally inseparable—is at the top of a hill that once dominated all Moscow.

You are now in the square, so walk to a position at about the centre of the State History Museum. With your back to the Museum, look over to the Kremlin on your right. The red flag that flutters over the Kremlin is above a cupola of the building that houses the Council of Ministers—the group of top government officials who run the Soviet Union.

Now let us get oriented.

You are standing on the north side of Red Square. The square got its name in the seventeenth century, when the Russian word *krasnaya* meant both "red" and "beautiful"; eventually, however, it lost the latter meaning (expressed today by a derivative form, *krasiviy, -aya*).

The first thing you notice is its tremendous size. When Moscow celebrated its 800th anniversary in 1947, an estimated *two million* people gathered here. This great plaza is 2,280 feet long and has an average width of 426 feet. As you can easily see, it is not a square in the literal sense at all, but a great oblong.

Now, as you look towards the south side of the square, you will see that masterpiece of Russian architecture, **St. Basil's Cathedral.** On your left is a two-story building with plate glass windows that stretches the entire length of the square opposite the Kremlin. This is G.U.M. (pronounced "goom"), the biggest department store in the Soviet Union. To your right is the Lenin Mausoleum and behind this is the Kremlin Wall, where the Soviet great lie buried.

Before moving off across the square, glance immediately to your right at the three-story Nikolskaya Tower. It was through the gates of this tower that the Bolsheviks poured into the Kremlin in 1917 to overpower the White Guards. Nowadays only officials use these gates as an entrance, and tourists are politely directed away.

On your right, the **Lenin Mausoleum.** Designed by the Soviet architect Alexei Shchusev in 1930, this sombre structure is a massive truncated pyramid of great blocks of red granite. Above the bronze doors the main portal bears the name of Lenin in dark purple. A two-man guard of honor (who will take no notice of you) stand stiffly erect with rifles, bayonets fixed, at their sides. The guards change every hour, day and night, a precise maneuver that is enthralling to watch. (See page 86 for visiting hours.)

Continue walking south towards St. Basil's Cathedral. On your right is the main Kremlin tower, the **Spasskaya**, a much-photographed symbol of Moscow. The tower's Spassky Gate—or the Saviour's Gate, as it is known in English—is the main entrance to the Kremlin. Before the Revolution, anyone passing through this gate had to uncover his head before the picture of the Saviour which used to be over the entrance.

The Spassky Gate was designed by the Italian architect Pietro Solari in 1491. It was an Englishman, Christopher Holloway, who added the Gothic tower in 1625, and placed a clock in it.

What "Big Ben" is to London, so the ten bells of the Kremlin Chimes are to Moscow. The chimes are broadcast daily over Radio Moscow, and Russians set their clocks by them. It is worth looking through the gate. On the hour, the soldiers who guard the Lenin Mausoleum leave from this point, marching in a kind of goose-step that is guaranteed to send bumps up your spine.

If you turn your back on the Spasskaya and look slightly to your right, you will then face the Cathedral of St. Basil the Blessed, one of the architectural wonders of the world. Originally known as the Pokrovsky Cathedral, it was built by Ivan the Terrible to commemorate the conquest of Kazan. An army of masons and carpenters completed St. Basil's in just six years, 1555 to 1560.

According to legend, the Tsar ordered the architect blinded so that he could never duplicate his work. Until 1957 it was thought to be the work of two

architects named Postnik and Barma. Records discovered in that year revealed that it is the work of
Postnik Yakoviev, nicknamed Barma.

As you look up, count the domes—there are nine of
them, each different from the others; the strange forms,
bulbs, pineapples, and onions painted in rainbow
colors, and with twisted or serrated spirals. The sight
of St. Basil's apparently annoyed Napoleon, who is
said to have exclaimed: "Destroy this monstrosity!" He
profaned it by allowing his troops to stable their
horses within it.

Fantastic though the building is on the outside, the
interior is a disappointment. The Cathedral has long
been desacralized and is now a museum. The interior
consists of ten small chapels, dark and gloomy within,
and you wander from one chapel to another, wondering
where all the space disappeared.

Go back at night, however, when the Cathedral is
all illuminated, and you will realize how the city has
made St. Basil's a truly national shrine, a monument
to Russia's independence and its national spirit.

As you leave the Cathedral, you are bound to notice
the monument to Minin and Pozharsky sculpted by
Ivan Martos in 1818. The two gentlemen atop the
plinth were early liberators of Moscow (1612). The inscription on the pedestal reads:

> *To Citizen Minin and Prince Pozharsky*
> *from a grateful Russia, Summer, 1818.*

If you stand with your back to St. Basil's, then walk
to your right, you will come to an unadorned round
platform built of white stone. This is the **Lobnoye**

Mesto, the Place of the Skull. In medieval times hundreds of people were put to death here—and in the most horrible manner imaginable. The victims were not only hanged, but were whipped to death with the knout, scalded in boiling water, and—in the case of traitors—had molten lead poured down their throats. Ivan the Terrible had his political enemies executed here. It is said that he spent his mornings in bell-ringing and prostration; during the midday meal he would read the lives of the saints; and in the afternoon watch his victims being tortured at the Lobnoye Mesto.

As you walk past the Lobnoye Mesto, you will see, opposite the Lenin Mausoleum, the G.U.M. (State Universal Store). This vast department store was completed in 1888 in the pseudo-Russian style, at a cost of more than 15 million roubles. In its day it was one of the wonders of Russia and, architecturally speaking, the forerunner of all those enclosed shopping malls that sprang up in the USA during the 1950's. (More details about G.U.M. on page 260.)

And here is where we end our first walk.

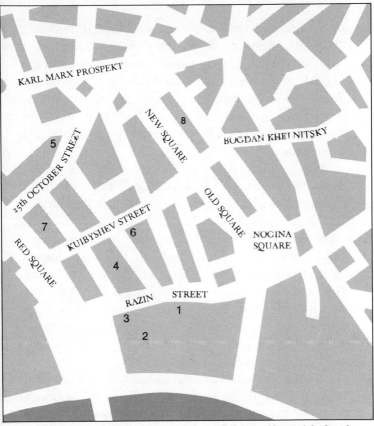

1 House of Boyars Romanov
2 Hotel Rossiya
3 Church of Conception of Anne
4 Gostinny Dvor (Old Trading Hall)
5 Printing House of the Synod
6 Old Stock Exchange
7 G.U.M.
8 Polytechnic Museum

Walk Two: Into the Inner City
(Time: 45 minutes)

Leaving the pigeons and the tourists in Red Square, we shall now explore one of the most fascinating parts of Old Moscow, the Kitai-Gorod, or Chinese City.

As already noted, Moscow grew outwards from the Kremlin. The Kitai-Gorod was the place where scholars, merchants, and foreign ambassadors lived, the second "ink-blot" on the developing map of Moscow.

It was here, in the narrow streets behind where G.U.M. now stands, that Ivan Fyodorov produced the first books in Russian, and the very first Russian newspaper was published under Peter the Great. Many of the buildings date back to between the sixteenth and eighteenth centuries.

Why was it called the "Chinese City"? Although some old guide-books mistakenly call this "Moscow's Chinatown," it is just not so. The fact is that *kitai* is actually a Mongol word for "central," which the Russians subsequently borrowed as their name for China (taking their cue from the traditional Chinese concept of that country as the center of the world). *Kitai-Gorod*, then, originally meant "Central City," in allusion to its location between the Kremlin and outlying settlements. Depending upon whom you want to argue with, either the Kitai-Gorod was built by the Mongols or it was their chief trading area.

Like the Kremlin, the Kitai-Gorod was once a walled enclave. Most of the brick wall, built in the sixteenth century, was removed during the reconstruction of Moscow in the mid-1930's. But you can still see remains of it as you wander around—particularly at a spot near the Hotel Metropole in Sverdlov Square, from which a long stretch of the old wall is visible.

Take a glance at the map. The sinews and muscles of the old inner city are formed by three parallel streets running from east to west into Red Square. Bisecting these streets at right angles are a maze of tiny lanes, whose names often give clues to their past—

Khrustalny (Glassware) Pereulok, Rybny (Fish) Pereulok, and so on.

In the nineteenth century, Moscow's chief trading
centre was in the area between what is now called 25th
October Street* and Razin Street. Beneath many of
these buildings are vast warehouses (and, some say,
tunnels that lead in and out of the Kremlin), made
possible because of the area's elevation above the
Moscow River.

Because many of these streets nowadays house government offices and ministries, they are always crowded.
A good time to visit the inner city is either early morning or early evening. From G.U.M. walk down to 25th
October Street and turn right.

Three centuries ago this was not so much a trading
street as the centre of intellectual and religious life in
the city. Just where you made the turn from Red Square
there once stood Kazan Cathedral. It was demolished
after the Revolution.

First look at No. 9, which long ago was the **Za-
Ikono-Spassky** (Behind the Icon of the Redeemer)
Monastery, founded in 1660. Here, in the late seven-
teenth century, was housed Russia's first institute of
higher learning. It was in this place that Michael
Lomonosov, founder of Moscow University, studied.

There were once many churches and monasteries
on this little street. Most are now gone, but the
Epiphany Monastery's eighteenth-century baroque

* In commemoration of the Bolshevik seizure of power
on that date in 1917.

church has survived. You will find this on your right, down Kuibyshev Pereulok.

Continuing along 25th October Street, you come to No. 15. This is the Printing House of the Synod, the oldest such establishment in Russia, founded in 1562 by Ivan the Terrible.

Take another look back down this charming street. The walls are peeling, the brickwork needs fixing up, and there is altogether too much traffic, but it remains one of the most lovable streets in Moscow. One hopes it will be preserved.

Looking down the street, you can see New Square. Until 1930 the street was blocked by the ancient Illinskiye Gate in the Kitai-Gorod wall; this was all knocked down during the modernization of New Square. Do not continue down the street but turn around and walk to the corner where the old Stock Exchange stands. This is Rybny Pereulok—"Fish Lane."

Go down this little alleyway, which provides a pleasant reminder of Old Moscow. Here Muscovites once bought their sturgeon, carp, and caviar. In the winter months the fish would be heaped up and shaped into walls, the interstices being filled with snow. Lyall, in his *History of Moscow*, recalls seeing a prodigious Beluga sturgeon, weighing 2,450 pounds, in this market.

Nowadays Rybny Pereulok is only a short cut for pedestrians and traffic. At its end you come to Razin Street.

Of the three main thoroughfares of the Kitai-Gorod, Razin Street is the one lying furthest south. Nowadays the houses on this street are almost all used as office buildings for various government enterprises.

At No. 18 is an old Russian boyar house, reputedly

the birthplace of Michael Romanov, the first of the Romanov tsars. It was built in 1565, but what you now see before you is a heavily restored version of the original building. Inside is an interesting exhibition of Russian art of the seventeenth and eighteenth centuries.

Next door is the former **Znamensky Monastery,** dating from the seventeenth century.

Now if you retrace your steps, you will find yourself on the south side of Red Square. Turn left, and continue downhill towards the river.

On your left now will be the enormous white jumble of stone and glass that is the Hotel Rossiya (Russia). Once more, it is worth recalling that you are on top of a very ancient hill. During the excavations for the Rossiya, archaeologists uncovered artifacts dating back to mediaeval times. A treasure trove of ancient Russia from the twelfth to the seventeenth century was recovered from this site. Today, the imposing Rossiya stands here within a landscaped miniature park.

At one time, also, there stood here some of the most fetid slums in the world. Before 1917 this district, then known as Zaryadiye, was a breeding ground of vice and disease, a terrifying place at night.

From the steps of the Rossiya, look towards the Kremlin. Directly in front of you, on the rise of the hill, is a beautiful apricot-hued church that has been lovingly restored in recent years. This is the tiny sixteenth-century **Church of the Conception of Anne, the Church of the Georgian Virgin.** It is no longer an active place of worship.

The Rossiya stands on the Moskvoretskaya Embankment. On your right, as you continue towards the river, is the Kremlin Embankment. Directly ahead is the

Moskvoretsky Most (Bridge), completed in 1936. It was designed by Alexei Shchusev, the architect whose most famous work is the Lenin Mausoleum.

During the Revolution this area was the scene of bitter fighting as workers from the industrial district on the far side of the bridge fought their way across on their way to the Kremlin.

If you care to take a photograph, you can get one of the best views of the Kremlin from this vantage point.

A leisurely stroll up the hill will bring you back to Red Square.

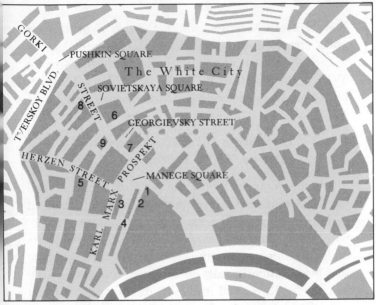

1 Tomb of the Unknown Soldier
2 Alexander Garden
3 Central Exhibition Hall
4 Trinity Bridge
5 Tchaikovsky Conservatoire
6 Moscow Art Theatre
7 Council of Ministers
  Building
8 City Hall
9 Central Telegraph Office

Walk Three: Manege Square, Herzen Street, and Gorkovo

(Time: 1½ hours)

This walk takes you through the Byely Gorod, or White City, the third great division of ancient Moscow. Today a stretch of green boulevards has taken the place of the whitewashed wall that, in the sixteenth century, surrounded the White City. As you can see by a glance at the map, the shape is roughly that of a horseshoe, with its ends running into the Moscow River.

From Red Square, walk north and bear left at the

State History Museum, where there is a little street going steeply downhill. Follow this and turn left.

Directly in front of you, at the corner of the Kremlin Wall, is the **Tomb of the Unknown Soldier**. Here lies buried one of the defenders of Moscow who died during World War II. The inscription reads:

> *Thy name is unknown, thy exploit is immortal. To the Fallen, 1941–45.*

We are going to follow the western Kremlin Wall via the **Alexander Garden**, perhaps the most beautiful park in all Moscow. It is exceptionally well maintained, with vivid plantings of flowers and shrubs. As you pass under the lime trees, you are actually walking where the old Kremlin moat once flowed. This was the Neglinnaya River, and it didn't just disappear. Around 1820, Tsar Alexander I ordered it put under ground in conduits, and that is where it is today.

The enormous square on your right is the **Manege** ("Riding") **Square,** and the large mustard-colored building with 80 white columns is the **Central Exhibition Hall**. It was built in the first quarter of the nineteenth century to commemorate Russia's victory over Napoleon in 1812. A hundred years ago Hector Berlioz conducted an orchestra and choir of 700 under its rafters. An audience of 12,000 applauded him. Wrote Berlioz later: "It is the biggest impression I have ever made in my life." In the 1890's, Nicholas II turned the building into a drill hall for his troops, and when Lenin came to power, the government turned it into an indoor parking garage for a period.

As you continue your walk through the Alexander Garden, observe that it is actually divided into two halves by the looming white bridge ahead of you. This is the **Trinity (Troitskaya) Bridge,** which once spanned the now-buried Neglinnaya River. As you can readily see, it connects the **Kutafya Tower** (to your right and leading to the street) and the **Trinity (Troitskaya) Tower,** the Kremlin's tallest (262 feet to the top of the red star). It was across this bridge that Napoleon's troops entered the Kremlin for what turned out to be only a brief stay.

When you go under the bridge, exit to your right. Cross the street towards the Central Exhibition Hall, but *don't jaywalk*—you can get an instant fine from the militiaman on duty. You should now have the rear of the Exhibition Hall on your right. Keep on walking and cross **Karl Marx Prospekt** towards the Metro entrance across the street. You are going to your right, but pause for a moment in front of the building next to the Metro, directly opposite the Exhibition Hall. Here are located the **Reception Rooms of the Presidium of the USSR** and the setting for many diplomatic gatherings.

Although the road is wide, the sidewalk is narrow here, and you will have to get used to Moscow jostling. Crowds will be one of your lasting impressions of this city, and this is a particularly busy spot. People are in a hurry, so watch out for their elbows.

Proceed down Karl Marx Prospekt in the direction of Manege Square. On your left, about a hundred yards along, is what might be described as the downtown branch of Moscow University. The correct title is **Moscow State University, Old Building,** and in the courtyard is a statue of its founder, Michael Lomonosov. Alexander Pushkin said of Lomonosov: "He established our first university. To put it better, he himself was our first university." Built at the end of the eighteenth century by the great Russian architect Matzvei Kazakov, it is in the classical tradition.

Take another look at Manege Square again before you move off. Imagine what this is like on November 7, when the Soviet armed forces stage their massive parade. The Manege then becomes an enormous staging area filled with rockets, tanks, and troops by the thousands.

Turn left at the next street corner. This is **Herzen Street**, named after Alexander Herzen, the liberal socialist whose anti-tsarist writings forced him to spend much of his life in exile.

This is uphill all the way, but if you are feeling hungry you can get a hot pie, a soft drink, or an ice cream from a street vendor here. You get the authentic feeling of Moscow along this street: old men with shaven heads reading wall newspapers, students hurrying between lectures, shoppers in pursuit of this or that bargain.

In the wedge of land between Karl Marx Prospekt and Tverskoy Boulevard is a tangle of lanes and tree-shaded streets lined with old family homes that Tolstoy once described in *War and Peace*. This is the true old Moscow of the merchants and aristocratic families.

Let us proceed up Herzen Street. You will find the **Tchaikovsky Conservatoire** about halfway up the street on your left, at No. 13. It was once the mansion of a duchess. Notice the statue of Tchaikovsky, then observe the railing that is designed in the form of musical notes from his work. This is Moscow's Carnegie Hall, where just about everyone in the world of Russian music has performed. David Oistrakh studied here, as did Rachmaninoff, Khachaturian, Rostropovich, and Scriabin. Tchaikovsky himself was a professor of music here.

Keep heading up the street and you will come to **Tverskoy Boulevard**. At this corner once stood the Nikitsky Gate, and here too was the old wall of the White City. Centuries ago this was the beginning of the great highway to Novgorod, the oldest of all Russian cities.

Turn right here on your way to Gorkovo. Moscow boulevards are not simply streets planted with trees (part of the city's anti-pollution program) as is the case in Paris; they are long strips of real parks running along the central section of wide streets. Notice how they are railed off from the traffic.

So now here we are at the intersection of Tverskoy and Gorkovo. Directly ahead, across Gorkovo, is **Pushkin Square** with the statue of Russia's greatest poet. Cross the street by means of the underground walkway. Here there is a small park with plenty of benches.

No one has ever successfully translated Pushkin's poetry into English, and no one ever will. But give a moment to Pushkin before leaving this square, for he was his country's Walt Whitman, Carl Sandburg, and Thoreau in one, a prodigious human being whose writings echo the soul and fire of essential Russia.

You are now on your way back to Red Square. Walk south on Gorkovo, which runs rather steeply downhill at this point. **Gorkovo**, or **Gorki Street**, was formerly known as the Tverskaya.

After 1917 the Soviets renamed it after the celebrated writer Maxim Gorki. This street is both the Broadway and the Fifth Avenue of Moscow. During the

1930's the street was widened and, through an ingenious building technique, many of the buildings were moved as much as 160 feet back from their original locations.

As you stroll down Gorkovo notice, on the left-hand side of the street, **Yeliseyevsky's Food Shop**, at No. 14. Nowadays it is simply called Food Shop No. 1, but before the Revolution, Yeliseyevsky's was the most renowned food shop in Moscow, frequented by the very wealthy. If you don't want to shop now, at least duck your head in the door and look around at its unusual interior. (See page 274.)

The bookstore called **Druzhba** (Friendship) is on the opposite side of the street. Here you can find marvellous art books (amongst many other kinds), all for a few roubles apiece.

A few hundred feet down on the left you come to **Sovietskaya Square**, the Square of the Soviets. The statue is that of **Yuri Dolgoruky** (George Long-Arms), a feudal lord who is regarded as the founder of Moscow. Behind is a public garden, and beyond you will see a statue of Lenin, in front of the **Lenin Institute**, the principal center for the study of Lenin and Marx in the USSR.

Stand in front of the statue of Yuri Dolgoruky and turn around. The purple-red-hued building opposite is the **Mossoviet**, the House of the Moscow Soviet, the town hall of Moscow.

Small though it is, it has seen a lot of history. Before 1917 it was the palace of Moscow's Governor-General. It was originally built in the eighteenth century with stones from the wrecked wall of the White City. Lenin often spoke from the small balcony on

the second floor,* and De Gaulle also spoke from this
same spot during one of his visits to Moscow—a
tremendous honor in Soviet eyes.

Cross Gorkovo to the City Hall side and proceed in
the direction of Red Square downhill and southwards.
This is a good place to take a photograph, for the street
really slopes downhill at this point.

The large, Victorian-looking apartment houses on
your right were actually completed in 1950. A lot of
what the British refer to as "Top People" and Americans as "V.I.P.'s" live in these apartments. Take a
look at the polished granite that has been used to face
the street level. A quarry full of these polished stones
was captured by the Russians toward the end of World
War II; the Nazis had planned to use them for a monument celebrating the downfall of the Soviet Union!
With a fine sense of irony, Moscow city planners used
them instead in postwar reconstruction or new construction.

Further down the street on the right is an enormous
gray building with large windows and a clock and a globe
above the entrance. This is Ivan Rerberg's **Central
Telegraph Office**, designed in the constructivist style of
the early Revolutionary period. When Ian Fleming,
author of the James Bond books, was a young reporter
covering the Moscow Trials in the 1930's, it was in this
office that he filed his reports. To this day, every
foreign correspondent who works in Moscow uses the
building. Inside, reporters wait their turn each evening
for a telephone connection to their offices around the

* The second floor to Americans, the first to Britons.

world. If you wish to send a cable overseas, this is the place.

Directly across from the Telegraph Office is one of Moscow's most famous theatres—on a side street with the jaw-breaking name of Proyezd Khudozhestvennovo Teatra (Art Theatre Lane). This is Stanislavsky's **Moscow Art Theatre**.

The next side street as you continue down Gorkovo —you enter through the archway—is Georgievsky. Here will be found the **Glinka Central Museum of Musical Culture** (see page 167). The house once belonged to the Troekurov boyars, one of Moscow's wealthiest merchant families, and is a marvellous example of seventeenth-century architecture.

Return to Gorkovo; across the street on your right is the new Hotel Intourist, and on the corner next to it is the charming old Hotel National. In the stretch of Gorkovo between the Telegraph Office and the National there are a number of quick-service restaurants. Here you can buy a meat pie or a glass of buttermilk for a few kopecks. Also worth remembering is the **International Post Office**, located on the ground floor of the National. Here you will be able to send and receive foreign mail (see page 21).

As you reach the junction of Gorkovo and Karl Marx Prospekt, look at the large gray building opposite the Hotel National. Here are the offices of the Council of Ministers—the administrative nerve center of the Soviet Union. It is from here that the country's superbureaucrats give day-to-day direction to its affairs, in accordance with the decisions and policies laid down within the Kremlin. If the grain harvest fails in Kazakhstan, if steel production falls, if consumption of consumer goods rises too rapidly, you can be sure that some minister in this glum-looking building will be on the telephone.

From this corner you can take the underground passage that will lead you under Manege Square into Revolution Square and the entrance to Red Square.

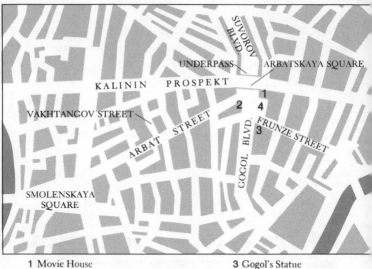

1 Movie House
2 Praga Restaurant (entire corner)

3 Gogol's Statue
4 Arbatskaya Metro Station

Walk Four: Kalinin Prospekt, Old Arbat, and a river ride to Gorki Park

(Time: 3 hours)

Follow the route of Walk Three as far as the corner of Kalinin and Karl Marx. Proceed north up Kalinin Prospekt. On your right is a somewhat old-fashioned department store. Across the street is the **Lenin Library**, the country's largest library.

Comparable to the Library of Congress in its scope, the Lenin owns a copy of *everything* published in the USSR—and a good deal else besides. A Western journalist (who may well be biased) says that this is the only place in Moscow with a back file of *The New York Times*; to read them, you need special permission. He says they are filed away under "Pornography."

There are more than 25 million books here in the 89

languages spoken within the Soviet Union's far-flung borders. There are 22 reading rooms, and about as many people come here in a single day as report for work at Ford's gigantic River Rouge plant—9,000. The Library, as you can see, occupies an entire city block and fronts four streets: Marx, Kalinin, Marx-Engels, and Frunze. Beyond the new building can be seen the outlines of the magnificent old library, known as **Pashkov House**.

As you may surmise from the buildings around you, what is now the beginning stretch of Kalinin Prospekt is one of the city's oldest thoroughfares.

The Sheremetyev family once lived in feudal splendor at No. 8, on the right-hand (east) side of the street. This mansion was built in 1780 by Guarenghi in the classical style. The airport where you arrived, Sheremetyevo, is built on only a fraction of the millions of acres that this enormously wealthy family once owned.

Few Muscovites are aware that this building now houses the **Kremlin Hospital**, where top party and government officials and Soviet leaders receive medical treatment.

Across Kalinin is a most interesting house. This is No. 5, built in 1787 by one of Imperial Russia's greatest architects, Matzvei Kazakov. The house is described in *War and Peace* as the home of Pierre Bezukhov. Today it is the **Alexei Shchusev State Architectural Research Museum**, well worth a visit if you are interested in the development of Russian architecture. In Tolstoy's day this was the most fashionable quarter of Moscow.

Continuing your stroll up the left-hand (west) side of Kalinin Prospekt, you come to No. 9, described in Tolstoy's great novel as the **Bolkonsky house**, and once the home of Prince Volkonsky, Tolstoy's grandfather.

Notice the odd-looking house across the street. It was built in the last century by a merchant family called the Morozovs. It has been described as Portuguese Renaissance in style, but no one from Portugal would be likely to recognise it as such. In any event, the Morozovs clearly had a good time building it. Immediately after the 1917 revolution the house was turned into a headquarters for the "Proletkult" group of Soviet writers and artists. Nowadays it is known as **Friendship House** and is used to entertain foreign visitors to the Soviet Union. If you are with an official delegation, you will almost certainly visit this place.

Keeping to the left-hand side of the street, you will come upon a cinema with the almost unpronounceable name of **Khudozhestvenny** (Art). The first Soviet sound film, *A Start in Life,* had its debut here in March 1930. At all times of the day there are flower sellers here with small bouquets of roses and gladioli wrapped in cellophane for a rouble or so a bunch. Fresh flowers are a rarity in Moscow and florists practically nonexistent, so every faded bloom is worth its weight in roubles.

To our left ahead of us is the **Arbat,** a quarter of Moscow that looks as though it came full-blown out of one of Gogol's novels. And no wonder, for Gogol lived and worked here, and so did many other writers and artists. Arbat takes its name from an ancient Arabic word meaning "district"; centuries ago this was the trading place of merchants who bought or bartered with the Near East. At the present time there seems to be a head-on collision brewing between old Arbat and brand-new Kalinin Prospekt. A good deal of the old quarter has been knocked down to make way for productions of the new egg-crate school of architecture.

But the planners have promised that what is left will be preserved.

You are now at **Arbatskaya Square,** which is the focal point of a semicircle of famous boulevards that make up the **Boulevard Ring.** Before crossing Gogol Boulevard, let's briefly explore the street to your left. This is Frunze Street, named after one of Lenin's top generals (he died under mysterious circumstances after Stalin came to power). Dostoevsky was a lodger on this street; you'll find his old house at No. 9. A bit closer to the square is No. 14, where Tchaikovsky and Nikolai Rubinstein lived. As you head back to the square, you are fairly certain to notice soldiers walking about on various errands. The reason is simple: on the corner of Frunze Street is the Ministry of Defense, and it is jammed from floor to roof with bemedalled generals. About a block away is the Navy Department.

At Gogol Boulevard, you will see the statue of the writer. This is a new work of art put up in 1952, for the writer's centenary. The powers-that-be thought the old statue looked much too gloomy, so they added a smile and a bit of energy to the new version.

There is another bit of history you might be interested to learn. You are standing on almost the exact location where, in 1812, the vanguard of Napoleon's army entered Moscow. In those days the walls of the White City were between this point and the Arbat Gate. It was here that the French positioned their cannon and destroyed the Trinity (Troitskaya) Gate of the Kremlin.

If you want to see the original Gogol statue, you can make a quick diversion. Cross Kalinin Prospekt by means of the pedestrian tunnel (see map) and, in the inner courtyard of No. 7a Suvorov Boulevard, you will discover the older version, which portrays the author of *Dead Souls* in deep melancholy. It was in this house that Gogol wrote *The Inspector General* and many other masterpieces.

To get across Gogol Boulevard in any direction, you use the pedestrian tunnels. If you do not visit Gogol's residence, then directly across from where you are standing is the corner of **Arbat Street** and **Kalinin Prospekt.** The corner building, which occupies the entire block, is the well-known **Praga Restaurant** (see page 219). Arbat Street is the district's chief commercial artery; it begins here and runs west to **Smolenskaya Square.** Where Kalinin stands today there was once an extension of old Arbat Street, barely more than 7 feet wide. The great thoroughfare of today is 260 feet wide. Walk up Arbat, leaving Kalinin behind. You are now entering one of the oldest quarters of the city. Settlements of craftsmen and "His Majesty's outbuildings" were located here in the sixteenth and seventeenth centuries. The Tsar's cooks once lived on old Povarsky Street (*povar* meaning "cook"). You will also find streets named Kalashny (a fancy kind of bread); Skaterny (table-cloth); Stolovaya (dining room); Plotnikov (carpenter); and Serebryany (silversmith).

These side streets and those beyond, along the higher reaches of Arbat Street, are well worth exploring. They are filled with old mansions and well-kept gardens that once belonged to the nobility. A Soviet guidebook notes that: "The Soviet Government turned these mansions of the aristocracy over to the children, museums, institutes, and public organizations." (As for the aristocrats, many of them ended up driving taxi-cabs in Paris.)

You might want to pause for a moment at No. 12: Pushkin lived here in 1826. Across the street, at No. 11, is the home of Alexander Scriabin, now a museum.

About halfway up Arbat Street are the cross-streets **Maly** (Little) **Nikolopeskovsky** and **Bolshoi** (Great) **Nikolopeskovsky.** These form the borders of a characteristic old aristocratic corner of Moscow, the **Sobachaya Ploshchadka** (Dog Square). The name is derived from the kennels of the Tsar's estate, which were located here in the seventeenth century. Bolshoi Nikolopeskovsky has been renamed Vakhtangov Street, after the great actor-director of the early Soviet theatre.

The whole of the Arbat area has a prevailing yellowness. Whole streets of houses are painted yellow. In between are other houses painted apricot, pistachio, or chocolate-brown. You are now in the heart of what the Russian writer Isaac Babel called "tavern Moscow" —only the taverns have long since vanished. Communists don't approve of excessive drinking; the horrendous "vodka palaces" of yesteryear are no more.

Walking along Arbat will give you a vivid sense not only of the pre-Revolutionary past but of the Soviet present. Notice the banners, the slogans and signs, that are everywhere around you. Moscow (as we have observed before) is a puritanical, hard-working city, where achievement is measured by performance. One slogan that is a particular favourite is СЛАВА КПСС!— GLORY TO THE COMMUNIST PARTY OF THE SOVIET UNION!; you will see it in every part of the city.

Nowadays Arbat Street is chiefly a shopping thoroughfare, full of interesting shops. You can buy antiques and second-hand items at the two special commission-shops (see page 266) on the left-hand side of the street —No. 19 and No. 32.

If you continue all the way up Arbat to **Smolenskaya Square**, the only building of interest you'll find there is the skyscraper of the Foreign Ministry, built in the Stalin Gothic style. But it is not really worth the visit. Retrace your footsteps towards Kalinin Prospekt. Just a few yards from the Praga Restaurant, on your left, is the best poster shop in the city.

Kalinin Prospekt

Some Muscovites call it the city's "false tooth." But others point with pride to this mile-long grand concourse as Moscow's liveliest quarter. Built in 1963, it runs from Karl Marx Prospekt westward, connecting the centre of the city with Kutuzovsky Prospekt and the Mozhaisk Highway. It is named after Michael Kalinin, who for nearly a quarter of a century was Chairman of the Presidium of the Supreme Soviet.

Turn left at the Praga Restaurant and proceed up Kalinin. On your left you can see a group of four 24- and 25-story apartment and office buildings flanking the street. You may walk around Moscow for weeks, but never see so many stylish, attractive girls as you'll espy here. Further along, also on your left, is the **Arbat** (АРБАТ) (see page 214), one of Moscow's best, and most expensive, restaurant-cabarets. Downstairs is a cocktail bar, usually crowded with young, well-dressed Muscovites. Well worth a visit.

Cross the street via the underground pedestrian tunnel hard by the Arbat, and you emerge almost directly in front of the city's largest bookstore, **The House of Books** (ДОМ КНИГИ). Inside you will find a wide selection of books (many in foreign languages), records, posters, and postcards.

Next door is the 2,500-seat **October** (ОКТЯБРЬ) movie house. Take time out to look at the huge mosaic mural that forms its façade. The subject is the birth of the Soviet state (for the Soviet people, October is a month of special significance, a symbol of universal progress). The mosaic compositions—like film sequences—reproduce historic events: the storming of the Winter Palace, the Civil War, the early Five Year Plans, and so forth.

If you were to continue along Kalinin, you would come to Kutuzovsky Prospekt. It is recommended that you turn around, however, and return slowly towards Red Square. Just beyond the House of Books on your left is the city's newest supermarket. Built along Western lines, it has checkout counters and shopping baskets (but no sales promotions). Nothing to prevent you from walking inside and doing some comparison shopping of your own (you can buy French cognac and fine wines here at reasonable prices). Other shops in the vicinity include **The Enchantress** (ЧАРО-ДЕЙКА), a barber shop with 30 chairs (average price for shave, haircut, and shampoo: 4 roubles); **Gifts** (ПОДАРКИ); **Salon for Newly-Weds** (САЛОН ДЛЯ НОВОБРАЧНЫХ); **Clothes à la Mode** (МОДНАЯ ОДЕЖДА); and **Amateur Cameraman** (ЛЮБИТЕЛЬ ФОТОГРАФ). All of these shops are, of course, run by the state. The only private enterprise you will see in Moscow is the street vendors who sell vegetables and flowers from the kerbside.

Kalinin to the Moscow River

You are now confronted with multiple choices:

(a) You are tired and want to return to the hotel. In that case, hail a taxi—there are plenty hereabouts.

(b) You want to skip the river ride and walk back to Red Square. Easy: just continue in your present direction and retrace footsteps down Kalinin Prospekt, across Manege Square, and along the sidewalks adjacent to the Alexander Garden, and you are back where you began.

(c) You still have enough energy to walk to the **Kievskaya River Station** (about thirty minutes). Proceed up Arbat Street, through Smolenskaya Square, across the Borodinsky Bridge, and bear left. About four minutes from the bridge you reach the embarkation point. Can't be missed.

(d) You want to take a taxi to the river station. Ask Intourist (or an English-speaking clerk in the House of Books on Kalinin Prospekt) to write out the address for you. Show this to the taxi driver. The ride will cost about 1 rouble.

Kievskaya River Station to Gorki Park

This is an inspiring ride on a summer's day. At the embankment, take a motor boat going to the right. On your left you will see the spires and towers of the **Novo-Devichy Convent.** As the river turns, you notice the **Lenin Hills** with **Moscow University** in the distance. Then comes the **Lenin Stadium** and the river turns once more. The motor boat glides beneath the **Andreyevskaya Bridge** and to your right is Moscow's most beloved patch of greenery—Gorki Park. (For a full description, turn to page 172.)

Of course, if you only want to enjoy the ride, you can stay aboard the motor boat. A few minutes more cruising on the river will bring you to the Kremlin (on your left) and you can leave the motor boat at the **Moskvoretsky Bridge**. From here it is but a few minutes' walk to Red Square.

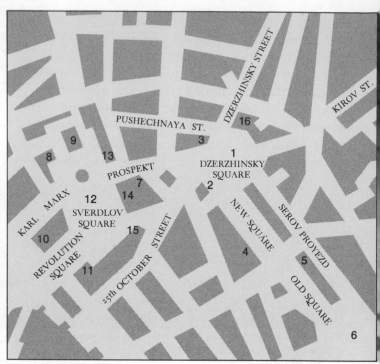

1 Memorial to Dzerzhinsky
2 Dzerzhinsky Square Metro Station
3 Detsky Mir (Children's World)
4 Museum of History of Moscow
5 Polytechnic Museum
6 Plevna Monument
7 Memorial to Ivan Fyodorov
8 Children's Theatre

9 Bolshoi Theatre
10 Hotel Moskva
11 Lenin Museum
12 Marx Statue
13 Maly Theatre
14 Hotel Metropole
15 Kitai Gorod Wall
16 Lubyanka

Walk Five: Eight Squares in Central Moscow
(Time: 4 hours)

Leaving Red Square behind you, walk down **25th October Street** (see the map), keeping to the right-hand side of the street. At the first corner come to a full stop.

Directly ahead is **Dzerzhinsky Square**; to the eye,

more like a traffic circle than a square, because no less than nine streets converge at this point. What the traffic is whizzing around is the 36-foot high statue of **Felix Dzerzhinsky**—the man who played Lenin's J. Edgar Hoover as head of the Cheka, the forerunner of the KGB and, as it is known to party members, "the sword of the Revolution."

Beyond the statue you will observe, on the rise of a hill, a mustardy-yellow building that stands quite alone. Notice the neat white curtains at each window, the shiny brass fittings on the doors. It looks like (and at the time was) a turn-of-the-century insurance office. But this is the notorious **Lubyanka**, a fearsome place in Stalin's day.

Nowadays it is the headquarters for the Central Administration of State Security of the USSR (KGB), with its internal prisons and interrogation rooms. In the United States particularly, but throughout the Western world in general, we have all got an obsession with the KGB. Like the CIA, M.I.5, or Deuxième Bureau, it is responsible for counterintelligence, espionage, and security. It was the KGB, for instance, who trapped the British spy Greville Wynne. He was brought to this building on Lubyanka Street in 1962, eventually given eight years hard labor, and released in exchange for a Russian spy after two years in prison. In his book, *Contact on Gorky Street*, Wynne describes the daily routine inside Lubyanka, including exercise on the flat roof that you see ahead of you. From this, and other buildings in Moscow, the KGB fulfills the same functions as the Central Intelligence Agency; at the same time it possesses police powers like those of the FBI.

It is the absence of a tradition of judicial independence that makes the KGB loom larger in Soviet society than its counterparts do in the West. During the 1930's especially—the Stalin era—this agency had enormous power and the building at 22 Lubyanka Street was, quite literally, a symbol of national dread.

You are standing almost in front of **Dzerzhinsky Square Metro Station.** Turn right, walk past it, and you come to **New** (Novaya) **Square,** which is actually more a street than a square. It is wide and well laid out and leads to the **Old** (Staraya) **Square.** Both squares extend along the walls of the old Kitai-Gorod. As you proceed in the direction of the Old Square, you pass the **Museum of the History and Reconstruction of Moscow** on your right. This is well worth a brief visit, an absolutely fascinating exhibit of Moscow's growth during the last eight hundred years.

On your left is another of those vast architectural hulks, a building in the old Russian style called the **Polytechnic Museum.** This is the Soviet counterpart to Washington's Smithsonian. One of the most interesting exhibits here is a fully working model of a coal mine. In 1917 the Moscow Military Revolutionary Committee (the military group that directed the workers in their assault on Tsarist positions) was headquartered here.

Passing the museum, you cross **Kuibyshev Street.** Here begins **Old Square.** It is long and narrow and slopes gently towards the Moscow River. Contrary to popular opinion, Leonid Brezhnev does not work in the Kremlin, but in this square where, at No. 4, you will find the offices of the **Central Committee of the Communist Party of the Soviet Union.** Next door are the

Moscow Regional and Moscow City Committees of the CP. The Red Flag always flies above these offices.

The Old Square runs into Nogina Square and you start back through Nogina to return to Dzerzhinsky Square. Off Nogina is a wide boulevard, **Bogdan Khelnitsky**. Notice the monument on the corner, in front of the Polytechnic Museum. This commemorates the Russian dead who fell in the battle of Plevna during the Russo-Turkish War of 1877–8.

Walk down Bogdan Khelnitsky (the Polytechnic Museum is on your left across the street) and cross over, turning left on **Serov Proyezd**. Intourist may be correct in saying that this street is named after a famed Soviet flier; many Muscovites, however, believe it is named for Ivan Serov, a prominent KGB official who was once head of SMERSH (James Bond readers are familiar with that interesting counterespionage organization). In the Khrushchev era Serov was Chairman of the KGB, the direct counterpart of Allen Dulles at the CIA.

On the left-hand side of Serov Proyezd, at No. 3, the great poet **Vladimir Mayakovsky** had his study from 1919 to 1930. It was Mayakovsky's habit to leave his apartment in the Brik house (see page 166) and walk several miles each day to this apartment, which he used as a kind of poetry studio. He would compose as he walked, jotting lines and phrases down in a pocket notebook. He was always having chats with inanimate objects, which gave his work an anthropomorphic quality. As he strode down Gorkovo to just about where you are standing at the present moment, this marvellous "poet of the Revolution" would compose such poems as "PARIS (A Chat with the Eiffel Tower)":

> *Come to Moscow!*
> *Moscow*
> *is so*
> *spacious.*
> *You,*
> *everyone will want in their street!*
> *Everyone*
> *will adore you.*
> *A hundred times a day or so*
> *we'll polish your steel and copper*
> *like the sun.*

Now you are back in Dzerzhinsky Square. All around you is workaday Moscow going about its business. Across from where you are standing is Kirov Street. But we are not going this way. Instead, we cross the square to visit **Detsky Mir** (Children's World) with its eight glass arches. This is a unique department store catering only to youngsters. (See page 288.) Join the crowd and look around inside. From the upper floors you can get an overall view of Dzerzhinsky Square and see as far as the Moscow River. Between the fifteenth and eighteenth centuries the site of Detsky Mir was occupied by the Moscow Cannon Works. In fact, the street that runs along the east side of the store is still named **Pushechnaya** (Cannon) **Street**. The great Tsar Cannon on the Kremlin grounds was cast here.

Leaving Detsky Mir, go to the right down Karl Marx Prospekt. Across the street, at the corner of 25th October Street, is the statue of **Ivan Fyodorov**, Russia's first printer. He founded the Tsar's printer's yard in 1562 and the first printed Russian book, *The Apostle*, came off its presses in 1563. In 1703 it was the printing plant of the first Russian newspaper—*The Bulletin of Military and Other Affairs.* No more than fifty books were printed in Russia during the sixteenth century; today every fourth book printed in the world is a Soviet book—a reminder that Russia's is a very print-oriented culture.

Take a quick glance at the map and get your bearings. In front of you is the nearest thing Moscow has got to compare with Broadway or the West End. Before the Revolution this was known as Theatre Square. After 1917 it was renamed **Sverdlov Square,** in honor of one of Lenin's close revolutionary associates. This is a fine place to visit on a summer evening and just sit and enjoy the people and activity around you. Americans, in particular, never cease to be amazed that a visitor can sit here at any hour of the day or night and never be molested.

Turn right into the square. Ahead of you is the **Bolshoi Theatre.** Make your way down to it and stand under its great portico. The tall stuccoed columns are surmounted by four rearing horses harnessed to the chariot of Apollo. This delightful edifice is a monument to the Imperial Age. Inside, it is all gilt and red plush. There are hundreds of stories about the Bolshoi. In the 1850's Richard Wagner conducted here and amazed Muscovites by facing the orchestra instead of the audience (as was the custom in Russia at the time). Nicholas and Alexandra once sat in the theatre's Royal Box, and Lenin made his last public address from its stage on November 20, 1922.

With your back to the portico, look around the

square. On its right-hand side, where it joins Karl Marx Prospekt, is the famous **Children's Theatre** (Detsky Teatr), where plays written for children are often acted and performed by them.

Now, head down the left-hand side of Sverdlov Square towards Karl Marx Prospekt. On your left is the **Maly Theatre** (remember that *Maly* means "little," *Bolshoi* "big" or "great"). The Maly is occasionally called Ostrovsky House, for it has produced nearly all the plays of this greatly loved Russian playwright, whose statue stands in front of the theatre.

You are now at the corner of Karl Marx Prospekt: the square, as you can easily see, has two public gardens. Cross the street. In front of the larger of the two gardens there is yet another monument, a 220-ton job unveiled in 1961 to honor Karl Marx. The sculptor, Lev Kerbel, won the Lenin Prize for it. The granite represents the great man as The Greatest Teacher. Marx is leaning on a rostrum passionately affirming the idea of Communism. His well-known slogan, "Workers of the world, unite!" is inscribed on the plinth.

Turn into the green park, and you are confronted with ordinary Muscovites enjoying the sunshine. Here you will see a rather nice fountain dating from 1835 and designed by Ivan Vitali. To your left, occupying the entire block, is the dear old **Hotel Metropole,** a vast, green-hued, turn-of-the-century piece of architecture. Completed in 1903, it was then the latest word in hotel design. It has any number of interesting features, including the offices of Chase Manhattan, the first American bank to open in Moscow after President Nixon's trip in 1972. Make your way across the street—watch out for the traffic!—and stare up at the large majolica mural that ornaments the façade. Known as "The Dream Princess," it is a replica of a drawing by the Russian painter Michael Vrubel. A closer look reveals a most curious inscription above the second floor:

The old story again—on completing a house, you discover that you've learned something.

For a time shortly after the October Revolution the Metropole was used as the Second House of the Soviets. The American journalist John Reed covered many of Lenin's speeches here. In recent years Intourist has been trying to modernize the place, but inside, among the patchwork of renovation, you can still enjoy some of the old splendor. In the great dining room are crystal chandeliers with plenty of sparkle, cut-glass mirrors, Art Nouveau lamps, and lots of palms. Lunch here is a nostalgic reminder of a bygone era.

As you leave the Metropole, look to your left, where there is an almost perfect view of the old red brick Kitai-Gorod wall with its swallow-tail battlements.

With your back to the Metropole walk to your left, cross the street and continue walking away from the hotel. You are now approaching **Revolution Square** (consult the map), which, like New Square, is more a street—as you can see—than a square. The letter M above the building ahead of you on your left indicates the Metro station. The building next door is the **V. I. Lenin Museum** (see page 160). It is hard to tell where Sverdlov leaves off and Revolution Square begins; they merge at the Metro. The Lenin Museum (formerly the Moscow Duma), built in 1880, is in the pseudo-Russian architectural style. In 1917 there was a ferocious battle fought in this spot as White Guards loyal to the Tsar held off the Communists for days. Finally a Communist artillery battery near the Bolshoi Theatre put an end to their resistance.

Across the street is the old **Grand Hotel** (today a part of the Hotel Moskva). In its heyday it was the finest hotel in the city. Tchaikovsky, Rimsky-Korsakov, and Anton Chekhov signed the guest register. So too did Theodore Dreiser (who once wrote from Moscow: "I have seen the Future, and it works!"). You can buy postcards and magazines at the street kiosks around the Metro station (notice the cards with illustrations of Russian movie stars and cosmonauts). Flower sellers also traditionally station themselves here with their carnations, gladioli, and roses.

As you pass the Lenin Museum, turn left and you will find yourself back in Red Square.

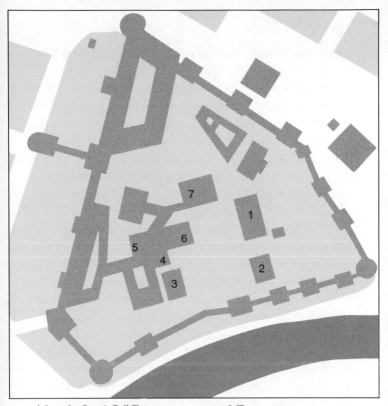

1 Ivan the Great's Bell Tower
  (and adjacent building)
2 Cathedral of the Archangel
3 Cathedral of the Annunciation
4 Granovitaya Palata

5 Terems
6 Cathedral of the Assumption
7 Patriarch's Residence
  & Cathedral of the
  Twelve Apostles

Walk Six: A first look inside the Kremlin—
from the Spassky Gate to Cathedral Square
(Time: 2 hours)

The Kremlin is at once the seat of government and
holy ground to all Russians. For long centuries it was
a forbidding and forbidden place. During Stalin's lifetime the "No Admittance" sign was up for everyone
except those who had official business. But nowadays
millions of visitors a year crowd the cobbled streets

within the Kremlin walls. Daily, from 10 a.m. to 6 p.m., you may enter freely. There is no admission fee.

It is an excellent idea to visit here with your Intourist guide. But one major purpose of this book is to give you a little independence of movement. You may want to preview your guided tour, or you may want to follow it up with a more leisurely walk-around on your own. As you will quickly observe, there are usually a number of guides showing tourists around at any given time, and you can always eavesdrop at the edge of the crowd.

From Red Square you enter the Kremlin through the Spassky Gate. Beyond it you find yourself in a city in miniature: cathedrals, palaces, theatres, and official buildings are here all squeezed within nearly two miles of unbroken walls. There are 19 decorative towers (built in the seventeenth century, when Moscow had ceased to be a fortress) and five gates.

Before proceeding, a word of caution: the Kremlin is not merely a tourist attraction; it is also the working place of the Soviet leadership. Consequently, quite a bit of it is out of bounds. Observe the white lines. If you step beyond them, be prepared for a warning whistle from a militiaman. Also keep off the grass, which is another forbidden zone.

Entering from Red Square, you walk up the cobble-stoned open space formerly known as the "Square of the Tsars." Just inside the gate, you will see on your right the **Kremlin Theatre**. This building was once—in Nicholas II's Russia—the Voznesensky Nunnery.

From here you can see, directly ahead of you, the Kremlin's highest structure, the 265-foot white-stone **Bell Tower of Ivan the Great**. It was built by Boris Godunov in 1600, and is contemporaneous with the

Taj Mahal. For centuries this was Moscow's tallest building and served as a watchtower. Napoleon and his marshals climbed to the top to get a twenty-mile view of the burning city. In Baedeker's time, visitors were allowed for twenty kopecks to do the same. Alas, you are no longer permitted to follow in their footsteps.

Near the base of the white Bell Tower is one of those marvellous believe-it-or-not sights that pop up everywhere in the Kremlin: the **Tsar Kolokol**, the "Tsar of Bells." It is over 20 feet high, weighs more than 200 tons, and is almost 60 feet in circumference. It is easily the biggest bell in the world, a tribute to early Russian gigantomania, and it has only a single flaw—it has never worked. This silent bell, which took two years to cast (1733–1735), was cracked during a great fire in 1737. All the same, there is something about it. Watch, and you will observe that almost everyone who views it feels compelled to touch its glossy crack.

Now that you have looked inside the world's largest bell, you are ready for the other half of the conversation-piece. Walk *back*, keeping to the grassy kerb, and you will arrive at the **Tsar Cannon**. It was cast in 1586 for Tsar Theodore, the feeble-minded son of Ivan the Terrible. The cannon balls are at least a yard in diameter, but no one ever fired the gun for fear it would blow up. If you examine it closely, you will find the Tsar's likeness engraved upon it.

Before proceeding, turn around, and you will see a triangular-shaped yellow building over which the Soviet flag is flying. Since 1918, this has been the seat of the Soviet government, but in Tsarist days it was the meeting place of the Imperial Senate. The building was designed by Matzvei Kazakov in 1788.

It was here that Lenin lived and worked. If you are a distinguished guest of the Soviet government, you can get permission to visit his third-floor study and private apartment. (If you're an ordinary visitor like the rest of us, don't despair—a replica complete in every detail can be seen in the Lenin Museum; see page 160). On this third floor today, the USSR Council of Ministers meets in much the same manner that the Cabinet meets with the President of the United States in the White House.

Cathedral Square

The heart of the city is the Kremlin, and the heart of the Kremlin is Cathedral Square, the oldest square in Moscow.

Walk around the Tsar Cannon and you will see a footpath that leads you gently downhill into the center of the square. On your right will be the **Cathedral of the Twelve Apostles**.

Stand with your back to the Cathedral and look into the square. Clockwise from left to right you will see:

1. The Bell Tower of Ivan the Great.
2. The Cathedral of the Archangel (almost facing you).
3. The Cathedral of the Annunciation (known as the Blagoveshchensky Cathedral in Russian).
4. The Granovitaya Palata (which adjoins the Grand Kremlin Palace at its rear).
5. The Terems (Women's Apartments). But note: all that can really be seen are the eleven golden domes.
6. The Cathedral of the Assumption (the Uspensky Cathedral in Russian).

7.   The Patriarch's Residence and the Cathedral of the Twelve Apostles.

All of what you see before you was completed by the eighteenth century. The tsars of Russia called this "Parade Square"; emperors were crowned here, and here foreign ambassadors made their first official appearance. Now let's explore the square.

The Bell Tower of Ivan the Great   The inscription around the golden cupola notes simply that the Bell Tower was erected in the year 1600 by Tsar Boris Godunov. Actually, work on the whole ensemble—the Bell Tower proper and an adjoining structure—was begun in 1505 by an Italian architect named Bon Friazin. In the vertical center of the latter building you can see the enormous, 70-ton Uspensky Bell. Napoleon's gunners knocked the top off this structure, and a near miss turned the Bell Tower proper slightly askew, giving it a nickname: "Ivan the Tipsy."

The Cathedral of the Archangel   Now make your way to the burial church of the tsars of Russia, whose respective likenesses are painted on the walls above each of their 46 tombs. Built in 1505–9 by the Italian architect Alevisio Novi, it is a mixture of traditional Russian architectural forms with the ornateness of the Italian Renaissance.

Once inside, be sure to examine the murals that represent the Last Judgement. Among the religious figures the artists have mingled various portraits of Russian tsars and princes.

All that was mortal of Imperial Russia's ruling figures is here entombed. Peter the Great is buried here. Close

by is the tomb of Ivan the Terrible and his elder son (killed by his father). As you gaze at these sepulchres, take a moment to ponder the fate of these men who stood at the pinnacle of Russian society. Few of this large collection of tsars, grand dukes, and princes seem to have died of natural causes; murder—by knife, by poison, by smothering—was usually the means of their precipitous exit from this world.

Make a point of examining the Iconostasis, or icon wall. The icons are of exceptional merit, the work of Andrei Rublev, Theophanus the Greek, and Prokhor of Gorodets.

The Cathedral of the Annunciation This is the wedding church of Russian princes and tsars, and also the place of their christening. The smallest of the Kremlin cathedrals, it is perhaps the most attractive. It contains magnificent murals dating back to the early sixteenth century. Do examine the iconostasis, which is a precious work of art. The icons of its second and third tiers were painted in 1405 by Andrei Rublev, and include an especially outstanding representation of the Archangel Michael.

Look down at the floors. As might be expected in an emperor's private church, these are composed of blocks of precious agate jasper—a present from the Shah of Persia.

As you leave, glance at the white stone portals which are adorned with carvings; then pause for an overall view of this nine-cupola gem that dates from the fourteenth century.

The Granovitaya Palata (Palace of Facets) The Granovitaya Palata, which fronts Cathedral Square, is the oldest public building extant in Moscow. Strongly reminiscent of the Pitti Palace in Florence, it was constructed in 1487–1491 by Russian craftsmen working under the direction of the Italian architects Marco Ruffo and Pietro Solari. It was here that Ivan the Terrible celebrated his victory over the Tatars at Kazan.

Within—now closed to visitors—is the former audience chamber of the Tsar. Today, official receptions and government ceremonies take place here.

Above the carved portal there is a grilled "lookout" from which the ladies of the royal family watched crown receptions, for custom then banned women from such occasions.

The Terems You are still viewing from the other side of the square. Crowded in among the older buildings behind the Granovitaya, and a little to your right, are the *Terems*, which were the women's quarters of the palace. For centuries, until Peter the Great "Westernized" Russia, the Tsarina and her ladies-in-waiting had to live in a separate part of the Kremlin. Scholars are generally agreed that the early Russians acquired this custom from the Mongols. Curiously enough, in a country that boasts of having developed a Communist model of women's liberation, the wives of top officials rarely appear in public with their husbands. It is still difficult for a Western journalist in Moscow even to find out whether a Soviet leader is married or not.

The Cathedral of the Assumption   Don't forget that each of these cathedrals had a particular purpose: one for burying, another for marrying, and this—the most magnificent of all—for coronations. Beneath its five golden domes the Tsars of Muscovy, and later the Tsars of All the Russias, were crowned.

Incredibly Russian in appearance, it is hard to believe that it was done under the supervision of Aristotele Fioravanti, an Italian architect who had made a lengthy study of Russian church design before essaying this masterpiece in 1475–1479.

Napoleon played havoc when he arrived here in 1812. His troops not only turned the interior into a stable, but stole 600 pounds of gold and more than 5 tons of silver. The Cossacks later caught up with the loot; in commemoration they presented the Cathedral with a 46-branched silver chandelier that weighs 880 pounds and now hangs from the dome.

This is the church where Moscow metropolitans and patriarchs lie buried; their shrines, of bronze and silver, represent the summit of Russian applied art.

Behind the solemn white stone façade is an interior really worth visiting and appreciating. The proportions are perfect, spacious, lofty, and bright, with arches supported by round pillars. It's a treasure house. Just a few of the marvels you should look out for are: 1. The South Doors, plated with black-lacquered copper sheets with twenty Biblical themes embroidered in gold.

2. The carved throne of Ivan the Terrible made in 1551; a triumph of the magnificent craftsmanship of Russian wood-carvers.

3. The open-work bronze shrine of Patriarch Germogen (tortured to death by Polish invaders in 1609).

4. The Iconostasis, or icon wall. This vermilion-hued gallery of icons is a group portrait of five rows of saints encrusted with precious stones.

5. The frescoes to the right and left of the entrance. Restored in the Soviet era, they represent the Last Judgement.

Patriarch's Residence and Cathedral of the Twelve Apostles The Patriarch's Residence is another reminder that in Imperial Russia the Kremlin was the spiritual, as well as the secular, heart of the nation.

In this mini-Vatican lived the Patriarch of All the Russias. Nowadays it is a museum of applied art. Within its walls are rare books, manuscripts, fabrics, and old jewellery. If you want to know what life at the top was like in the seventeenth century, take a look inside this rather chilly place.

The Cathedral part, really a church on the second floor, is dedicated to the Twelve Apostles and was completed in 1656. There are said to be secret passages within the walls. As you gaze at the Residence, it is worth recalling that Tsars and Patriarchs rarely got along with one another. As a matter of fact, Peter the Great, in his day, abolished the Patriarch's job. So you can imagine the sort of intrigue that went on between the prelates in this building and the nobility across the way in the Granovitaya Palata.

The Church That Nobody Knows There is one last building of note in Cathedral Square. Look to the right of the Granovitaya Palata, and you will see, set back from the square, a small jewel of fifteenth-century Slavonic church architecture. This was once the private church of the Patriarchs. Intourist calls it the **Church of Priestly Ordination** *(Rizopolozheniye)*. Its ancient name was the **Church of the Deposition of the Virgin's Dress,** and it really is one of the Kremlin gems. Like so many public buildings in Russia it makes no attempt at all to hide its voluptuous drainpipes, which hang like chicken ribs around every wall.

Don't go further today. Time now to leave the Kremlin and head back for Red Square.

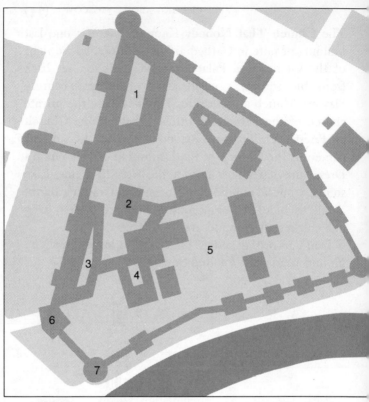

1 Arsenal
2 Palace of Congresses
3 Oruzheinaya Palata
   (The Armoury, Kremlin Museum)
4 Grand Kremlin Palace
5 Cathedral Square
6 Borovitskaya Gate
7 Vodovzvodnaya Tower

Walk Seven: A second look inside the Kremlin —the Kremlin Armoury, Palace of Congresses, Grand Kremlin Palace, and the Arsenal
(Time: 3 hours)

You are now ready for the rest of the Kremlin. From Red Square walk through the Spassky Gate, turn in the direction of the Kremlin Armoury (see map).

The Armoury (Oruzheinaya Palata)

Before setting out on your own, you should remember that a visit to the Armoury is almost certain to be part of your Intourist arrangements. It is highly recommended that you join this tour for a first visit.

The Armoury is also called the **Kremlin Museum**, although there are in fact several museums within the Kremlin walls. Considered the finest museum of its kind in Russia, it contains an overwhelming display of absolutely everything amassed by tsars and tsarinas down through the centuries.

First thing to greet you as you enter is the cloakroom. Here you must discard your overcoat and umbrella, and put on a pair of canvas overshoes with no backs to them. This slows your touring pace down to a snail's crawl, but also prevents you from slipping and breaking your neck on the beeswaxed parquet floors.

Peter the Great started this massive collection. Since he loved costumes and armour, the first rooms you enter are jammed with pre-twentieth-century battle gear. Press on to the Trophy Room, where you will see 15 thrones that belonged to various tsars. None look too comfortable. Among these: the Diamond Throne, studded with 2,000 diamonds and amethysts; the Ivory Throne, brought by the Constantinople princess who married Ivan III; Boris Godunov's golden throne; and the unusual double throne of the twin tsars—Ivan and Peter the Great—which has a section cut out of the back. During audiences their eldest sister, Sophia, would hide behind the drapes and whisper the right responses to the young tsars.

The Room of the Crowns In this room you will find the headgear and other regalia of seven centuries of Russia's rulers: the Siberian Crown, made of gold lace and glittering with gems, dating from the seventeenth century; the Kazan Crown, made in 1553 for the last tsar of Kazan; the walking sticks of Peter the Great and other tsars; the coronation robes of Catherine II, Elizabeth, Peter the Great, Peter II, and Paul I; the Imperial Orb; and the diamond-encrusted scepters of various tsars.

The State Coach Room This is a long corridor that looks like a toy shop at Christmas-time and never fails to delight youngsters. There is an incredibly elaborate coach given by Queen Elizabeth I of England to Boris Godunov, the sedan chair of the Swedish King Charles XII, the gala coach of the Russian Tsarina Elizabeth I which is at least 30 feet long. They have been beautifully maintained; when you look inside them the velvet trimmings look as though they were made yesterday. Several are elaborately decorated with scenes of war and peace, children, nymphs, and other fantasies. One of the most enchanting is the enclosed sleigh that Elizabeth I used to travel to her coronation in 1742; it looks like a miniature house, complete with tiny doors, and fourteen mica windows. The interior of this early mobile home is upholstered in green cloth, has chairs, tables, divans, and a charcoal heating system. It took a total of twenty-three horses, in relays, to draw it from St. Petersburg (now Leningrad) to Moscow.

The Silver Room Here are six centuries of the art of the silversmith. Also you can get an idea of what kind of presents tsars and tsarinas liked to receive. Your

Intourist guide will probably tell you that the Kremlin
has a finer collection of sixteenth- and seventeenth-century English silver than can be found in London. She
is correct: Cromwell melted down much of the good
stuff—the Russians kept theirs.

So here you can look at two life-size panthers, another
gift of Queen Elizabeth of England to Boris Godunov
Beyond are some delightful oddities. Keep an eye open
for the fumigators in the shape of Danish palaces, the
coconut goblet, Ivan the Terrible's tableware, and some
of the most enormous drinking cups you will ever see.

This vast treasure house is, in the end, exhausting.
If you are intent on "doing" the Kremlin Museum,
you must make at least half a dozen more visits. In
the hope of whetting your appetite to return, here are a
few remembered mental snapshots:

1. The collection of Fabergé bibelots, some of the
world's most expensive knick-knacks. These include a
platinum-and-gold super-miniature of the Trans-

Siberian Express complete with a NO SMOKING sign too small to be seen by the naked eye. This *inside* an Easter egg!

2. The boots of Peter the Great, made by the Tsar himself, and as tall as a small man. (Peter was six feet eight inches tall.)

3. Napoleon's camp bed, captured in 1812.

4. An incredible piece of carving in the form of an ivory eagle on a rock of ironwood. This was a wedding gift from the Mikado of Japan to Nicholas and Alexandra.

5. A horse-robe made of the feathered skins of five hundred yellow parrots.

6. Russia's biggest Bible, encased in diamond-encrusted gold.

7. The Clock of Glory, made in the eighteenth century for Catherine the Great; each five seconds an eagle dropped pearls into the beaks of its young; music played and a waterfall sprang to life.

A pair of towers

As you leave the Museum, stand with your back to it and look right. To the south is the **Borovitskaya Gate**. The tower above it is pyramidal in shape and is crowned by a kind of inverted ice-cream cone.

Now if you glance to the left of the Borovitskaya, you will see what many people consider to be the most beautiful of all the Kremlin towers: the **Water-Raising (Vodovzodnaya) Tower**, some 200 feet high. Built in 1805, wrecked by the French in 1812, it was restored in 1819. (If you want to check out of the Kremlin at this stage, simply walk down to the Borovitskaya Gate and you will be back in workaday Moscow.)

The Grand Kremlin Palace

One of the loveliest of all the Kremlin buildings, it stands on the crest of the Kremlin hill. It is almost the only truly Russian building within the Kremlin and enjoys an architectural harmony with all that surrounds it. Built one hundred years ago, it incorporates several old residences of the Tsars. Here were located the private apartments of the Imperial family during their visits to Moscow.

Alas, unless you have special connections, the Grand Kremlin Palace is out of bounds for visitors. Nowadays the Supreme Soviet holds its sessions here. The 1,443 representatives, elected by about 150 million voters, meet only twice a year for a period of about a week each time. It is really not possible, of course, to compare the Supreme Soviet to the U.S. Congress, British Parliament, or any other democratic assembly.

The Palace of Congresses

Built in 1961 in the modern style, this is the nearest architectural equivalent to the Kennedy Center in Washington. An all-purpose building, it is used for various kinds of conventions. It is also the summer home of the Bolshoi.

Inside, take a look at the lobby decorated with the emblems of all 15 Soviet republics. If you are a summer visitor to Moscow, chances are good that you will spend at least one evening at the ballet here. You will not be disappointed: this is one piece of auditorium architecture that really works. The acoustics are marvellous, the seats are comfortable, and there is not a single column to block the view of the airport-size stage.

The Arsenal

A splendid bit of eighteenth-century design. This long, two-story, orange-and-white building once housed the Kremlin's gunpowder and much else. Nowadays it is used as a barracks for the special detachment of security troops who guard the Kremlin. During the 1917 Revolution troops loyal to the Tsar made a last stand here. Surrounding the building are the 875 cannon captured from the "twenty nations" who invaded Russia with Napoleon in 1812.

You are now near enough to the Trinity Gate (see map) to make your way to Manege Square.

Taxi ride to one of the world's most interesting cemeteries
(Time: 2½ hours)

A visit to a cemetery is not ordinarily an appealing prospect, but you would be missing quite an experience if you passed up the famous **Novo-Devichy Cemetery,** a six-minute taxi ride from Red Square. As special in its own way as Britain's Westminster Abbey, or Hollywood's Forest Lawn, the Novo-Devichy Cemetery is a Who Was Who of Russia's famous.

Intourist has no organized tours that include this remarkable place, but they will willingly assign a guide to escort you. This, however, is not really necessary as long as you get someone in the Service Bureau to write out the address to show the taxi driver.

There is a small flower shop at the gates. Walk inside. As you wander the gravelled paths, you will see the graves of Chekhov, Gogol, Mayakovsky, Esenin, and Ehrenburg. In a setting of trees and flowers are such musicians as Anton Rubinstein, Scriabin, and

Prokofiev. A row of white marble busts portrays a group of generals purged in the wake of Stalin's death (they all died, you will note, in 1953).

A special corner is devoted to the graves of former actors of the Moscow Art Theatre. The great theatrical directors Konstantin Stanislavsky and Vladimir Nemirovich-Danchenko rest here. Not far away is the grave of the anarchist revolutionary Peter Kropotkin. The Tretyakov brothers, Pavel and Sergei, who founded the gallery named after them in Moscow; the wife of Alexei Kosygin, Nadezhda; former premier Nikita Khrushchev; and the great film director Sergei Eisenstein, are all memorialized with simple tombs.

Standing alone, in a vest-pocket corner lot, is the dignified white sculpture of Stalin's wife, Nadezhda Alliluyeva Stalina, who shot herself.

Strikingly absent are such symbols as weeping angels or crosses. The Memorial Impulse is largely expressed through life-sized marble and granite busts of the deceased. In the 1930's many pioneering Soviet airmen were buried here. Running alongside Area 1 is a wall almost entirely devoted to the memories of the 37 men who died in the famous crash of the tri-winged *Maxim Gorki* in 1935. Another plaque records the crash of one of the first Soviet-built zeppelins, and yet another records a transport plane's crash into the White Sea.

From here you can walk into the **Novo-Devichy** Convent (the exact translation is "The New Monastery of the Virgin").

Novo-Devichy Convent

This convent was founded in the first quarter of the sixteenth century, after Grand Duke Vasily III had returned Smolensk to Russia and vowed to build a new cloister.

Today it forms part of the Museum of History, but, as you will notice when you walk inside, there is a "working" church inside its walls. Many funeral services take place here, and respect should be shown if you enter the church during such a service.

As you enter, notice the crenellated wall with its 12 battle towers. Centuries ago this convent-fortress shielded Moscow from enemy raids.

It was here that Boris Godunov was elected tsar in 1598.

In Peter the Great's time, the convent served as a place of confinement for the disgraced Tsarina Eudoxia and Peter's sister Sophia, who had conspired against her brother.

The Convent is a bit weedy and overrun these days, but it is full of atmosphere and can send a shudder up your spine when you consider what Peter actually did to his sister. Having locked her up here, he proceeded to hang 300 *streltsy* (troops) who had supported Sophia right outside her cell window. Not content with this, he then chopped off the hand of her principal supporter, Prince Khovansky, and had it nailed to her door. You can get the main details of the story from your Intourist guide in the museum which is inside the main church—the **Smolensk Cathedral**, also known as the **Church of the Smolensk Mother of God**. If you are doing this trip on your own, the pictures and other artworks within the museum graphically illustrate Sophia's fate.

The Smolensk Cathedral, with its five golden domes, resembles the Uspensky Cathedral in the Kremlin. Within are the tombs of Eudoxia (died 1731), the first wife of Peter the Great, and of his sisters, Catherine, Eudoxia, and the ambitious Sophia (died 1704).

Don't overlook the mural paintings and the altar-piece; these are the work of the best painters of the seventeenth-century Moscow School, and have been restored in recent years.

Alongside the Cathedral stands the baroque **Church of the Transfiguration of Christ**, whose slender belfry, also in the baroque style, is one of the most beautiful in Russia.

Before you leave the Novo-Devichy, you might care to do some shopping. Across the street from the main entrance is one of the largest and best Beriozka (birch tree) stores in Moscow. It is well worth a visit. (See pp. 261–2 and pp. 269–88 *passim*.)

To return to Red Square, you can easily hail a taxi hereabouts. If you would rather return by Metro, con-

158)

sult one of the English-speaking clerks in the Beriozka
for directions to the **Sportwnaya Station** nearby.

backgrounder: soviet architecture

If you are interested in the architecture of the Soviet
era, put aside a morning and ask Intourist to arrange
for a car and a guide. (Oddly enough, though, Intourist tends to underplay post-October Revolution
architecture.)

A good beginning is a ride up Kalinin Prospekt,
where the current generation of Soviet architects is
showing its mettle. Pause for a moment by the **Comecon**
headquarters and look across the Moscow River at the
Hotel Ukraine.

Here in a single glance is the revolution that has
taken place in Soviet architecture since the Stalin
years. The Comecon headquarters is all glitter and
glass; the Ukraine represents the heavy monumentality
of the Stalin years, a period that the poet Voznesensky
—an ex-architect—calls "cowsheds with cupids."

Before we proceed, a brief historical survey may be
in order.

The year 1922 marked the end of the long Civil War
in Russia, the true beginning of the Soviet era; it was
a remarkably innovative period in the arts, and nowhere
was this so evident as in the new architecture. Buildings were to reflect the outlook and aspirations of the
machine age. The latest materials were employed:
steel, glass, concrete, aluminum, and even plastics. The
architects aligned themselves with the painters, called
themselves "constructivists," and based their designs

on the cube, the circle, and the spiral. If we look at these buildings today, we can readily see how far in advance of their age these Soviet designers of the twenties were.

In the year 1932, all this experimentation came to a full stop. Stalin had decreed that Soviet architecture should return to its classical heritage. One of the last great designs of this unique era in Soviet life was the offices of the party newspaper, *Pravda*, designed by Ivan Golosov and built between 1929 and 1935. Ironically, it was from these offices that the major attacks against the modernist spirit were launched. By the end of 1932, constructivism as an idea was finished; work in that style was strictly forbidden. Henceforth architecture had to be monumental and decorative, to reflect "the greatness of Socialist construction." In many ways this was a wasteful approach in a society short of so much. When you enter the Metro, you can see many vivid examples of this ornate and lavish style.

After Stalin's death, the reaction in civic architecture was swift, and the extravagance of the recent past was condemned by the government. By the 1970's, Moscow and other Soviet cities contained contemporary buildings that could be compared favorably with modern design in other countries. As you walk through Moscow, you can see many such examples around you: the Hotel Rossiya, the October Cinema, the Palace of Congresses in the Kremlin, and the Comecon headquarters with its open plaza.

museums & galleries

Moscow's museums and galleries are a treasure-house of Russia's past. The major ones you will find on Intourist's regular schedule. But there are quite a number that are not on the beaten track. You may wish to visit these either on your own or with an Intourist guide. Admission is usually 30 kopecks.

Revolution

Lenin Museum 2, Revolution Square. This is a fascinating place to visit if you want to learn about the life and tumultuous times of the founder of the Communist Party and of the world's first socialist state. The museum contains over 7,000 exhibits: newspapers, documents, books, photographs, congratulatory postcards from American workers and a marvellous Rolls-Royce that Lenin commandeered during the Revolution. The rooms are arranged in such a manner that you follow in sequence the life of Lenin from birth to death. One of the most interesting exhibits is the replica of Lenin's Kremlin study.
Open daily 11–7. Closed Monday.

Lenin's Funeral Train At Paveletsky Railway Station, 1, Kozhevnichesky Square. Here in a special memorial pavilion you can see the engine (Y–127) and carriage in which the coffin of Vladimir Ilyich Lenin was brought to Moscow on January 23, 1924. It looks as good as new. You can walk around it and examine the display which tells the story (in Russian) of that last journey.

Museum of the Revolution 21, Gorkovo; near Mayakovsky Square, in a three-storey red building that in pre-Revolutionary days housed the English Club (notice the stone lions that stand on either side of the gateway). Here you can trace the various phases of the Revolution from 1905 onward. Allow about 45 minutes to see an extraordinary collection of posters, pamphlets, serf-chains, home-made bombs, illegal printing presses, and the first decrees of the Soviet Government on peace and land measures.

Open Monday, Wednesday, Friday 12–8; Tuesday, Saturday, Sunday 10–6. Closed Thursday.

Museum of Karl Marx and Friedrich Engels   5, Marx-Engels Street. Metro station: Kropotkinskaya. Not for everyone, but if the study of Communism is your interest, then do visit this exhibit. Judging by the wealth of manuscripts, letters, and documents, neither Marx nor Engels ever had a lazy day off in their lives. Here too are Marx's personal belongings, including his armchair and the easy chair in which he died on March 14, 1883.

Open Monday, Wednesday, Friday 1–7; Thursday, Saturday, Sunday 11–5. Closed Tuesday.

History

State History Museum   Red Square. Moscow's oldest museum, it is reputed to contain more than three million items. The 42 rooms provide a vivid historical panorama of Russian history from the Stone Age to the end of the nineteenth century. You will find Novgorod birch-bark scrolls dating to the tenth century, samples of the arms of Kiev Rus, garments of Ivan the Terrible, and Napoleon's bed which he abandoned during his flight from Russia. If you are a coin collector, you will find here a unique collection of coins and medals.

Open Monday, Thursday, Sunday 10:30–5:30; Wednesday, Friday, Saturday 12–7. Closed Tuesdays and last day of the month.

Kremlin Armoury   A full description of Russia's premier museum can be found on pages 149–52.
Open Sunday through Thursday 9:30–6:30. Closed Friday.

History and Reconstruction of Moscow Museum   can be found at 12, New (Novaya) Square. If you are staying at any midtown hotel—the National, Intourist, Rossiya, Metropole, Bucharest, or Minsk—you can walk to this little jewel of a museum in ten minutes. A visit here is a fine way to begin your stay in Moscow; it will give you a graphic idea of how the city has grown during the past 800 years. Engravings, lithographs, mock-ups, and photographs reproduce Moscow's appearance at different periods of its history. Open Saturday, Sunday, Monday, Thursday 10–6; Wednesday, Friday, 2–9. Closed Tuesdays and the last day of each month.

Battle of Borodino Panorama   38, Kutuzovsky Prospekt. Metro station: Kutuzovskaya. This is one of those take-it-or-leave-it propositions. Once inside you see a vast circular painting—all done by hand, you are told—of the famous battle. Nearly 400 feet long, almost fifty feet high. The foreground of the painting is composed of three-dimensional figures in full size. Just the spot for a rainy day.
Open daily 9:30–8. Closed Friday.

Soviet Armed Forces Museum   2, Kommuny Square, is a smashing place to take small boys or anyone interested in World War II. There is a standard reprise of the history of the Soviet Army, of course, but what really counts are the imaginative displays that portray the tremendous struggle against the Nazis in what the Russians call The Great Patriotic War. One display has thousands upon thousands of Iron Crosses scattered on the ground, and about them the Nazi regimental standards. Here, too, are the flags of the Soviet Army that once flew over the Reichstag. Elsewhere can be seen the parachute, forged papers, pistol, and other items taken from U-2 pilot Francis Gary Powers. When your feet tire, there is a small restaurant downstairs for a cup of tea and a cigarette.

Open Tuesday, Friday, Saturday, Sunday 10–7; Wednesday, Thursday 12–8. Closed Monday.

Frunze Central House of Aviation 14, Krasnoarmeiskaya Street. You will need the help of Intourist on a visit here, but if you are interested in aviation it is worth the effort. There's much to marvel at in this history of flight from the Soviet viewpoint. The exhibits include Kostovich's models of an airship (1883–84), and the inevitable "world's first airplane," constructed long before the Wright Brothers heard of flight, by Mozhaisky (1882). N.B. This museum is open by invitation only; your Service Bureau has the details.

Science and Technology

Polytechnic Museum 3/4, New (Novaya) Square, offers a good morning's workout for the ardent science buff. Here are some 20,000 exhibits distributed throughout 55 rooms. Among the more interesting: the laboratory of M. V. Lomonosov (founder of Moscow University); also, the much-disputed "first" radio receiver designed by A. S. Popov. In addition, there are dozens of prototypes of modern automobiles, motorcycles, and engines of every conceivable variety. Nearly 21,000,000 visitors have trudged through these same rooms over the years, so join the crowd.

Open Sunday, Wednesday, Friday, 10–5. Tuesday, Thursday, Saturday 1–8. Closed Monday and the last day of each month.

Darwin Museum 1, Malaya Pirogovskaya Street. Metro station: Frunzenskaya. Acquaints you with the works and discoveries of Charles Darwin, and with the evolution of materialist teachings concerning the origin of life.

Open Monday to Friday 10–5. Closed Saturday and Sunday.

Museum of Anthropology 18, Marx Prospekt. More on the origin of man can be found here. The Museum contains one of the world's most outstanding collections of the osseous remains of primitive man, including examples of Pithecanthropus, Sinanthropus, Neanderthal man, and Cro-Magnon man.

Open daily except Sunday 9–4:30.

Zoological Museum 6, Herzen Street. Has a collection of 70,000 mammals, 90,000 birds, 20,000 reptiles and amphibians, and some 45,000 fish.

Open Sunday, Tuesday, Thursday, Saturday 10–6; Wednesday, Friday 12–8. Closed Monday.

Paleontological Museum 16, Leninsky Prospekt, is one of the oldest in Russia, having its origin in Peter the Great's Kunstkamera. Fossil vertebrae of past geological epochs are on display.

Museum of Mineralogy is at 14/16 Leninsky Prospekt. Experts agree that this is one of the world's
most outstanding collections of minerals, rare stones,
and gems of the USSR and other countries.

Planetarium 5, Sadovaya-Kudrinskaya Street. Metro:
Krasnopresnenskaya station. Be sure to take a good
look at the Planetarium building before you enter; it
is an outstanding example of early Soviet architecture,
a round building topped by a silvery, egg-shaped dome.
Inside you find yourself as if in the darkened universe,
a vast purple-blue void filled with stars and shooting
comets. In the halls are scale models of Soviet artificial earth satellites, a globe of the moon, and a relief
map of the moon that shows various Soviet space ex-
plorations. The lecturer (do try to have your guide
along to translate) usually presses a little switch during
the lecture and suddenly across the heavens flash the
trajectories of the Soviet sputniks and interplanetary
rockets. Nary an Apollo or a Gemini in sight.
Open daily, except Tuesday, 12–7.

Botanical Gardens of the Academy of Sciences are
located at 4, Botanicheskaya Street, Ostankino. If you
are a plant lover, you can happily spend an entire day
here walking around an area of 890 acres. Inside
Europe's biggest greenhouse are more than 15,000
tropical and subtropical plants. There is an aquatic
section with flowering lilies, Nile lotuses, and the Vic-
toria Regia.
A rosarium containing 16,000 bushes of 2,500 strains
of roses should delight rose-lovers. Keep an eye out for
one of the most unique flowers in the world: the rare
and ancient green rose from Bengal.

Another tactile experience is to walk through all the climatic zones of the Soviet Union, ascend the mountain range of Central Asia, and inspect the Far East with its lianas, Amur grapes, and giant 10-foot-high Sakhalin grass, ending in the Arctic tundra and Siberian taiga. Open daily 10–8. Closed Monday.

Botanical Garden of Moscow University 26, Prospekt Mira. Metro: Prospekt Mira. Begun in 1706 by Peter I for the cultivation of medicinal herbs, it was almost entirely destroyed by Napoleon's troops in 1812. Today this botanical garden is the oldest in Russia, and one of the oldest in the world. It contains 5,000 plants, and its hothouses contain a collection of 100 tall full-grown palms. A great tourist attraction is the miniature Japanese garden, whose trees, no taller than 20 inches, range in age from 50 to 200 years.

Literary, Theatrical, and Musical Attractions

Leo Tolstoy's House 21, Leo Tolstoy Street, is now a museum. This interesting street is full of old mansions that give you an idea of what life was like for the rich a hundred years ago. Tolstoy lived and worked here from 1872 to 1901, and you can see the simple study in which the writer created *Resurrection*, *The Death of Ivan Ilyich*, and other works. Open daily 10–4:30. Closed Tuesday.

Vladimir Mayakovsky's Apartment can be found at 15/13 Mayakovsky Pereulok. Here "the poet of the Revolution" lived in a *ménage à trois* with his great friends and patrons, the Briks. It is absolutely fascinating to visit his upstairs flat. His writing-desk, with all kinds of objects, is as he left it on the day he

committed suicide. By his bed is a travelling-case designed by Mayakovsky himself, and in a cabinet against the window wall is his tea-glass with a spoon in it.
Open Monday, Tuesday, Friday 12–8; Wednesday, Saturday, Sunday 10–6. Closed Thursday.

Dostoevsky Museum 2, Dostoevsky Street. Items of Dostoevskiana in this gloomy home.
Open Monday 10–4; Wednesday, Friday 1–9; Thursday, Saturday, Sunday 11–6. Closed Tuesday.

Museum of Literature 38, Dimitrov Street, is a gold mine for teachers and scholars interested in Russian literature. A superb collection of published and unpublished manuscripts, portraits, first editions of Russian writers. Recordings of the voices of Tolstoy, Mayakovsky, Esenin, and others.
Open Monday 11–4; Wednesday, Friday 2–9; Thursday, Saturday, Sunday 11–6. Closed Tuesday.

Glinka Museum of Musical Culture 13, Herzen Street, exists to preserve and promote musical history. (It is in the same building as the Tchaikovsky Conservatoire.) If you want to see one of the most astonishing collections of musical instruments—more than 1,500—ever gathered under one roof, this is an absolute must. In addition, there are musical scores and letters of Tchaikovsky, Rachmaninoff, Beethoven, Wagner, Liszt, Grieg, Ravel, Saint-Saëns, Glinka, Borodin, Rimsky-Korsakov, Prokofiev, Shostakovich, Khachaturian, and many other distinguished composers. There are also photographs, recordings, and paintings of eminent performers.
Open daily except Saturday 10–5:30; Saturday 10–3:30. Closed Sunday.

Puppet Museum   Sergei Obraztsov's Central Puppet Theatre, 32a Gorkovo, exhibits a unique collection of old and modern theatrical puppets. There are no puppets from the United States, although Mr. Obraztsov would love to add Kukla, Fran and Ollie to his collection. But there are puppets from nearly 40 different nations, as well as dolls from every corner of the USSR.

Bakhrushin Theatrical Museum   31/12 Bakhrushin Street. Metro: Paveletskaya Station.   All you want to know about the history of Russian drama, opera, and ballet from the eighteenth century to the present day. Theatrical costumes of famous Russian actors, playbills, programmes, manuscripts, personal belongings, and more than 200,000 photographs.
Open Wednesday, Friday 2–9; Sunday, Monday, Thursday, Saturday 12–7. Closed Tuesday.

Konstantin Stanislavsky's Home   is located at 6, Stanislavsky Street, off Gorkovo and close by the Mossoviet (City Hall). Stanislavsky, undisputed father of "method" acting, was the founder of the Moscow Art Theatre. His house is filled with souvenirs of the 1920's and '30's. Open Sunday 12–7; Tuesday, Thursday 3–9. Closed Monday, Wednesday, Friday, Saturday.

Art and Architecture

Tretyakov Art Gallery   10, Lavrushinsky Pereulok. Metro: Novokuznetskaya Station. This is Moscow's premier gallery and contains the world's largest collection of Russian paintings. There are between 5,000 and 6,000 paintings (no one knows exactly) in this dingy

Victorian mansion. Most of them seem to be jammed on the walls, piled up to the ceiling in a dizzy display. In recent years there has been at least some attempt to organize the chaos, but it is apparently a hopeless proposition. Latest rumor is that a new gallery will replace the Tretyakov shortly. Meanwhile, if you have joined its 1½ million yearly visitors, make straight for the masterpieces of Andrei Rublev, whose luminous icons are among the glories of Russia. Upstairs are the huge, wall-sized canvases of Ilya Repin and other nineteenth-century realists. The titles tell all: *Taking Leave of the Chief; The Wanderers; The Execution of the Streltsy; The Failure of a Bank*. Also here are hundreds of Stalin-inspired "socialist-realist" paintings—Polaroid art of the most tedious variety. If you find yourself fading, you can leave your group and enjoy orange crush and ice cream in the little courtyard outside.

Open daily 10–7. Closed Monday.

Pushkin Museum 12, Volkhonka Street, is where you will find the confiscated French impressionist paintings that once belonged to the capitalists Shchukin and Morozov. By Soviet standards this is a well-organized gallery, with far less clutter than you will have to plough through in similar museums. All the same, you have to walk through room after room of plaster casts of Greek epic figures before you reach the great moderns. Catch your breath: you will see 14 incredible Gauguins—including *Café at Arles*—and an extraordinary self-portrait. Nearby are several Van Gogh's, amongst them *Portrait of Dr. Rey*. There are 14 Cézannes, and nine pre-1914 Picasso paintings, including *Lady with a Fan*. Utrillo, Bonnard, Vlaminck,

Signac, and Toulouse-Lautrec are also well represented. Open daily 12–6:30.

Museum of Eastern Arts 16, Obukha Street. Metro: Kurskaya Station. Two major collections, both magnificent. The first is of Chinese art, and the exhibits range as far back as the first millennium B.C.: bronze animal- and bird-shaped bowls, remarkable jade, china, ivory ware, silk pictures, etc.; the second is of Indian art, dating from the sixth and seventh centuries to modern times. The museum also contains one of the world's finest collections of Japanese miniature sculptures, as well as artworks from Iran, Turkey, and the Soviet Far East.
Open daily 11–7. Closed Monday.

Andrei Rublev Museum of Ancient Russian Art 10, Pryamikova Street, is a comparatively new museum in a very ancient setting: the Andronikov Monastery, where Rublev lived, worked, and died. The monastery itself was built more than six centuries ago, and the oldest church in Moscow—the Archangel Church, built in the 1420's—stands in its grounds. You will not find many Rublevs here, however, since most were destroyed in the sixteenth and seventeenth centuries. What remains are either copies or fragments from the originals. Nevertheless, there are varied examples of early icon painting.
Open Monday, Thursday 1–7; Tuesday 11–3; Friday, Saturday, Sunday 12–6.

Museum of Applied Folk Art 7, Stanislavsky Street, is the place to visit if you like folk art. There are more than three centuries of individual articles made by peasant craftsmen—carvings in wood, delicate miniature paintings from Palekh, richly embroidered lacework, Daghestan gold inlays. Here, in contrast to the ostentatious trinkets in the Kremlin Armoury, is the art of the people.

Open Sunday, Monday, Wednesday, Friday 11–5; Tuesday, Thursday 2–8. Closed Saturday and the last day of the month.

Alexei Shchusev State Architectural Research Museum 5, Kalinin Prospekt (near the Lenin Library), is named after one of the most distinguished of early Soviet architects, the man who designed Lenin's Mausoleum. Within are drawings, paintings, and models that illustrate the history of Russian architecture from Imperial times to the Soviet age.

Open Monday, Thursday, Saturday, Sunday 11–6; Wednesday, Friday 1–8. Closed Tuesday.

Memorial Museums

Among the 150 or so museums that crowd Moscow are the dozens of mini-memorial institutions that celebrate this or that famous artist, author, poet, or scientist. Many of these are off the beaten path, but the Service Bureau will be glad to arrange a special tour for you if you tell them in advance. Amongst the better known:

Maxim Gorki Museum, 25a, Vorovsky Street

Chekhov Museum, 6, Sadovaya-Kudrinskaya Street

Alexander Pushkin Museum, 12, Kropotkin Street

Apartment-Museum of N. A. Ostrovsky, 14, Gorki Street

Apartment-Museum of Yevgeny Vakhtangov, 12, Vesnin Street

Apartment-Museum of Vladimir Nemirovich-Danchenko, 5/7 Nemirovich-Danchenko Street

Apartment-Museum of Alexander Scriabin, 11, Vakhtangov Street

parks & gardens

Moscow prides itself on being a "green city," and there are more than a hundred parks within a 10-mile radius of Red Square. The larger ones are known as "recreation parks" and contain everything from sideshows and Ferris wheels to outdoor dance halls. There are also a number of "forest-parks." These are located in the northern half of the city: Izmailovo, Sokolniki, Serebryany Bor, and Pokrovsko-Streshnevo.

Gorki Park is the place you are likely to visit if you have only a few days to spend in Moscow. It is the largest park in central Moscow, a combination of New York's Central and London's Hyde Park, a sprawling 272 acres of pleasure gardens. It is a marvellous place to visit on a warm summer evening—to stroll along its quiet paths, rest awhile at an outdoor cafe, go boating, visit the carnival grounds.

The park contains Moscow's biggest open-air theatre (Zeleny Teatr—"The Green Theatre"), seating 12,000. Admission is free, except on special holidays, when the going rate is about 30 kopecks.

Once there you can head for the midway, which has more than twenty side-shows. This is no Tivoli, but there is a Ferris wheel whose cabins gently ascend to a height of 165 feet (one of the few places in the city where you can get a really good panoramic picture of Moscow).

The park has five ponds for rowing and model-boating (take a boat with you) and plenty of grass to play games or picnic on.

One section of the park is known as Neskuchny Sad, or "Banish Boredom Garden." In another part of the park is a 35-foot-long portrait of Lenin made of 330,000 living flowers. Near the outdoor dance-hall is the **Pilzen** Restaurant, which serves Czech beer and dishes, and not far away is a cafe located in the former Hunter's Hut, a structure built in the eighteenth century. There you can get a samovar with a packet of charcoal for heating, and drink tea in the old Russian style out on the grass—but be sure to bring your own tea.

The park is currently undergoing large-scale expansion and reconstruction, a job that will take several years to complete. When this is finished, its area will be 680 acres (about three times the size of Hyde Park), and a suspension railway will run along its entire length. *How to get there*: 1. Take a taxi—it's about a seven-minute ride from central Moscow. 2. Take the Metro to the Park Kultury Station, but be careful, for there are two subway stations with that name—you must take the *Circle Line* from Revolution Square. Leave the Metro, cross under the traffic bridge, walk across the Krymsky Bridge, and you are at the main entrance. Open 10 a.m. to 11:30 p.m. every day.

Sokolniki Park This is really a full day's outing, the spot where Muscovites come on the weekends to get a bit of forest air. *Sokolniki* means "falconers" (*sokol* = falcon). Centuries ago, this was where the tsars took their falcons to hunt game. Most of the park's 1,500 acres are still in a natural state, and there are plenty of secluded spots where you can lose yourself for hours in the beautiful birch groves.

To the left of the main entrance is an amusement

area with a merry-go-round, funny mirrors, and an out-door dance-hall. Further into the park is a large dance-hall called *Vesna* (spring), which affords you a chance to meet Russian friends.

There is year-round ice-skating here; the park has an excellent artificial ice rink.

How to get there: An easy ride on the Metro to Sokol-niki Station. When you emerge, the park is directly in front of you.

Open daily 10 a.m. to 11 p.m.

Izmailovo Park must rank as one of the world's big-gest. Its area, 2,915 acres, makes it approximately five times the size of New York's Central Park.

Like Gorki and Sokolniki, it has outdoor dance-halls, a summer theatre, and lots of side-shows. There is a gallery for archers, and a riding academy (check with Intourist if you want to go horseback riding).

The main attractions, however, are the pine groves, birch woods, and lovely scenic vistas. This was once one of the Romanov estates, and Peter the Great spent his childhood here.

How to get there: Take the Blue Line direct from Revo-lution Square to the Izmailovskaya Station.

Open daily 10 a.m. to 11 p.m.

Hermitage Garden is a pleasant expanse of green in the middle of the city. It is a summertime centre for entertainment, with two theatres, a concert hall, a movie house, a restaurant, and a dance-hall.

How to get there: Take a taxi (about 1 rouble from mid-town Moscow) to 3, Karetny Road.

Open from May 1 to September 1 from 10 a.m. to 11 p.m. daily.

ZOOS

The Moscow Zoo Although comparatively old, this is a natural zoo in which animals roam around in open enclosures. Bring binoculars. There is also a children's corner with a panda, lion cubs, puppies, piglets, and bear cubs. (The entire zoo is due to be transferred in the near future to a new location on the city's outskirts.)

How to get there: 1, Bolshaya Gruzinskaya Street. Take the Metro to Krasnopresnenskaya Station, or trolleybuses 5 or 8.

Durov's Corner is one of the most charming miniature zoos in the world. Also known as the V. L. *Durov Educational Centre*, it is a teaching establishment, a "theatre of animals," and a museum. Very hard to classify, it has about 350 trained animals and 40 birds. If you think that the U.S. Navy is doing marvellous things in Florida with dolphins, then visit Durov's Corner and watch the tigers and canaries perform.

How to get there: Take a taxi (less than a rouble from midtown) to 4, Durov Street, near Kommuny Square. Open Monday, Tuesday, Wednesday, Saturday 11 a.m. to 5 p.m.; Thursday 11 a.m. to 3 p.m.; Sunday 10 a.m. to 5 p.m. Closed Friday. "Theatre of Animals" performances are given each Saturday at 1 p.m. and 3 p.m. and every Sunday at 11 a.m., 1 p.m., and 3 p.m.

backgrounder: city transit

One very striking aspect of Moscow is the lack of private cars and the abundance of public transportation. At a time when Western town planners are talking gloomily about urban death through traffic congestion, Moscow now looks like a model for the future.

Old Moscow had a tramway line built at the end of the nineteenth century, and tens of thousands of cabs. In the Soviet era the tram route has been considerably extended, especially on the outskirts, and is now more than 250 kilometres long. Buses and taxis made their appearance in the 1920's, followed by trolleys and river ferries in the 1930's. But the real solution to transporting millions of people lay under ground. Construction on the Metro began in 1932 (with an assist from American engineers). It is still not completed. Moscow's underground lines now total more than 100 kilometres in length, and there are nearly 80 stations. During the day and evening the Metro is the fastest way to get around.

If you want to cover the entire city, you will have to travel 40 kilometres from north to south, and 30 kilometres from east to west. Eight Metro lines and more than 280 bus, trolley-bus, and streetcar routes are at your disposal. The cost of travelling *any distance* by Metro or bus is 5 kopecks, by trolley-bus 4 kopecks, and by streetcar (a fast-disappearing sight) 4 kopecks. The charge for a taxi is 10 kopecks plus 10 kopecks per kilometre, making this one of the world's cheapest cab rides. There are also fixed-route taxis operating in the same manner as buses, though offering a little more convenience for double the bus fare. You will need a few simple Russian phrases (see pp. 50–2); one helpful procedure (as mentioned before) is to have a Russian friend, or someone at the Service Bureau, write out on a card exactly where you are going. This you can show to the bus driver or Metro attendant. You should

also have another card which says PLEASE DIRECT ME
BACK TO REVOLUTION SQUARE (a focal point of the system). After your first journey you will see just how
simple getting about by yourself really is. Public transport in Moscow is cheap, clean, safe. The only hazard
you may encounter is somebody falling over you after
a bit too much vodka on a weekend—though, as elsewhere, you should be prepared for the rush-hour crush.

the metro

Russians are proud of the Moscow Metro, and rightly
so; it is one of the finest in the world. The stations are
shiningly clean and a forced ventilation system changes
the air eight times each hour. Smoking is forbidden on
stations and in trains. At rush hours trains leave the
stations at intervals of 90 seconds. The first section in
any coach is reserved for elderly and crippled persons
and women with children. It is the custom in Russia
for parents to stand so that their children can sit. Many
of the stations are so elaborately decorated that you
will have some trouble finding your way to and from the
trains. (It is also worth noting that in the older stations
there are no public toilet facilities.) The Moscow Metro
moves three million passengers a day. It is recommended
that you avoid travelling during the rush hours. The
best time to tour the Metro is in the morning or early
afternoon, but preferably before 4 p.m.
A *word of caution:* Many of the stations in the city
centre are exceptionally deep. Banks of escalators take
passengers to and from platforms. If you have a heart
condition, you ought to avoid the Metro at Revolution
Square and Mayakovsky Square.

How to use the Metro

A Metro ticket costs 5 kopecks and is good in any direction. Metro service begins at 6 a.m. and stops at 12:30 a.m. Transfers are without charge.

When you enter any Metro station, one of the first things you will notice is a large schematic map of the entire Metro system mounted on the wall. You merely press a button for your destination on this map, and the route lights up. Anyone will find the map easy to follow. With its radial and circular routes, the Metro's underground network is a replica of the capital's above-ground lay-out.

Buy your ticket at the window, hand it to the attendant at the turnstile. If you are carrying luggage, you will have to pay 5 kopecks extra for each piece. Bulky luggage is prohibited (as are pets of any kind).

The length of any object (skis excepted) must not exceed 1 metre (39.37 inches) and the height and width 40 and 30 centimetres (just under 16 and 12 inches), respectively.

As with the London Underground, you must be careful when using the Inner Circle Line (see map in the back). It actually does go round in a circle; but there are other train routes that run through some of the Circle stations, and the only visible difference between them is the legend on the front of the train. So, unless you can read Russian, show a fellow passenger your card inscribed with directions in Russian to ensure you are on the right train.

How to tour the Metro

The Metro is the best tourist bargain in the Soviet Union. It is a breathtaking experience, and there's nothing like it anywhere in the world. The Soviet Union's finest architects, sculptors, and artists have built and adorned these underground palaces—and spent millions and millions of roubles in the process. Each station has its own unique design. The various artistic themes celebrate the building of a new society in the USSR, the creative work of the Soviet people, and important historical events of the past. From our point of view, however, it is the older stations that possess the most interest. For much of the splendor, paradoxically, was created during the Soviet Union's hardest years: the thirties and the wartime forties. John Gunther once described these stations as "promissory notes" on the future, which is quite accurate. The opulence, the sheer luxury, of the dazzling chandeliers, lavish marble mosaics, and porphyry columns had a purpose: to give the workers a psychological lift. The Metro is a symbol of the Communist future.

Head for the *Revolution Square* Metro. Take the Green Line (consult Metro map) to *Mayakovskaya*. Leave the train and explore the station. It was here, during the war, that Stalin held a big Communist Party rally while the Nazis were bombing the city. Named, of course, after the great Soviet poet of the 1920's, the station is a splendid example of Stalinist Baroque. Look closely at the richly colored mosaic ceiling murals which portray scenes from life in the thirties. Its vaults are supported by thin pillars finished in corrugated stainless steel.

Get aboard the train again, going in the same direction as before. The next stop is *Byelorusskaya*, a major railroad terminus. Here you transfer to the Circle Line, going in the direction of *Krasnopresnenskaya*.

You will now traverse about half the Circle Line route, passing such stations as *Kievskaya* (another rail terminal), then *Park Kultury* (this is where you get off for Gorki Park); then, in sequence, *Oktyabrskaya, Dobryninskaya, Paveletskaya, Taganskaya, Kurskaya* (another rail terminal), and *Komsomolskaya*. Here you get out and change trains.

But first take a look around at this station's rich decorations. It was designed by Alexei Shchusev, the architect of Lenin's Mausoleum and the most celebrated architect of his day. The elegant ceiling rests on 72 marble columns, and the theme of this station, embodied in eight huge mosaic murals, is the heroism of the Soviet people.

Now for your return trip: Take the Red Line. In sequence you will pass *Lermontovskaya, Kirovskaya, Dzerzhinskaya*. The next stop is *Ploshchad Revolyutsii* —Revolution Square. For this tour, allow yourself about an hour and a half.

buses & streetcars

Like the Moscow Metro, the bus and streetcar services are cheap, and offer a good way to see the city. But they are not easy to understand. There are no bus-route maps available, and few Muscovites (even if you can speak Russian) seem to know how to advise a stranger.

A good rule of thumb is: *Never* ask a group of people for advice. You will find they have as many suggestions as they have voices. And since you have no way of knowing who's right, you will find yourself totally baffled.

How to use surface transit

Most buses, trolley-buses, and streetcars do not have a conductor; passengers deposit their fares in the box provided. You drop the money in and tear off a ticket. The stops are announced by the driver over a loudspeaker. If you show him your card with directions when you enter, he will usually let you know your stop.

Motorbus Service begins at 6 a.m. and ends at 30 minutes past midnight. The fare one way, regardless of distance, is 5 kopecks.

Trolley-Bus Service begins at 6 a.m. and ends at 30 minutes past midnight. The fare one way, regardless of distance, is 4 kopecks.

Streetcar Traffic begins at 5:30 a.m. and ends at 30 minutes past midnight. The fare, one way, regardless of distance, is 4 kopecks. This is a vanishing form of transportation. There are no more streetcar tracks in the center of the city; they lie mostly beyond the Sadovoye Ring (Koltso). Remember: since you will usually not be able to make change, be sure to carry sufficient amounts of small change.

how to reach key points by metro or bus

Arbatskaya Square By Metro; trolley-buses 2, 15, 31; buses 6, 39, 89.

Byelorussian Railway Station By Metro; trolley-buses 1, 12, 18, 20; buses 10, 12, 27, 38, 63, 82, 116, 251, 263; streetcars "A," 5, 29.

Dzerzhinsky Square By Metro; trolley-buses 3, 5, 19, 23; buses 3, 18, 24, 43, 55, 74, 89.

Gorki Recreation Park By Metro to Park Kultury or Oktyabrskaya Station; trolley-buses "B," 10, 17, 28, 31; buses 8 and 108.

Kiev Railway Station By Metro; trolley-buses 2, 7, 34; buses 23, 45, 73, 89, 91, 119, 235, 267; streetcars 30, 31.

Komsomolskaya Square By Metro; trolley-buses 3, 14, 22; buses 19, 40, 85; streetcars 7, 32, 37, 50.

Kurskaya Railway Station By Metro; trolley-buses "B," 10; buses 40, 78, 81; streetcars 2, 20, 24, 33.

Kuznetsky Bridge (Most) To Dzerzhinskaya or Prospekt Marxa Metro station; trolley-buses 2, 9, 13, 23; bus 24.

Lenin Hills By Metro; trolley-buses 4, 7, 28; buses 1, 23, 57, 111, 114, 119; streetcars 12, 14, 22.

Lenin Library By Metro; trolley-buses 1, 2, 4, 8, 11; buses 3, 5, 6, 89.

Manege Square By Metro; trolley-buses 1, 2, 4, 5, 8, 11, 12, 20; buses 3, 5, 89, 107.

Mayakovsky Square By Metro; trolley-buses "B," 1, 10, 12, 20, 29.

Pushkin Square By trolley-buses 1, 3, 12, 15, 20, 23, 31; buses 5, 18, 87.

Red Square By Metro to Revolution Square (Ploshchad Revolyutsii) or Prospekt Marxa; trolley-buses 1, 2, 3, 4, 5, 9, 11, 12, 13, 20, 25; buses 3, 5, 18, 24, 25, 28, 87, 106, 111, 115, 211, 213.

Revolution Square By Metro; trolley-buses 1, 2, 3, 4, 5, 9, 11, 13; buses 3, 5, 18, 24, 87, 89, 107, 111, 115, 211, 213.

Sokolniki Recreation Park By Metro; trolley-buses 3, 14, 32; buses 40, 75, 80, 101, 216.

Smolenskaya Square By Metro; trolley-buses "B," 2, 10; buses 64, 89.

USSR Economic Achievement Exhibition By Metro; trolley-buses 2, 9, 13, 14, 36; buses 9, 33, 61, 82, 83, 85, 117, 265; streetcars 5, 7, 10, 11, 25.

taxis

Moscow, New York, and Paris have one thing in common: their taxi drivers are independent, sassy, fractious, and, apparently, beyond the power of any authority to regulate. Don't be surprised if they ignore your attempt to flag them down. Whether they choose to stop or not appears to be up to them.

The municipal taxi service uses dark-colored Volga, Pobeda, and Moskvich cars. By day they can be recognised by a checkered band on both sides and on the back and front of the engine hood. By night, watch for the green light in the top right-hand corner of the windshield; if the light is on, the taxi is free. You can call a cab from your hotel (25-00-00), but it's more convenient to have the Service Bureau do it for you.

Once inside, you pay 10 kopecks per kilometre, plus a 10-kopeck service charge. Any waiting time is reckoned at the rate of one rouble per hour. An average trip will cost from 50 to 70 kopecks. You pay according to the meter—not a kopeck more for extra passengers or for any baggage. Drivers gladly accept tips—the usual ten percent.

Fixed-route taxis

Not all taxis that zip by you are being deliberately nasty. There are *fixed-route taxis* that ply between the larger city squares. At each stand, a route taxi leaves approximately every five minutes. The best way to find a route taxi stand is to go to any square and look for a line of people, half a dozen of whom are trying to get into a single taxi. It is often easier to hail them en route. If there are empty seats, the driver is supposed to stop for you. At night, on an empty street, it is worth hailing any taxi, even if it is occupied. It may be a route taxi. Inside a fixed-route taxi the one-way fare, regardless of distance, is 10 kopecks.

Tipping in route taxis is an individual matter. Most drivers will accept a few kopecks, some don't seem to care, and others try to cajole you into paying in foreign currency. This is not recommended, however.

The time you really need your taxi driver is when you go out with Russian friends. Everything in Moscow closes down at half-past midnight. The only transportation then is either your legs or one of those green-light taxis. If you have just met your friends and they have invited you home—nowadays a not uncommon experience—keep in mind that this is a big city. Chances are they live in New Moscow, the great belt of new housing developments about 20 kilometres away. The soundest idea here is to have your friends negotiate a deal with the driver so that he will wait for you. Usually 5 roubles or so will sweeten his foul disposition. In that way he has made his nightly quota, and can have a good snooze in the taxi while you enjoy yourself.

A recent cartoon in the satirical magazine *Krokodil* suggests something of Muscovites' feelings about their taxi situation. It shows a covey of cabs lined up, bearing signs that read, respectively:

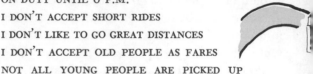

ON DUTY UNTIL 6 P.M.
I DON'T ACCEPT SHORT RIDES
I DON'T LIKE TO GO GREAT DISTANCES
I DON'T ACCEPT OLD PEOPLE AS FARES
NOT ALL YOUNG PEOPLE ARE PICKED UP
I ALWAYS TAKE MY LUNCH ON TIME

river trips

From May until October, more than a million people travel on the river annually. Most of them go to nearby scenic spots on the weekends, others take the more distant routes on vacation or business. You ought to treat yourself to a trip on the Moscow River; this is another of the city's travel bargains, costing about 20 kopecks each way.

The opening of the Lenin Volga-Don Canal in 1952 turned Moscow into a port with access to five seas: the Caspian, the Baltic, the White, the Black, and the Azov. What this means is that you have really quite a lot of choice. You can spend a few hours at the

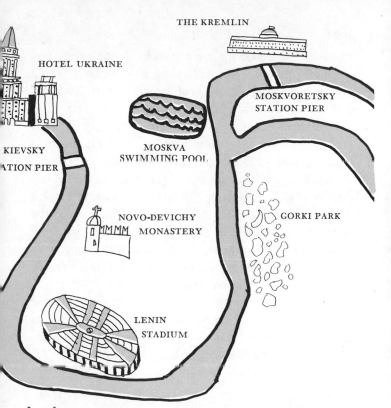

beach, or cruise up or down river for the entire day. Another alternative is to cruise through the center of Moscow, passing such sights as the Lenin Hills and the Kremlin.

Unless you speak Russian, it is advisable to have your Intourist guide along. It is easy to get on the wrong boat. The Service Bureau is always willing to assign you a guide if you give them 24 hours notice.

Here are a few possibilities:

1. Take the Metro to the *Rechnoi Vokzal* (River Terminal) station. You will cover the nine miles in less than 20 minutes. You emerge in front of the **Northern River Port Passenger Terminal,** the chief

embarkation point for river travel. If you wish, you can have quite an enjoyable time here without taking a ride, just sitting in the roof-garden cafe instead and looking out over the water.

Otherwise you can choose, with the help of your guide, from a wide variety of trips. You can board a leisurely three-deck motor-liner that looks as though it would be quite at home on the Mississippi, or you can take a breathtaking ride on a skimming Rocket or Meteor hydrofoil boat. Hydrofoils rise out of the water like seagulls and skim the surface at speeds of up to fifty miles an hour. A short ride will take you up the Moscow River to the **Khvoiny Bor** (Pine Woods) or the Birch Grove wharves.

2. If you don't want to make a day of it, then take the Metro from Revolution Square to Kievskaya (a matter of minutes). From Kievskaya walk down to the river. Here you may go in either of two directions:

Route One: Kiev Terminal–Lenin Hills–Gorki Park–Krymsky Bridge–Bolshoi Ustyinsky Bridge–Krasnokholmsky Bridge–Novospassky Bridge. This trip, about half an hour each way, takes you past the Novo-Devichy Convent, Lenin Stadium, Moscow University on the Lenin Hills, the Moskva Swimming Pool, the Kremlin, the Hotel Rossiya, the wedding-cake skyscraper on Kotelnicheskaya Embankment, Novospassky Monastery, and many other Moscow landmarks.

Route Two: Kiev Terminal–Krasnopresnensky Park–Kuntsevo Kryatskoye. This route takes you to Fili-Kuntsevo Park and the river beach. Allow 90 minutes each way.

day trips from moscow

It would be a pity to leave Moscow without spending a few hours in the country. There is a great deal to see beyond the city limits and it's a remarkably easy thing to do.

For one thing, you'll be surprised how *quickly* you can get out of the city (this is no London). Nowadays the traffic moves swiftly along broad prospects and highways, through new underpasses, across new overpasses, and soon enough the last of the putty-colored brick and concrete housing developments are behind you. *Thirty minutes* after you leave your hotel door you can find yourself deep in the unchanging, untidy, straggling Moscow countryside.

Your choice

You can travel alone with an Intourist guide, make up a small group (3–5 people), or join one of Intourist's regular bus tours. The choice is up to you. How much money you have to spend, of course, will govern your decision at least partly. Still, with a bit of ingenuity, you can ride in style. The best bet is to—

Rent a limousine Cheaper than you think. If you can get three to five people together, you can hire a chauffeur and a Chaika. This splendid limousine—which may remind you of a prewar Packard—is used by many Soviet big-wigs. You get a ten-hour day, including gas and driver, for less than $70. Of course, you need to book at least a couple of days ahead. If you don't feel up to the Chaika, Intourist has smaller cars available (see page 74). If you are travelling De Luxe or First Class, you have already *prepaid* individually for several hours of the services of an English-speaking guide. So if you are touring as a small group you can pool your time and obtain a guide for the entire day at no extra cost. The guide will make the necessary arrangements for meals, tickets, and so forth. If you plan your trip right you should be able to manage a picnic, buying all the necessary food, mineral water, and wine ahead of time.

Join a tour Less grand but cheaper is one of Intourist's bus tours. All of the places mentioned below are part of their itinerary.

You make arrangements in the Service Bureau at the TOUR desk. Tickets range in price from 2 to 15 roubles (depending on the distance) and usually include a meal if it is a day-long trip. In the peak summer period, May to September, it is necessary to book at least a day in advance.

Arkhangelskoye
(30 kilometres from Moscow)

Winter or summer, this is a perfect way to spend an afternoon. The Arkangelskoye estate comprises a peerless grouping of eighteenth- and nineteenth-century architecture, and has been called "the Versailles of Moscow County." Originally the home of Prince Yusupov, one of Imperial Russia's richest landowners, it looks today as it must have a century or so ago.

The Prince's palace is a masterpiece of wooden architecture covered with ochre-colored stucco. As you enter the gravelled courtyard, admire the elegant colonnades that surround the building.

Inside, attendants will ask you to slip canvas overshoes over your footwear to protect the parquet floors. Notice the extra-large windows—necessary in an age when candle-power rather than electricity was the chief source of illumination.

Here are dozens of rooms richly decorated with antique sculptures, tapestries, and porcelain. There are paintings by Van Dyke, Boucher, Tiepolo, among others; the rooms are luxuriously appointed with silk-canopied beds, crystal chandeliers, and elegant murals. No bathrooms are visible.

As director of the Imperial theatres, Prince Yusupov cut a great figure in Moscow society. It is not difficult to imagine how this great house looked when filled with guests.

Yusupov had thousands of serfs, and there is a theatre in the park where performances were given by serf-actors.

Don't miss the library upstairs. The Prince collected about 40,000 books in all European languages. Peek out of the library window for a beautiful view of the park, whose landscaping reflects a strong French influence. It is adorned with statues brought from Italy and France.

Open daily Wednesday through Sunday 11 a.m. to 5 p.m. Closed Monday and Tuesday. Admission is 20 kopecks.

Recommendation: If you have rented your own car, plan to arrive around 11 a.m. Tour the house and grounds, then go down the road (about a five-minute ride) to The Russian Hut (see page 225) for lunch. You will not be seated unless you have a reservation, so make sure Intourist books you a table before you leave Moscow. Quite an experience.

Vladimir Lenin House-Museum
at Gorki Leninskiye
(35 kilometres from Moscow)

This is where Lenin lived out the last years of his life. Here he died at 6:50 a.m. on January 21, 1924. Since that time the pilgrimage has never ceased to the lovely Moscow village of Gorki, associated forever with the leader of the Bolshevik Revolution.

Before 1917 this was the home of the wealthy Morozov family. It stands on a steep hill overlooking a rambling birch-filled park. As you walk through the well-tended grounds, your guide will point out Lenin's favourite bench, and the 18 cherry trees that were a gift from a delegation of textile workers who came to wish him a speedy recovery.

Inside the house his sparsely furnished room—inkwell, paper-knife, eye-glasses, books—is as he left it. The stream at the end of the garden is the Pakhra River, a tributary of the Moscow River.

Open Monday 11 a.m. to 5 p.m.; Wednesday through Sunday 11 a.m. to 7 p.m. Closed Tuesday. Admission free.

Zagorsk
(75 kilometres from Moscow)

The seat of one of the oldest Russian monasteries, the **Troitse-Sergiyeva Lavra** (Trinity Monastery of St. Sergius) and one of the treasures of ancient Russian architecture. Here you leave present-day Russia and step back into the Old Russia of the Middle Ages.

Founded in 1340, the Troitse-Sergiyeva played a major part in the history of Moscow. It was both a stronghold that defended the principal city of ancient Russia and a major seat of culture. Within this fortress-city lived master icon-painters, wood-carvers, silver-smiths, and many other craftsmen. A wall almost six feet thick encloses no less than 13 churches. These include the white-stoned **Cathedral of the Holy Trinity** (1423), **Church of the Holy Ghost** (1477), **Cathedral of the Assumption** (1559), **the Infirmary** (1637), and the Refectory (1686).

Before the 1917 Revolution this was the second-richest monastery in Russia, with a treasury valued at 650 million gold roubles. In those years more than 100,000 pilgrims a year visited this monastery. Today—although the Soviet state does not publicise the religious aspect—there are still many thousands of devout Russian visitors who make the pilgrimage.

You cannot walk up and down the main avenue of the monastery without being aware of the deep religious atmosphere of the place: old women cross themselves frequently, and the walls by the main entrance have been kissed almost coal-black by the devout.

Today the Troitse-Sergiyeva is one of the few places where priests of the Russian Orthodox Church are still trained. Look around, and you will see many of these bearded young men in their black flowing gowns walking through the grounds.

As you enter through the main gate, there is a small office on your left where you can buy postcards. On your right stands the five-domed **Uspensky (Assumption) Cathedral** built in the reign of Ivan the Terrible in the sixteenth century. This is an "active" church; the interior smells of beeswax, and wax tapers are always burning. If you make too much noise, you will be hushed by one of the many black-clothed women who act as custodians. Consecrated in 1585, the

Uspensky is a virtual copy of the Kremlin's Uspensky Cathedral. As you enter, notice the **Tomb of Tsar Boris Godunov** to the right of the door. Seventeenth-century frescoes and an eighteenth-century iconostasis (icon wall) have been preserved inside.

You are now close to the central square, with its 290-foot belfry designed by the Italian architect Rastrelli in 1741.

Walk south in the direction of two more churches. These are the **Church of the Holy Spirit** (1554) with a single dome, and the white-stone **Cathedral of the Trinity** (1422), the most revered because it contains the sarcophagus of St. Sergius. There is always a dense crowd of pilgrims here, chanting hymns as they file past the relics of the saint.

Some of the finest and most representative examples of ancient Russian painting have been preserved here. Take special notice of the iconostasis paintings and the murals—the work of the greatest of all medieval Russian painters, the monk **Andrei Rublev** (1370–1430).

Walk back towards the main gate, where you entered. On your right is a large building painted with multi-colored lozenges in the manner of the "facets" of the old Kremlin Palace. At one time this was the refectory; it has since been converted into a church, and the main religious services are held here. If you visit Zagorsk on a Sunday, it is a tremendous experience to work your way inside (it is always crowded) and listen to the magnificent singing.

As you walk around the monastery, don't be surprised to find a Hollywood-sized movie crew filming scenes here. Zagorsk is a favourite location for Mosfilm, most especially for costume pictures. In recent years, location shooting for such films as *The Brothers Karamazov* and *Andrei Rublev* has been done here. Open daily 8 a.m.–6 p.m. Admission free. Allow a full day for your visit.

Recommendation: Pack a picnic lunch, unless you are part of a bus tour. You can obtain ice cream and soft drinks outside the gates, but there is no decent restaurant for miles.

The Home of Tchaikovsky
(90 kilometres from Moscow)

Fifty-five miles northwest of Moscow is the old Russian town of **Klin**, founded in 1318. Here for many years the great Russian composer Pyotr Tchaikovsky made his home. "I cannot imagine living anywhere else," he once wrote. "The Russian village, the Russian landscape, and this all-pervading quiet I need so badly, have enchanted me." Everything in this house has been kept exactly as it was during his lifetime.

In the study and sitting room you can see Tchaikovsky's books and music. His last music lies on his desk, and in the centre of the room stands his grand piano. Here the composer wrote *The Sleeping Beauty*, the Hamlet Overture, and his Fifth Symphony. Twice a year, on the anniversaries of his birth and his death, the finest Soviet pianists sit down at his piano and play his music. The American pianist Van Cliburn once visited Klin and he, too, was given the honor of playing on Tchaikovsky's piano.

Open daily 11 a.m. to 6 p.m. Closed Wednesday. Admission 20 kopecks.

Recommendation: Pack your own lunch, because there is no restaurant or coffee shop nearby.

Yasnaya Polyana: Home of Leo Tolstoy
(200 kilometres from Moscow)

This is a long day's journey by car, but certainly a memorable one. The great writer Leo Tolstoy (1828–1910) was born, and spent most of his life, on this estate, where he is also buried. *War and Peace* was written here, *Anna Karenina, The Power of Darkness,* and much else.

It is a perfect place to visit in the summer and fall. You approach the house through an avenue lined with old birch trees. On your right is the park, on your left the garden.

You will be fascinated by the house. As you step inside, you can almost hear the quiet shuffling of servants.

On the ground floor are the guest rooms and a vaulted chamber that occasionally served as a study. On the upper floor are the library, where the manuscripts of Tolstoy's works used to be copied (often by Mrs. Tolstoy), and the drawing-room. Most of the family life of the Tolstoys passed in this latter room.

On the same floor are the reception room and the study, where Tolstoy wrote most of his books; from it a door opens onto the balcony, where you can get a fine view of the park and Yasnaya Polyana.

Keep your eyes open for the portrait of Henry George in the study. Tolstoy was deeply impressed by George's ideas on land nationalization and the single tax. The writer is buried in a forest glade about half a kilometre from the house.

Open daily 11 a.m. to 5 p.m. Closed Tuesday. Admission 20 kopecks.

Kolomenskoye
(12 *kilometres from Moscow*)

The village of Kolomenskoye is a true gem of Old Russia, with its quaint timber houses and its fine churches. Now a museum, it lies within what was formerly one of the tsars' suburban estates. It is less than twenty minutes' drive from midtown Moscow.

Kolomenskoye was built around the end of the sixteenth century and is picturesquely situated on the banks of the Moscow River. The village contains three outstanding examples of ancient Russian architecture: the **Church of the Resurrection** (1531); and the **Church of John the Baptist** (1529); and—easily the most remarkable—the **Church of the Ascension** (1533), the finest example of a "pyramid" (*shatior*) church in Russia. "Greatly wonderful in height, beauty, and brightness," wrote an old chronicler about the church, "the like of which has never yet existed in Russia." Within easy walking distance is the **Sokolin (Falcon) Tower,** where the tsars' hunting falcons were kept. Here you will find a museum of ancient Russian art that includes valuable collections of Russian tiles, wood carvings, and authentic examples of the ancient Russian timber houses, including the little house of Peter I (the Great), moved from its original site in Archangel.

eating and drinking

You may return home singing the praises of Russian cooking, but nowhere in Moscow will you find *grande cuisine*: this is decidedly not Paris. The truth is that the gourmet tradition is alien to Soviet man. This is a town where shashlik is considered an adventurous meal, beef Stroganoff laced with sour cream a treat, and fish salianka (the head winking out of the bubbling broth) a culinary landmark.

And yet, in one culinary dimension, the USSR is actually ahead of the United States: There is no Muzak in Russian restaurants; also, franchised food is unknown and so food in Russia tastes like real food and not like wet newspapers.

the cuisine

As befits a country with ferocious winters, the cuisine is heavy and freighted with starches. It is also somewhat rich to a modern diet-conscious palate. This has a purpose. As an ancient Tsar of Russia once observed: "The joy of Russia is drinking. She cannot do without it." In contrast to France, where wine is considered an accompaniment to a perfect meal, in Russia the meal is thought of as the natural accompaniment to drink.

Nevertheless, Moscow's reputation for indifferent food is a bit unfair, and standards have risen considerably during the past few years. The problem in Russia is how to enjoy dining while enduring the painfully slow service. Here we run into the famous *nichevo* spirit again: Russians enjoy sitting around the dinner table drinking and talking by the hour. A three-hour meal is commonplace. The Russians believe this aids the digestion; they shake their heads at foreigners who insist on rushing through a meal in less than two hours.

The food that I like eating in Moscow, and which is unsurpassed, is. fresh Beluga caviar served on small pieces of white bread; cold smoked salmon; all Russian fish, particularly sturgeon; beef Stroganoff; chicken zatsivi; Russian ice cream with berry jam; and most Russian cakes.

If you enjoy a cocktail before dinner, I strongly recommend that you have it in your room. You will have to buy the ingredients (the Beriozka store in your hotel—see page 261), but it will save you agony later. Russian restaurants do not serve cocktails. They do serve wine, champagne, brandy, and vodka.

You should start your meal with *zakuski* (appetizers) such as fresh caviar, smoked salmon, cold sturgeon, or cold chicken salad, and then have as your entree beef Stroganoff, chicken Kiev, or shashlik Caucasian-style, followed by ice cream for dessert. Instead of *zakuski* you might try a bowl of borshch or fish salianka. Steaks are very good, but they are not a familiar cut of meat.

Eating a green salad with your meal is unheard of in Russia, and anyway fresh green vegetables are scarce. You can obtain a tomato salad (САЛАТ ИЗ ПОМИДОРОВ —sa-LAHT eez pa-mee-DOR-av) upon request, if you wish. Ice (ЛЁД—LYOD) also has to be requested; butter (МАСЛО—MAZ-la) likewise, and you will be charged extra for it.

Wines are moderate in price and sometimes moderate, sometimes quite high, in quality. Champagne is inexpensive and comparable to U.S. domestic brands. You probably won't care very much for Russian beer (ПИВО —PEE-va), which tastes flat and tepid. Occasionally, however, you can find Pilsner Urquell, a world-famous Czech beer. Worth inquiring about.

Most hotel restaurants and cafes are open from 8 a.m. until 11 p.m. Breakfast hours are from 8 until 10 a.m., lunch is served from noon to around 3 p.m., dinner from 6 until 11 p.m. After 11 p.m. you are out of luck except for the "dollar" dining rooms that can be found in most, though not all, of the larger hotels. As you can guess, in these restaurants, as in the dollar bars, you have to put away your roubles and meal coupons and pay in hard currency. The advantage is that they stay open usually until about 1 a.m. and they are rarely crowded.

One other practical hint: The multilingual menus found in hotel dining rooms should not be taken too seriously, because less than a third of the items mentioned are ever available. What follows are the main dishes that are almost always on hand:

Cold appetizers

CAVIAR (ИКРА—ee-KRAH) A great bargain; though not cheap, it is roughly half the world market price in Moscow. Caviar has been prized as a delicacy since Aristotle's day. Though eggs from many species of fish are sold as caviar (most typically, black-dyed lumpfish from Iceland), only sturgeon roe is worthy of the name; and in Moscow you get the real thing. (More on the subject can be found on page 275)

SALMON (СЁМГА—SYOM-ga) Smoked and salted, and served in thin slices.

CHICKEN SALAD (САЛАТ ИЗ КУРИЦЫ—sa-LAHT eez ku-REE-tsy) Arrives in a small, square dish, decorated with egg-halves and cucumbers, and mixed with potato salad and mayonnaise.

STURGEON (ОСЕТРИНА—ah-SEET-ree-na) It comes sliced as thickly as roast beef, and the taste is delicate and distinctive—closer to chicken than to any other species of fish. A perfect accompaniment to vodka.

HAM (ВЕТЧИНА—vee-CHEE-nah) No particular merit can be found in Soviet ham, which has a tendency to fattiness.

Soups

BORSHCH MOSCOW STYLE (БОРЩ ПО-МОСКОВСКИ Borsh po-MOS-kov-ski) Beet soup with ham, beef, tomatoes, and chopped cabbage added. Sour cream on the side.

FISH SALIANKA (РЫБНАЯ СОЛЯНКА REEB-na-ya sa-L'YAN-ka) Several varieties of white fish in a soup made from stock with onions, bay leaf, and egg whites added.

MEAT SALIANKA (МЯСНАЯ СОЛЯНКА MIS-naya sa-L'YAN-ka) Beef and ham in a soup made from stock with vegetables added.

SHCHI (ЩИ—shee) There is an old Russian saying: *Shchi da kasha, mat nasha*—"Shchi and kasha, that's our mother." This is cabbage soup thickened with flour and often with a lump of meat served separately. You will not find *shchi* in the big hotels, but rather in the cafeterias, or *stoloviye* (see page 223).

Sturgeon

The most popular fish is the sturgeon from the Sea of Azov. In first-class Moscow restaurants you can have it in the form of a salad (with cold potatoes) in aspic

(on the menu this will be described as "sturgeon jelly"),
or served cold with a horseradish sauce. For a main
course it comes boiled, in tomato sauce, fried, or gar-
nished Moscow-style, which means grilled and decorated
with dill and parsley.

STURGEON SALAD (САЛАТ ИЗ ОСЕТРИНЫ   sa-LAHT eez
ah-SEET-ree-nee)

STURGEON WITH HORSERADISH (ОСЕТРИНА С ХРЕНОМ   ah-
SEET-ree-na ss-khre-NOM)

STURGEON JELLY (ОСЕТРИНА ЗАЛИВНАЯ   ah-SEET-ree-
NA za-LEEV-na-ya)

STURGEON IN TOMATO SAUCE (ОСЕТРИНА В ТОМАТНОМ
СОУСЕ   ah-SEET-ree-na v to-maht-NOM SAW-oos-yeh)

BOILED STURGEON (ОСЕТРИНА ОТВАРНАЯ ah-SEET-ree-NA
art-VAR-na-ya)

STURGEON MOSCOW-STYLE (ОСЕТРИНА ПО-МОСКОВСКИ
ah-SEET-ree-na po-MOS-kov-ski)

FRIED STURGEON (ОСЕТРИНА ЖАРЕНАЯ   ah-SEET-ree-NA
zhar-REE-na-ya)

Meat and Fowl Dishes

BEEF STROGANOFF (БЕФ-СТРОГАНОВ   beef STRO-ga-noff)
The classic dish of Russian cuisine: sautéed beef with
mushrooms and onions. In Moscow this is very good
indeed—partly because of the addition of sour-cream
sauce, partly because of the ravishing taste of the locally
picked mushrooms. The dish is served with straw potatoes scattered on top of the plate.

BEEFSTEAK ANGLISKI (БИФШТЕКС ПО-АНГЛИЙСКИ   BIF-
steks po-an-GLEE-skee) Can be ordered rare (С КРОВЬЮ
SKRO-vyu), medium (СРЕДНИЙ SRED-nee), or well done

(ХОРОШО ПРОЖАРЕННЫЙ ka-RO-shaw pra-ZHAR-ree-nee).
Invariably excellent, the meat is grilled and is about the
size of a tournedos.

SHASHLIK CAUCASIAN-STYLE (ШАШЛЫК ПО-КАВКАЗСКИ
SHASH-leek po-kaff-KASS-ski) Grilled, skewered lamb.
The marinated meat is strung on long skewers, meat
alternated with chunks of onion, then grilled on a stove
and served with raw tomatoes.

LULJA-KEBAB (ЛЮЛЯ-КЕБАБ loo-LA-kee-bab) Pretty much
like shashlik: lamb in chunks, with onions, green pep-
pers, but minus the skewers and served on a bed of rice.
Very tasty.

CHICKEN KIEV (КОТЛЕТЫ ПО-КИЕВСКИ Kot-LE-ty po-kee-
YEV-ski) Possibly the most popular dish in Moscow.
Reliable and always well-prepared. Served with pastry
baskets holding a thimbleful of peas, and accompanied
with a mound of straw potatoes. What is it? A chicken
breast, deboned, filled with an oblong of butter, then
dipped in bread crumbs and egg and fried. Be careful!
As the prongs of your fork touch a perfect chicken Kiev,
you will be greeted by a spurt of hot melted butter.

CHICKEN TABAKA (ЦЫПЛЯТА ТАБАКА see-PLA-TA ta-ba-KA)
A Georgian dish. The chicken is prepared by removing
the backbone, which in itself is quite an art. The bird
is then flattened and fried under a heavy weight. Served
with a prune sauce and accompanied by pickled cabbage.

CHICKEN ZATSIVI (ЦЫПЛЯТА САЦИВИ See-PLA-TA Sa-
TZEE-vee) Boiled chicken in a walnut sauce with coriander
and other herbs. It is a very spicy dish.

Desserts and Cakes

ICE CREAM AND BERRY JAM (МОРОЖЕНОЕ С ВАРЕНЬЕМ ma-ROZH-no-yeh sva-rayn-YEM) Many lovers of ice cream rank Russia's version as the best in the world. In restaurants it comes only in one flavor—vanilla—and is made from pure eggs and pure cream with nothing but sugar added in the manufacture. It arrives at your table in a silver dish with a meringue biscuit and topped with freshly made berry jam.

BLINY (БЛИНЫ —BLEE-nee) Russians have been eating them for a thousand years. They can be eaten for dessert, but you may also find them appearing with caviar at the beginning of a meal. For dessert they are served with berry jam. On all occasions they arrive at tableside accompanied by butter and sour cream. You choose one or the other—never both—and then top with caviar or jam, as the case may be.

CAKES (ПИРОЖНЫЕ pee-ROZ-nee-ya) Russians make the kind of cakes that small English boys adore. They are heavy, fruit-filled, and enriched with nuts. After a normal Russian meal they may be too rich for your palate, but after an afternoon about town they are delightful with a steaming cup of tea.

A great favourite with Russian schoolchildren is *pampushky*—doughnuts filled with jam. These can be bought in the city's cafes or luncheonettes (see pp. 223–5).

A *word about Russian bread* (ХЛЕБ **Khlyeb**)

It is a popular myth that Russian bread is black. In fact, it is only when you travel to the Soviet Asian republics that you find such a bread. In Moscow, the bulk of the baking is done with rye or whole-wheat flour (much of it from the USA and Canada) and it is either white or light brown. It never comes thinly sliced but is eaten in thick slabs, usually without butter. It is when you leave the hotel dining room and visit some of the restaurants that specialize in regional cuisines that you will encounter different breads.

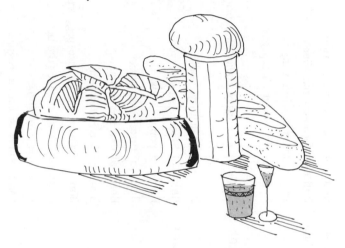

drink

In most Moscow restaurants you can enjoy vodka, champagne, a choice of Soviet wines (some very good indeed), or cognac with your meal. But if you crave mixed drinks or scotch, bourbon, or gin, you will have to visit a dollar bar (see page 226). Liquor is sold either by the bottle or by weight. It is *never* sold by the glass in a dining room. Vodka, for example, costs about one cent a gramme. With any liquor, 100 grammes is approximately three drinks, and 200 grammes enough for three people. More serious imbibers order by the bottle. Here are some typical prices, in roubles and kopecks:

ГРУЗИНСКОЕ БЕЛОЕ ВИНО	Bottle of Georgian white wine	2.85
ГРУЗИНСКОЕ КРАСНОЕ ВИНО	Bottle of Georgian red wine	3.00
БЕЛОЕ ВИНО	100 grammes of white wine	0.38
СУХОЕ СОВЕТСКОЕ ШАМПАНСКОЕ	Bottle of dry Soviet champagne	3.38
ПОЛУСЛАДКОЕ СОВЕТСКОЕ ШАМПАНСКОЕ	Bottle of semi-sweet Soviet champagne	3.90
СТОЛИЧНАЯ ВОДКА	Bottle of Stolichnaya vodka	4.45
СТАРКА (КРЕПКАЯ) ВОДКА	Bottle of Starka (strong) vodka	4.50
ПЕРЦОВКА	Bottle of pepper vodka	2.60
КОНЬЯК	Bottle of three star cognac	6.00
« — »	Bottle of four star cognac	6.75
« — »	Bottle of five star cognac	7.80
ДВИНСКИЙ КОНЬЯК	Bottle of Dvin cognac (see page 215)	12.30
ЕРЕВАНСКИЙ КОНЬЯК	Bottle of Erevan cognac (the best)	12.75
КОНЬЯК	100 grammes of three star cognac	1.20
ЕРЕВАНСКИЙ КОНЬЯК	100 grammes of Erevan cognac	2.55

If you want ice with your drinks, you must specify by saying лёд!—*lyod!*, pronouncing each letter. Mineral water is another peculiarity that you have to get the hang of. It is usually served chilled. It comes in a variety of tastes. If you want something akin to plain soda-water, specify НАРЗАН—*Narzan* (which in Kabardian, a Caucasian language, means "the water that gives you strength"). On the other hand, if you wish to clear your head, ask for БОРЖОМИ—*Borzhomi*, a mineral water that has the tang of iodine. Mineral water costs an average of 13 kopecks a bottle.

A few words about vodka

A lot of nonsense has been written about this crystal-clear spirit. So here are the true facts: It has been distilled in Russia since time immemorial from fermentable carbohydrates, usually grain—wheat, corn, or rye. It can be distilled from potatoes, but most Russian vodka is grain-based. Vodka is made in the same way, and from the same ingredients, as whisky, gin, or akvavit. But it is more thoroughly filtered than any of these, so as to be as nearly without flavor as possible. Long considered a top-of-the-head remover, vodka is in fact one of the gentlest drinks known to man. Stolichnaya, the most famous Russian vodka, is filtered through quartz sand and a special charcoal made from birch trees. As a result the congeners—fusel oil, acid, esters, aldehydes, and tannins—which cause hangovers have been removed.

How to drink vodka   Properly, it is never sipped, but taken in one quick swallow, followed by a bite of salt herring or caviar. In Moscow you will find it is served in very small glasses that hold less than a half-ounce. Many Russians follow each glass with a long gulp of mineral water. If you adhere to this procedure, and drink in moderation, you will wake up with a clear head the next morning.

Although clear vodka is by far the most popular, there are at least 10 or 15 different kinds. At the Hotel National, for instance, you can get Starka, an aged rye vodka the color of caramel that is slightly stronger than average. Also widely available are Zubrovka, a flavored vodka made by steeping buffalo grass in the bottle, and pepper vodka, which is laced with red pepper.

Wines and champagne

When you ask for wine in Moscow, nine times out of ten you will receive Georgian wine. The little Georgian Republic, traversed by the great Caucasus Mountains, is the Soviet Union's Napa Valley and Burgundy all rolled into one. The wines are excellent. This is how to order:

БЕЛОЕ ЦИНАНДАЛИ	WHITE Tsinandali No. 1
КРАСНОЕ ТЕЛИАНИ	RED Teliani No. 2
БЕЛОЕ ГУРДЖИАНИ	WHITE Gurdzhiani No. 3
КРАСНОЕ МУКУЗАНИ	RED Mukuzani No. 4
КРАСНОЕ САПЕРАВИ	RED Saperavi No. 5
БЕЛОЕ КАХЕТИНСКОЕ	WHITE Kakhetinskoye No. 8
БЕЛОЕ ТВИШИ	WHITE Twishi No. 19
КРАСНОЕ ХВАЧКАРА	RED Khwanchkara No. 20
БЕЛОЕ ТЕТРА	WHITE Tetra No. 26

If you want to be safe and sure, you cannot go wrong by sticking to Tsinandali No. 1 for a white wine, and Mukuzani No. 4 for red. Both possess a clean, fresh, dry flavor. Be careful when ordering. It has happened and will happen again: the finger is raised to the waitress or waiter to indicate the number of the wine desired. The guests are surprised to get twenty-six bottles of No. 1 instead of one bottle of No. 26!! To be on the safe side, point to the menu.

About Soviet champagne very little can be said. It ought to be tasted, it is remarkably cheap, and if you drink enough of it you will have a fearsome hangover.

manners & customs

It is not absolutely unknown in Russia for a three-course meal to be served in an hour. But it is rare. Hotel restaurants, especially, are notoriously slow in service. In fairness, as mentioned previously, this is an age-old Russian tradition. Put simply: Russians have very different dining habits from you and me. Knowing this, try then not to become frustrated. You came to Russia to see a different way of life. This is just one example of another nation's folkways.

Of course, if you are part of a group tour, you will normally encounter no difficulties. Intourist arranges a permanent table for your group. It is rather like being aboard a cruise ship. You show up at scheduled times and are fed from a scheduled menu. Should you find yourself with a group that is being served far too slowly there is something you can do about it. With the consent of your fellow visitors, you work out a simplified menu, with precise items, for lunch as well as dinner. Hand this list over to your guide at 8:30 a.m., suggesting the times you wish your meals. This method has been known to work successfully.

If you are travelling independently, or if you choose to dine out, you are very much on your own. Restaurants are nearly always crowded in Moscow. On entering, your best approach is to catch the eye of any waitress or waiter and see if he or she can offer you a table. If not, you can head for the nearest empty table, making sure that there is no "Reserved" (ЗАКАЗАНО) sign on it. If you are alone, it is the Soviet custom that—with the exception of a table occupied by a large group or delegation—you can join any table where there is an empty chair.

If you are planning to go to the theatre or the ballet, see your guide in the morning (or the Service Bureau), who will arrange for an early dinner on your behalf. It is practically impossible to enter any Russian restaurant after 9 p.m.

The point bears repeating: It is important to take Russian dining philosophically. Time has little meaning, with a single important exception—closing time. At that hour (usually 11 p.m.) service stops, even if you are in the middle of your meal. Nothing except the most ferocious banging of plates will help you.

It should not come as a surprise to you if you wait thirty minutes for a menu. Allow another thirty minutes for the table to be reset. Allow an additional half-hour before the first course arrives. Once you have the menu in your possession, it is highly recommended that you order everything at once. A word you will hear waiters using all the time is СЕЙЧАС—Sey-CHASS! or, abbreviated, CHASS! Its literal meaning is "within the hour," but it is used in the same sense that we use the phrase "right away." Strictly speaking, there is no word for "immediately" in the Russian language, so be calm when told "Within the hour!"

Like to dance? Many restaurants have "live" music, usually a four- or five-piece orchestra with a girl vocalist; the repertoire is middle-of-the-road stuff and exhibitionism on the dance floor is frowned upon. Though Russians adore dancing, prancing and swirling are not favored and it is by no means uncommon for the band to stop playing if the dancing becomes too exuberant.

There are some basic rules of dancing etiquette that are well worth remembering: It is perfectly O.K. in the Soviet Union for a girl to ask a man for a dance. You can also ask anyone—accompanied or not—for a dance, although it is not good form to ask twice.

Tipping is not customary in the USSR. All the same, if the service has been extremely good, leaving the small change on the plate is a nice gesture.

restaurants

Moscow is not a great restaurant town and never has been. Still, you can enjoy yourself hugely if you visit any of the restaurants listed below. The best way to get to them is to have your Russian guide write down the name and address of the place in Russian, have the Service Bureau make a reservation (absolutely a must where so indicated), and then off you go. Hail a taxi, show the driver the note; in due course you will arrive. If there is a queue outside the restaurant, don't join it. Just go to the door and knock. The doorman will let you in. A word of caution: the expense account is alive and well in the Soviet Union. All good restaurants are crowded, mainly with Russians. Be patient. In time you will get your table.

Cafe Arbat *(Kalinin Prospekt 291–14–03)*

One of the city's best and most expensive restaurant-cabarets. It has modern furniture and a bustling, efficient staff to go with it. Windows are discreetly lace-curtained. Through them you get a view of busy Kalinin Prospekt. At lunch-time you are surrounded by the people who really keep Russia going: civil servants from the various ministries or from Comecon (the Eastern European equivalent of the Common Market) whose offices are close by. At night the atmosphere is sophisticated. One visits the Arbat for the cabaret; this is one of the few places in Russia with a chorus line. A rare opportunity to watch a dozen slender Russian girls together. Food is on the hearty side. The menu has been designed by the Moscow Food Trust, so don't expect brilliance. Surroundings, however, are tops. Prices expensive. Dinner from 5 to 15 roubles, depending on choice. Reservations mandatory.

Aragvi *(6, Gorkovo 229–37–62)*

One word sums up the Aragvi—terrific! Quite possibly Moscow's most popular restaurant. The "in" place for top Russians and foreigners alike. The cuisine is Georgian and so is the service. Georgians are famously hospitable people and the waitresses with their lustrous, dark large eyes make you feel at home at once. You dine under low arches decorated with murals. The speciality is chicken zatsivi, the highly spiced cold chicken dish which comes smothered in walnut sauce (see page 205). There are more than thirty dishes on the menu—chicken tabaka, broiled sturgeon, shashlik, among others. As an appetizer, try the sulguni, a crisp, deep-fried cheese, with warm, round, freshly baked bread as an accompaniment. Georgian wines are fine, especially the Mukuzani (which is often hard to find in Georgia because of Moscow's demands for it).

Prices expensive. Dinner from 7 to 20 roubles, depending on choice. Reservations mandatory.

Ararat (4, Neglinnaya Street 223–57–46)

Ornate, mysterious—Peter Lorre in a white suit would fit quite nicely into the Ararat's rich atmosphere. Much more earthy in flavor than Aragvi, this restaurant is the capital's mecca for Armenians whom you can see all around you enjoying roast lamb, pilaf with raisins, and *chebureki*—Armenian meat pies fried in deep fat—all washed down with Algeshat, a sweet Armenian wine. After the meal, try one of the pungent Armenian brandies. The most potent of these are *Dvin* (100 proof) and *Erevan* (114 proof).

Medium-priced. Dinner from 4 to 12 roubles, depending on choice. Reservations necessary.

Baku (24, Gorkovo 127–32–83)

Loaded with atmosphere. This eating house, which takes its name from the capital of Azerbaijan, is a delight. The rooms are small and intimate. There are stained glass windows, brass lamps, carpets on the walls. For a Soviet restaurant, service is remarkably speedy, yet no one rushes you. Azerbaijanis, who nowadays are chiefly oil men, lend to the oriental mood.

If you compliment the manager, he may well show you into his crowded office, where in his wall safe he keeps a tattered copy of *Life* Magazine with a color photo of his wonderful establishment. Specialities: twenty different kinds of pilafs (lamb, chicken, beef, milk, eggs, etc.). For a first course, try *Baku's Piti*, a soup which is prepared and served in a clay bowl. Other first courses include *dovta*, a sour milk soup with meat, and a nut soup with chicken. The Baku is also known for its *golubtsy* (chopped meat and rice cooked in grape leaves) and *narkurma* (lamb roast with pomegranates). Medium-priced. Dinner or lunch from 4 to 12 roubles. Reservations necessary.

Comecon *(Kutuzovsky Prospekt)*

Not on the beaten tourist path exactly. If you want to see how middle-level Soviet officials dine, come to this modern restaurant behind the soaring new Comecon building. Decor is modern and service is quick. Middle-of-the-road Moscow cuisine: chicken Kiev, salianka soups, etc. Moderate prices. Dinner or lunch from 3 to 7 roubles. No reservations required.

Metropole *(1, Karl Marx Prospekt 228-40-60)*

The Grand Hotel tradition lives on here. The main restaurant is on your left and up the stairs as you enter. Generations of Americans—from John Reed to Lillian Hellman, who lived here during the war—have dined here. It's an excellent place for lunch, a bit gloomy during the dinner hour. The room is decidedly pre-1914 in its spaciousness. One imagines doves fluttering about in the gloom up beyond the enormous crystal chandeliers. Palm trees, mirrored walls, and an eight-piece orchestra on a distant stage all add to this *fin-de-siècle* mood.

Service can be disastrously slow. The food is better than average, but the menu does not vary. You will find the regular standbys: chicken Kiev, beef Stroganoff, chicken tabaka, and various fish dishes. Upstairs, on the fourth floor, the management has opened what they call a tea room. Despite the name, you can get wine and bliny here—one of the few spots in the city where those delicious thin pancakes can be found. As you eat there is balalaika music, and girls in peasant costume to wait on you. Only dollars or hard currency are accepted here. Both restaurants are medium-priced. In the main dining room, dinner or lunch will range from 4 to 10 roubles. No reservations necessary, but try to avoid rush hours.

Moskva (7, Marx Prospekt [Manege Square] 292-62-60)
The view is the thing here. The Hotel Moskva is where Soviet officials stay when they have business in Moscow. You take an elevator to the tower restaurant. A fine, big-window view of the Kremlin. The menu is standard Moscow fare. There are always chicken Kiev and beef Stroganoff. Service is slow.
Medium-priced. Most of the main dishes are reasonably priced. Dinner or lunch from 3 to 9 roubles. Reservations necessary.

National (1, Gorkovo 203-55-95)
One of the oldest restaurants in the city. Lenin once lived on the floor above the dining room, and almost every important visitor to the city has dined here at one time or another. If you are lucky enough to get a table by the window, the Kremlin is across the Manege Square and is illuminated until midnight. Crowded at all times; the food is good but not distinguished. Caviar is always available. Excellent cold sturgeon, better-than-average chicken Kiev, beef Stroganoff. Beef Angliski, a thick slice of steak, also first rate. In recent years the service (which used to be appalling) has made some improvement.

As you while away the time waiting for your waiter or waitress, admire the elegant painting on the ceiling. For a brief period each evening there is an orchestra which plays Russian pop music plus a soulful soprano who goes along with such hits as "Moscow Nights" and "Orchi Chornya."

There are, in fact, seven separate dining rooms on the same floor, and two of them will not take roubles or Intourist meal tickets, only dollars or hard currency. Make sure you enter the right room.

The menu runs to over a hundred dishes, but only a few of the items mentioned are ever available. Recommended: the crab salad; chicken Kiev; beef Stroganoff. Also, the National serves the best steak (English beefsteak) in Moscow. If you enjoy soup, try the fish salianka. You can usually obtain fresh caviar at about 1½ roubles a portion, and the ice cream is delicious.

As mentioned earlier, do not be offended if a stranger joins your table. At the National, space is hard to find. Likewise, if you are alone, simply move in on any available table.

The men's and ladies' rooms are down the corridor to your left as you leave the restaurant. If you leave during your meal, be sure to let someone know at the door or you will have a hard time reentering.

Medium-priced. Dinner or lunch from 4 to 12 roubles. Reservations necessary.

Pekin   (1/7, *Bolshaya Sadovaya Street* 253–83–65)

A quite extraordinary evocation of Old China. Here you sit amidst the red lacquer bamboo screens and Chinese lanterns and there is not a Chinese face in sight. One can imagine this restaurant in the glowing era of cordiality between the two powers. Nowadays only the plates and the furnishings are a reminder of the days before the Sino-Soviet rift.

As you listen or dance to a standard Moscow seven-piece band, examine the menu. Your waitress may recommend the *Druzhba* (Friendship) salad. With a straight face she will tell you this is a typical Mandarin appetizer. It includes cold pork, squid, pickled hard-boiled eggs, lettuce, shrimp, carrots, and noodles. You can also order a shark's fin omelet—pike in sweet and sour sauce. Regrettably, the management ran out of Mai-Tai just after the Cultural Revolution, so you'll have to settle for vodka.

If you find a very old man waiting on your table, he could be Yakov Usakov, the oldest waiter in the capital. Through an interpreter he will tell you he once upon a time waited on Maxim Gorki and Alexei Tolstoy.

Medium-priced. Dinner or lunch from 4 to 12 roubles.

Praga   (2, Arbat Street 290–61–52)

If you have been to London, this may remind you of the Lyons' Corner House in the Strand: Several restaurants inside. Old-fashioned atmosphere and a certain faded gaiety. Greville Wynne, the British spy who worked with Oleg Penkovsky, used to dine here and didn't like it. On the other hand, Premier Khrushchev once declared it the finest restaurant in the world. You will have to make up your own mind. The whole place looks like a converted movie theatre. There are seven restaurants within, and the main dining room has a glass roof, potted palms, and ornate tiles with a Czech motif. Your dining companions are likely to be Soviet army generals (GHQ is around the corner), German businessmen, Rumanian party bosses. Some of the most attractive girls in Moscow seem to eat here, and the food—though not recognizably Czech—is excellent. The menu is multilingual, though a great many tempting items are not in fact available. From time to time the Praga will have roast pork (a rarity in Moscow), served with dumplings and sauerkraut. There is also a hot sausage, called a *vuršty*, that is served with potato salad. Pilsner Urquell, the famous Czech beer, is available. The rest of the menu is Russian and not too dissimilar to that of the National. Food apart, the Praga has more ambience and atmosphere than most Moscow restaurants, and is well worth a visit. After dinner there is dancing. For a businessman, this is an excellent place to entertain Russian colleagues.

Prices expensive: 6–20 roubles, depending on choice. Reservations necessary.

Rossiya (1, *Moskvoretskaya Most 298–05–52*)

What the Rossiya's main ground floor restaurant has going for it is one of those gigantic swing bands of the 1950's, all dressed in gold lamé coats, and playing such hits as "Take the A Train." Although the restaurant seats 1,000 people (and there is another one elsewhere in the hotel the same size), with 3,000 bedrooms above you the dining rooms are understandably packed.

The atmosphere is reminiscent of Las Vegas: lots of noise, clinking glasses, banging trays, and overworked staff. The food is well prepared but the menu is standard fare—chicken Kiev, beef Stroganoff, and so forth. You may find yourself surrounded by delegations of earnest molecular biologists attending some conference. If the doorman refuses to let you enter, simply say *Delegatsiya* in a firm tone and the glass doors will open. After that you are on your own.

Medium-priced. Dinner or lunch from 4 to 12 roubles.
Reservations necessary, unless you arrive very early.

Seventh Heaven *(TV Centre, Ostankino)*

The most spectacular dining room in Moscow, situated two-thirds of the way up the city's TV tower. You
can watch the clouds roll by from your table. This
rotating three-story restaurant seats 300 and is always
crowded. For a minimum of 8 roubles you are served
a fixed menu with no substitutes allowed. Drinks are
extra. Under house rules, each person must finish his
meal within 2 hours to make room for new customers.
Reservations necessary.

Slavansky Bazaar *(13, 25th October Street 228–48–45)*

This is the Slav equivalent of a restaurant like the
Baku, long on atmosphere. An ideal setting for young
Russians in love. Recently a new interior decoration
was added to the faded splendors of the old Bazaar: an
electrically illuminated mural based on an old Russian
folk tale. This eating house dates back to the nineteenth
century, and Gogol once supped here. Excellent Russian appetizers *(zakuski)*, cucumber salad with sour
cream, sturgeon, and jellied pike.
Medium-priced. Dinner from 4 to 12 roubles. Reservations necessary.

Tsentralny *(10, Gorkovo 229–72–35)*

Founded in 1865 as the Filippov Cafe, it became
part of the Hotel Tsentralny before the Revolution.
This old-established haunt with its starched white linen,
golden ornaments, caryatids, and crystal chandeliers is
today one of Moscow's best restaurants.
Specialities: crab salad (САЛАТ ИЗ КРАБОВ sa-LAHT ees

KRA-bov), *kholodets* ХОЛОДЕЦ ko-LOYD-dyets), an appetizer of beef, veal, and chicken in gelatin served with a mustard sauce, and *charlotka* (ШАРЛОТКА shar-LOT-ka), a creamy vanilla and raspberry-puree dessert.

Medium-expensive. Dinner or lunch from 6 to 18 roubles. Reservations necessary.

Ukraine   *(Kutuzovsky Prospekt 243–32–97)*

A restaurant that serves Ukrainian dishes: borshch, chicken Kiev, and a special dumpling dish called *varenyki*. Wash it all down with a Massandra wine from the Crimea or a muscat called Krasny Kamen (Red Stone) which seems to be served only here. There is an orchestra, dancing, and service is fair.

Medium-priced. Dinner or lunch from 4 to 10 roubles.

Uzbekistan   *(29, Neglinnaya Street 221–31–77)*

You are in Central Asia. Spacious, cool interior. The tiled walls are magnificent, and everything is served on Uzbek porcelain and pottery. The food is extraordinarily good, and served with warm, aromatic Uzbek bread that almost makes a meal in itself.

The menu is superb. For openers, try *tkhum-dulma* (ТХУМ-ДУЛМА tkoom-DOOL-ma), a boiled egg inside a fried meat patty, or *mastava* (МАСТАВА ma-STA-va), a rice soup with specially prepared chopped meat. For a main course: *maniar*, a strong broth with ground meat, egg, and bits of rolled-out dough. Another excellent dish is shashlik Uzbek style—marinated, then broiled over hot coals. Uzbek wines are on the sweet side. Two of the most popular are Aleatiko and Uzbekistan.

This is a wonderful place for either lunch or dinner. A very popular restaurant, and you'll have to work hard to get booked here, but it is well worth the effort. Medium-priced. Dinner or lunch from 4 to 12 roubles. Reservations mandatory.

Warsaw (Varshava) *(2/1, Oktyabrskaya Proyezd 236–80–63)*

You can have a wonderful time here. It is a place where Russians go to enjoy themselves. Be warned, the atmosphere is noisy in the extreme, the air-conditioning nonexistent, the place filled with smoke, the toilets an absolute horror. But here you have the kind of place where hard-working people let off steam. Everyone seems to know each other (but welcomes strangers). The waitresses try to serve dinner but the attempt is all but hopeless in the wash of ribaldry and loud cheer. To add to the confusion, there is a raucous five-piece band belting out "Moscow Nights" and other favourites. You'll love it. To reach the restaurant take the elevator to the top floor.
Medium-priced. 3–10 roubles. Reservations necessary.

inexpensive eating

There are hundreds of self-service restaurants in Moscow. These luncheonettes, or *stoloviye* (singular *stolovaya*—СТОЛОВАЯ), are places where workers can get a warm meal at a reasonable price. If you are in a hurry, they are worth your attention and you can find them everywhere. On Gorkovo, for example, there are more than a dozen such *stoloviye*. Inside the choice is fairly limited, ranging from, say, a hot pie to a bowl of cabbage soup. The food is served up cafeteria-style from behind a long counter. You point to the item you want and pay either the person serving you or the cashier.

The most popular *stolovaya* dish seems to be a fried meat patty called a *kotleta* (КОТЛЕТА) which is often served with a side order of potatoes. You can lunch for under a rouble in these places. Neither wine nor beer is available as a rule. Instead, most *stoloviye* serve *kvass*, a non-alcoholic, mildly sweet-tasting brew made out of fermented bread.

A different class of restaurant again are the cafes. These are open from 8 a.m. until 11 p.m., and they serve light snacks, cakes, and desserts, and wines. A few serve hard liquor such as vodka and brandy, but this is the exception rather than the rule. These cafes, simple in decor and flavored with the personality of their clientele, are well worth a visit. Muscovites, like Parisians, like to *s'encanailler*—immerse themselves in the mob scene of city life. In modern Soviet movies a cafe scene is almost obligatory, and it is in the cafes, thick with the acrid and pungent aroma of Russian tobacco, that you can see and share the human face of Moscow. There is always plenty of action in the National Cafe in the hotel of that name, 1, Gorkovo, a spot that is popular with the theatre crowd. Poets and writers favor the Arbat quarter, especially the newer cafes along Kalinin Prospekt (see pp. 213 ff.)

Here are a few of the better-known Moscow cafes. They are always crowded, and you may have to wait in line.

Ararat 4, Neglinnaya Street
Cosmos 4, Gorkovo
Druzhba 5, Petrovka
Kholodok 10/34, Strastnoi Boulevard

Khrustalnoye (Crystal) 17, Kutuzovsky Prospekt
Krasny Mak (Red Poppy) 20, Stoleshnikov
  Pereulok
Landysh (Lily of the Valley) 29/3, Kirov Street
Leningradskoye 38, Arbat Street
Lira 17, Gorkovo
Mars 5/6, Gorkovo
Molodyozhnoye (Youth) 41, Gorkovo
Moskovskoye 8, Gorkovo
National 1, Gorkovo
Ogni Moskvi (Lights of Moscow) 7, Marx Prospekt
Prokhlada (Cool) 3, Marx Prospekt
Raketa (Rocket), 6, Gorkovo
Romantiky (Romantics) 40, Komsomolsky Prospekt
Russky Chai (Russian Tea) 13, Kirov Street
Sever (North) 17, Gorkovo
Snezhinka (Snowflake) 60/2, Leninsky Prospekt
Sokol (Falcon) 61, Leningradsky Prospekt
Sputnik 78, Leninsky Prospekt
Uyut (Cosy) 34, Leninsky Prospekt
Yunost (Youth) 40, Prospekt Mira

outside moscow
The Russian Hut *(Near Arkhangelskoye)*

Though you can eat Russian food everywhere in
Moscow, this is the only dining spot that serves the
traditional country cuisine. A visit here cannot be
recommended too highly. Specialities include *ukha*
(УХА), a fish soup flavored with herbs and seasoning;
meat boiled in *kvass* and served with *kasha* (buckwheat
groats); and *shashlik* (ШАШЛИК), which is cooked out-
doors. Bear meat is served in season.

Guests sit at long wooden benches and eat from red-and-gold enameled wooden vessels (the kind you can buy at any Beriozka store, incidentally).

About an hour's drive from the city center. A visit here can be combined with one to the country estate of Prince Yusupov (see page 190). The restaurant, a traditional log cabin, is situated on a lake surrounded by a birch forest.

It is always crowded, proximity here being considered a virtue. Food is served in generous portions. As the wine, vodka, and home-made *kvass* flow, the guests get a bit on the jolly side. Only open during the day, from noon until 6 p.m. You absolutely need an interpreter here, mainly to get through the crush at the door.

Medium-priced. 4–12 roubles. Reservations mandatory.

moscow after dark

Street-cleaners, journalists, marketmen, and policemen work through the night. Otherwise Moscow is abed by midnight. It is a wonderful time to take a walk. Street crime is virtually unknown, and it is safe to walk in any direction. Patrolmen in a police car may look at you suspiciously, but otherwise you will not be disturbed. Moscow is an enchanting deserted stage set by moonlight and should not be missed.

There is not much night life in Moscow, but then taxi drivers from Paris to New York lament "There is no night life anywhere." Here, however, it is programmed that way. How else can the USSR overtake the West economically by the year 2000? Yet don't give up hope. Prompted by the need for hard currency, the Soviets have, in recent years, opened a number of the so-called "dollar bars" previously described (see page

60). Few Russians here, only your fellow Intourists in search of company. Try the following late-night pubs. They usually close at 2 a.m.

The National Bar (Hotel National, 1, Gorkovo)

The action begins around 10 p.m. here and continues until around 2. The bar gives the impression of having never recovered from last night's hangover. Once the home away from home for foreign correspondents, today it is the haunt of Finnish businessmen, London sharpies, lost American ladies looking for a little excitement, and young lads and lasses who have heard that this is the place for action. There is a Polish jukebox with no song titles: you pay your money and take pot luck. Ladies tend the bar and are very sweet. They will give you change in any currency that comes to hand, so look twice—you may get Austrian schillings or Polish zlotys in exchange for your ten dollar bill or five pound note.

Drinks are now in the neighborhood of a dollar apiece, but be warned: there are no posted prices. The girls seem to charge by your looks.

You may be approached by an African student from Patrice Lumumba University with an offer to buy him a drink. It seems that foreign students get their stipends once a month, blow it all in a few nights, then rely on "Intourists" for the rest. Occasionally a Russian girl shows up here. This is very much frowned upon by the authorities. Several have, in fact, found the National Bar the first step towards a stay in a labor camp for "wayward" behaviour. There is a great shortage of chairs and tables, so help yourself and join a group. The bar is on the second floor of the National.

Turn right at the head of the stairs and head for the noise.

The National Late Night Restaurant *(1, Gorkovo)*

One of the few places in Moscow where you can get a four-course dinner at 1 a.m. But it will be expensive— hard currency only. Atmosphere intimate and quite elegant. The restaurant is on the second floor. Turn right, and it is the first room on your left. After supper you can cross over to the bar for a nightcap.

The Labyrinth Bar   *(Hotel Intourist, 3, Gorkovo)*

The newest and noisiest. No Soviet journalist could do justice to the scenes of mayhem and drunkenness around 1 a.m. on a midsummer's evening.

The decor is Soviet Modern and reminds one of Hitler's bunker: raw concrete walls, with lamps, which must weigh fifty pounds each, loosely anchored to the walls, directly above your table. The mini-skirted waitresses have a hard time getting through the service door—which isn't surprising, considering that it's several hundred pounds of ponderous concrete. Ever tried opening a 300-pound door with a table knife? Even so, the Labyrinth has a certain boozy charm. There are several interconnecting rooms here, and for Moscow the lighting is positively sexy.

At the bar madness prevails as a dozen different nationalities scream for "visky," "zhin," and "wodka."

No posted prices. During the rush hour—1 to 2 a.m.— the bar girls' pricing of drinks gets erratic. You may be asked for 50 cents, a dollar, or a dollar and a half for the same drink. Best practice is to proffer a fair price in the rush hour.

The management might consider posting prices in the interests of international goodwill.

Never have there been so many tourists seeking so little solace at such high prices. It's a seller's market.

If you decide the Labyrinth is for you, the path is downstairs through the Hotel Intourist's lobby. Fair warning.

Metropole Bar   *(Hotel Metropole, 1/4, Marx Prospekt)*

Compared to the Labyrinth, this after-hours spot resembles a Philadelphia club on Christmas Day. To be heartily recommended if you want a quiet nightcap in pleasant surroundings.

Open until 2 a.m. The bar service is pleasant and correct.

Pechora Cafe   *(Kalinin Prospekt)*

Where the under-thirties gather. Popular with the young, hip, and adventurous. Dixieland music. Down-

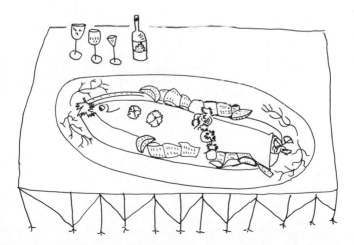

stairs is a beer bar, one of the few in Moscow, and a good place to meet young Russians of both sexes. Both places close around midnight.

The Railway Stations offer food and shelter on a 24-hour basis. The buffets serve sausage rolls and hot tea. Head for Komsomolskaya Square, where you have a choice of terminals: Leningrad, Yaroslavl, and Kazan Terminal, all within brief walking distance of each other. See people arriving, departing.

Sobering-up Stations Drunks are not welcome on Moscow's streets. The city fathers have arranged for special motor-cycle patrols to pick up the light-headed. Should you be one of them, expect to find yourself in the side-car and whisked away to a *vytrezvitel,* a sobering-up station. You will be charged 10 roubles for the evening and released next morning with a warning.

entertainment

Moscow excels in things to see and do. The arts flourish here. It is a city boiling and bubbling with cultural life (and at very little cost). There are no breaks between seasons. In Moscow it is always theatre time.

Twice a year the city holds festivals of the performing arts: the Moscow Stars Festival, May 5–15, and the Russian Winter Festival, December 25–January 5. Both feature opera, ballet, and drama by Moscow's finest theatre companies, and recitals of such outstanding musicians as Richter, Oistrakh, Gilels, Oborin, Rostropovich.

In summer, when many of the capital's theatrical groups go on tour, the stages of Moscow are turned over to the best theatrical companies of other Soviet cities. Outdoor theatres in parks and gardens feature variety concerts and festivals of song and music.

In short, you will find plenty to choose from. At any given moment there are, at a guess, some thirty plays running, a dozen major concerts, half a dozen ballets or opera performances, and movies by the hundred. To discover what is going on, buy a copy of the English-language *Moscow News* and check the entertainment page. Or else go to the THEATRE desk in the Service Bureau. The Intourist clerk there always has a copy of the weekly calendar of events.

A word of advice: Don't wait in lines to obtain tickets. In this as in all matters, Intourist takes very good care of visitors. The Service Bureau will willingly get you the best seats in the house, at no extra charge.

backgrounder: the theatre

You can't appreciate theatrical life in Moscow without at least a quick glance backwards historically. *Vsevolod Meyerhold*, who founded his own theatre in 1920, anticipated virtually every development of world theatre down to the present. The pop-rock musical *Hair* would have held no surprises for him—much about its staging and lighting was familiar in his own productions.

Performances with the audience on the stage or with actors placed in the audience, fireworks, circus turns, motion pictures used as part of the stage action, "theatre-in-the-round," montage, "living newspapers"— all these techniques were developed in the early Soviet theatre. The best-known playwright of the era was undoubtedly *Vladimir Mayakovsky*, whose brilliant satirical comedies, *The Bedbug* and *The Bath House*, lampooned the new bureaucracy.

In the 1930's the "golden age" of the theatre was ended by Stalin; by 1935 "Socialist realism" was the ruling idea. Lost in the Stalin purges were dozens of producers, dramatists, actors, critics—among them Isaac Babel, Meyerhold, Bulgakov, Erdman, and Natalie Sats, the founder of the Jewish theatre.

It was the 20th Party Congress in 1956, where Khrushchev denounced the Stalinist excesses, that gave new life to a stagnant theatre. Mayakovsky's plays were rehabilitated; several new foreign plays were staged (including *Dial M for Murder*, called *The Telephone Call* in Moscow, since there is no *M* on any Moscow telephone).

The Khrushchev era produced a number of new theatres, the first of real significance being the Moscow

Sovremennik (Contemporary) under the brilliant leadership of the actor-producer Igor Yefremov. The current atmosphere, unfortunately, is not encouraging to artistic experimentation, and once again the Soviet theatre is beset by bureaucratic interference, censorship, and dull conformity.

going to the theatre

Still, if you enjoy the theatre, you can have the time of your life in Moscow—even without knowing a word of Russian. Of course you must make a choice, and it is recommended that you see what may already be familiar to you. The plays of Chekhov, for example, at the **Moscow Art Theatre.** It is a fine idea to bring with you to Moscow an English edition of some of the better-known Russian plays. A quick read before the performance will enable you to follow the action. The Taganka and the Sovremennik are for those who either understand Russian or are students of drama.

Ticket prices range from about 60 kopecks to 4 roubles. Although tickets are hard to get for Russians, visitors usually have no problem obtaining them. Check with the THEATRE desk in the Service Bureau (see page 42). Evening performances at theatres begin at 6:30 and usually end between 10 and 11. Concerts begin at 7 p.m. Matinee performances at 12 noon. The Puppet Theatre, 7:30 p.m. It is against house rules to wear outer garments within the theatre. The cloakrooms will be found as you enter. Tipping is not necessary. Don't lose the stubs.

The Moscow Art Theatre   (3, *Proyezd Khudozhestvennovo Teatra Tel: 29-25-46*)

The chief shrine of Russian theatre (commonly called by its initials, the "MKhaT"), the Moscow Art Theatre is known and revered everywhere. Three-quarters of a century old, it has been called a miracle of sustained creativity. Founded by the great Konstantin Stanislavsky in 1898, it is the birthplace of "method" acting, giving the world "the theatre of inner feeling." Its 34-play repertory today includes the great classics made famous by Stanislavsky, including Chekhov's *The Sea Gull* (the Art Theatre's emblem), *Uncle Vanya, The Three Sisters, The Cherry Orchard*. Another favourite: Maxim Gorki's *The Lower Depths*. The Theatre is famed for its classically simple sets, clear lighting—and magnificent ensemble acting.

Vakhtangov Theatre   (26, *Arbat Street Tel*: 41–07–28)
Until Eugene Vakhtangov's death in 1924, this was Moscow's Hebrew Theatre. Vakhtangov's forte was something called "fantastic realism." Today very much a mainstream kind of place.

Taganka Theatre   (76, *Chkalov Street Tel*: 99–19–92)
Under the direction of Yuri Lyubimov, the Taganka has become one of Moscow's liveliest theatres. This young theatre thrives on new productions and contemporary stagecraft. Sound, shadow, slide-projection, music, mime, are all part of the "Lyubimov touch." Definitely the first place to check out if you care for modern drama.

Maly Theatre   (1/6, *Sverdlov Square Tel*: 31–37–28)
Founded 150 years ago, the "Little" is a warehouse of Russian culture. Gorki called it "the Russian people's university." The Maly is still considered the best of schools in Russian elocution, and of that specific articu-

lation marking the Moscow accent with its sonorous "ah" sound.

Sovremennik Theatre   (1/29, *Mayakovsky Square Tel: 51–36–72*)

The "Contemporary" ranks with the Taganka as a liberally oriented theatre. Choice of plays tends to be non-political, funny, and very real to Muscovites.

Romany Theatre   (20, *Pushkin Street Tel: 29–43–76*)

In many ways the most interesting theatre in the city. Gypsy actors portray scenes from Romany life in plays bursting with music and dance.

Satire Theatre   (18, *Bolshaya Sadovaya Street Tel: 99–18–72*)

Occasionally a bit of mild satire seen here, attacking Soviet bureaucracy. The repertoire includes Maya-kovsky's *The Bedbug* and *Mystery Bouffe*.

Lenin Komsomol Theatre   (6, *Chekhov Street Tel: 23–96–68*)

An excellent place to study the theatre of propaganda. Primarily intended for youth audiences. It is also a stage for first-time plays of young dramatists.

Central Puppet . Theatre   (32a *Gorki Street Tel: 51–33–61*)

Also called the Obraztsov after its resident genius and founder, who may well be the most gifted puppeteer in the world. Although a great treat for children, the audience is well peppered with grown-ups who "ooh" and "ahh" with the youngsters over his elaborate productions.

Children's Theatres

Moscow has four of them:

Central Children's Theatre, 2/7, Sverdlov Square (Tel: 29-41-59);

Moscow Children's Theatre, 10, Pereulok Sadovskikh (Tel: 99-53-60);

Moscow Puppet Theatre, 26 Spartakovskaya Street (Tel: 61-21-97); and

Children's Musical Theatre, 17, 25th October Street, whose repertoire includes *The Wolf and Seven Kids,* based on old Russian fairy tales.

ballet

As everybody knows, Russia's artistic pride and joy is the ballet—always has been, always will be. To be sure, there was a time just after 1917 when some revolutionaries suggested that the ballet be abolished as a bourgeois relic of Imperial entertainment. Fortunately, wiser heads prevailed, and it was swiftly recognized as a national asset by the young Soviet state.

For years, both before and after 1917, Leningrad was a better ballet town than Moscow. Until the late thirties the Leningrad Ballet (officially the Kirov Ballet, after Communist Party boss S. M. Kirov) excelled the Bolshoi. This was due to the brilliant ballet teacher Vaganova, who trained such superb pupils as Semyonova, Dudinskaya, and the great Galina Ulanova. At the same time, Leningrad produced virtually all the ballet music composers: Prokofiev, Glière, Asafiev, Shostakovich. Among the outstanding works created during Leningrad's ascendency were Prokofiev's *Romeo and Juliet* in 1939, and Asafiev's *Flames of Paris* and *Fountains of Bakinchisarai*.

As compared to theatre and literature, Soviet ballet in the thirties was relatively less troubled by the demands for "socialist realism." Yet it did not entirely escape attack. In 1936, 1946, and 1948 tremendous controversy and debates broke out between the proponents of mime on the one hand, and the supporters of pure dance on the other. The chief accusation levelled against the purists was "formalism." Grandiose staging and acrobatic dancing became the signature of Soviet ballet in the 1940's; the Moscow-trained Olga Lepeshinskaya, a superb acrobatic dancer, became the ideal for a whole generation. Today, the Soviet ballet is a mixture of the classical tradition and cautious experimentation.

As a visitor, however, you need not be terribly concerned about doctrinal and theoretical matters. Even if you don't know a *pas de deux* from a *fouetté*, an evening at the Bolshoi will hold you spellbound. The Russians love grandeur in their dancing and decor. In *Swan Lake* and *Prince Igor*, you will see some of the most imaginative staging ever created. Thus in *Igor*, among other highlights, the Prince comes dashing in astride a real horse in full regalia, the sun rises, the sun sets, the moon pops out, and Igor's enemies set fire to the town.

Bolshoi Theatre   *(2, Sverdlov Square Tel: 29-17-51)*

The word *bolshoi* means "great" or "big." Founded in 1776, the year of the American Revolution, the Bolshoi—with its five-tiered red and gold hall, its stupendous crystal chandeliers, its enormous stage (almost as large as the auditorium), and its remarkable

acoustics—is simply magnificent. The present Bolshoi was built in 1856 by Bove and Mikhailov. If you go, be sure to rent glasses from the cloakroom. One minor advantage of doing so is that when you leave, you can jump the waiting lines to return the glasses, and so you also get your coat back a lot earlier.

Kremlin Palace of Congresses *(the Kremlin, Trinity Gate Tel: 27-83-63, 27-79-90)*

If you visit Moscow in summer, more likely than not this is where you will see the Bolshoi Ballet perform. They can squeeze 6,000 paying customers into this building. The acoustics are impeccable, the stage the size of a football field, and viewing is perfect from any seat in the house. In addition, the building is air-conditioned. The walk here, across the Trinity Bridge (see page 111) into the floodlit Kremlin grounds, is a fine bonus. During intermissions walk over to the marble hall, where you can enjoy an ice cream and a promenade.

Also appearing here from time to time are one or other of the 14 major ballet companies besides the Bolshoi.

Stanislavsky and Nemirovich-Danchenko Musical Theatre (*17, Pushkin Street Tel: 29–42–50*)

Classical and modern operas, ballets, and operettas. This was originally "the studio of the Bolshoi Theatre." The ballet troupe of the Bolshoi includes its "Filiale," or "Branch": over 220 artists and a kind of shock troop reserve of 300 pupils. It is here that you can meet these aspiring stars.

Operetta Theatre (*6, Pushkin Street Tel: 29–42–05*)

Capacity 2,000. Classics to Franz Lehar performed here.

comedy & variety

In tsarist days, Moscow was full of music halls; these were rowdy places where vodka flowed along with the entertainment. To liven things up, a tame bear would often be let loose amongst the convivial crowd. The tradition of cabaret continues, but—alas—the smoke-filled music halls (and the booze) have vanished. Today the comedy tradition has been largely transplanted to TV, and what's left is to be found in only a few theatres. They are listed below. *Note:* In summertime there are quite a few variety shows staged in Moscow parks. You might inquire at the Service Bureau's THEATRE desk about such performances (see page 42).

Variety Theatre *(20/2, Bersenevskaya Embankment Tel: 31–08–85)*

Heart and soul of Moscow's variety art. Satirical shows and reviews which make fun of everything from the Metro to Soviet bureaucracy. Comedy stars from all across the USSR play the Moscow equivalent of the Palace or the Palladium.

Moscow Theatre of Miniatures *(3, Karetny Road Tel: 99–66–01)*

Melodrama in the Chaplin mode, farce, Victorian songs, dance miniatures, blackout sketches. The audience, which appears to hugely enjoy the goings-on, is part of the fun.

Moscow Music Hall

Every summer from May to September—the mobile Moscow Music Hall makes the rounds of the city park, with a week or so at the Exhibition of Economic Achievements. A great ensemble. Check with THEATRE desk at the Service Bureau.

Moscow Circus *(13, Tsvetnoi Boulevard Tel: 28–82–31)*

It is a toss-up whether Ringling Brothers or the Moscow Circus is the best in the world. In any event, you cannot lose by visiting what is almost surely the most entertaining show in Moscow. When the lights go down, everything comes up superlatives: the most fantastic tame bears, the funniest clowns, the cleverest horses (watch for the "troika" show), and the Cossack riders. There is also a new, ultra-modern hippodrome, with multiple arenas, on Prospekt Vernadskovo, that is the largest in the USSR.

Tickets available through the THEATRE desk in the Service Bureau (see page 42).

Moscow Ice Ballet

A great winter-only treat. Some fans say it outranks the famous Viennese Ice Review. Decide for yourself. This troupe usually performs in the Palace of Sport, Lenin Stadium. Tickets and performance times from the THEATRE desk in the Service Bureau.

concerts

Moscow is one of the great musical centers of the world. From Mussorgsky to Scriabin, from Bach to Shostakovich, it is all to be found here. Every performance of the State Symphony Orchestra is a sell-out occasion. The Pyatnitsky Choir's rendering of old and modern Russian songs is well worth an evening. The Beethoven Quartet, the Osipov Russian Folk Orchestra, and the Soviet Army Choir are all world-renowned. The unsurpassed standard of performance is the result of considerable resources devoted to music by the State, and of extraordinary and intensive training.

In an average week (there is no particular "season" in this city) there are upwards of thirty concerts to choose from. Tickets and information on current concerts you can obtain from the THEATRE desk in the Service Bureau.

Tchaikovsky Concert Hall (31, *Gorkovo Tel: 99–03–78*)

Symphony concerts, solo recitals by musicians and singers, musical oratorios, and concert versions of well-known operas.

Tchaikovsky Conservatoire (13, *Herzen Street Tel: 29–74–12*)

This is the hub of Moscow's musical life. It is also the home of the International Tchaikovsky Competition. Seats 2,000. Among the professors who have taught and played in the Great Hall of the Conservatoire are Rachmaninoff, Scriabin, Tchaikovsky himself, Khachaturian, Richter, Rostropovich, and David Oistrakh. You reach here with a brisk eight-minute walk from the Red Square (see Walk Three).

Small Hall of the Tchaikovsky Conservatoire (13, *Herzen Street Tel: 29–81–83*)

The place to come for chamber concerts of organ music.

Hall of Columns of Trade Union House (1, *Pushkin Street Tel: 29–36–12*)

Formerly a club for the nobility, this house is right out of *War and Peace*, a superb example of eighteenth-century Russian architecture. The hall is used for symphonies and chamber music. In pre-Revolutionary days it was the scene of many a glittering soiree. In 1919 it was turned over to the trade unions.

Lenin made over 40 speeches here between 1919 and 1922, and in January 1924 it was here that his body lay in state while hundreds of thousands of Russians filed by. A gallery runs round the entire auditorium; above are enormous sparkling chandeliers between each pair of columns. Quite an experience.

Hall of Gnesin Music Institute (30/36, *Vorovsky Street Tel: 28–24–22*)

Chamber music.

Concert Hall at Scientist's Club *(16, Kropotkin Street Tel: 46–66–84)*
Often used for debuts of promising young musicians.

Concert Hall at Hotel Sovietskaya *(32, Leningradsky Prospekt Tel: 50–73–53)*
Classical and chamber music.

Concert Hall at the Central Railwaymen's Club *(4, Komsomolskaya Square Tel: 62–86–04)*
Small choirs and concerts.

cinema

Moscow's movie houses range in size from Roxy Palaces to Bijou flea-pits. Go, even though you may not speak or understand a word of Russian. Join the fourteen million Russians who attend the cinema every day.

More even than the other arts, cinema is closely watched and supervised by the Communist Party. Lenin himself was an avid movie fan. Indeed, he laid down three main tasks for Soviet cinema. It was to be informative but selective, "like the best Soviet newspapers," he wrote; secondly, it should educate "like a public lecture"; and finally, it should be "artistically entertaining."

Broadly speaking, whatever you see will fall into one or the other of four main categories: First, films of literary classics such as *War and Peace, The Brothers Karamazov, Hamlet,* and *Uncle Vanya.* Second, war movies that reflect, as one writer put it, "the truthful portrayal of the victory of Soviet arms." Sometimes it seems as if every movie house in the Soviet capital is celebrating World War II—or, as the Soviets call it, "The Great Patriotic War." Third, Lenin films. In recent years this has become a major subdivision of the industry, with such items as *Lenin in Poland, A Mother's Heart, A Mother's Loyalty, The Living Lenin,* and *Banner over the World.* Finally (and most interesting of all from a Western viewpoint), movies on contemporary social themes such as *Hooligans, Rain in July,* and *Dangerous Road Show.* Of course, some of the more interesting films are flawed from the viewpoint of party ideology. As a result, you may have to travel to an outlying suburb to discover them.

Going to the movies

English and French movies play the Moscow circuit with Russian subtitles. But if you want to see Russian movies, you will have to see them in Russian. Still, you can get a surprising amount from the experience even if you don't possess a word of the language.

You can, if you wish, get tickets to the major Moscow movie houses from the THEATRE desk in the Service Bureau. Normally, however—except for some of the more off-beat movies—you should have no problem getting a ticket simply by lining up at the cinema. Prices are cheap, usually under a rouble. One nice thing: there is no price hike for the latest, hottest, or most publicized movie of the hour. All tickets are numbered and reserved. When you enter, look for your particular seat. Tickets are sold for one performance only—when the film is over, you have to leave. Soviet movie manners are exemplary, so try not to talk during the showing. It is also considered very bad form indeed to leave in the middle of a movie.

Newsreels, which are dead in most other countries, appear to be alive and well in the USSR; they precede the main feature. Doors open at 9 a.m. in most houses, with the last show beginning, as a rule, at 10:45 p.m. There is no admission in the middle of a showing.

The bigger and newer cinemas are in the city's central area, and are very comfortable indeed. The largest are the *Rossiya*, in Pushkin Square, and its twin on the new section of Kalinin Prospekt, the *Oktyabr*; each audi-

torium seats 2,500. Be sure to check out the mosaic murals adorning the façade of the Oktyabr (October). The overall theme is the birth of the Soviet state, and the murals form a continuity very similar to that of film sequences: the storming of the Winter Palace, the Civil War, and so forth.

Another major movie house is the *Cosmos*, with a seating capacity of 1,600. It is located at 109, Prospekt

Mira. The *Mir* (the word means both "Peace" and "World"), at 11, Tsvetnoi Boulevard, is a Cinerama-style theatre, reputed to possess the largest screen in Europe.

A night here is quite an experience. The screen has a curvature of 150° like a wrap-around windshield, and the visual effects are accentuated by the stereo sound provided by 120 loudspeakers. The sensory impact is startling: you feel as though you're in the middle of a crate of oranges riding along a particularly bumpy road. The film subjects tend to be predictable travelogues.

Another cinematic curiosity is *Circarama*, at the Exhibition of Economic Achievements, which has been called the "wonder" of the Soviet cinema. Twenty-two screens are joined in a closed ring. The spectator is totally enveloped in the action projected on the screen. Well worth a visit.

Yet another odd movie house is the *Rekord* at the Lenin Central Stadium. This house specializes in stereoscopic 3–D movies projected on widescreen.

Here's a short list of Moscow cinemas with the type of film normally shown.

Barrikady (21, *Barrikadnaya Street*)
Children's films and cartoons.
Khudozhestvenny (Art) (14, *Arbatskaya Square*)
Widescreen. One of city's oldest movie houses.
War movies, romance, literary epics are the usual fare.
Khronika (Events) (4, *Sretenka Street*) Newsreels only.
Nauka i Znaniye (Science and Knowledge) (51, *Arbat Street*) Specializes in science and science fiction.
Novosti Dnya (News of the Day) (33, *Tverskoy Boulevard*) Newsreels and documentaries.

Povtornovo Filma Classics   (23/9, *Herzen Street*)
Weekly classic revivals from Eisenstein to Dovzhenko.
Stereo Cinema   (3, *Sverdlov Square*)
3–D movies and general releases.
Trud (Labor)   (18, *Sushchovsky Val*)
Features with working-class orientation. Farm epics.
Yuny Zritel (Young Viewer)   (39, *Arbat Street*)
Films on Youth.

television

As with the press in the Soviet Union, television is
part of the transmission belt between the Party and the
masses. It is heavily weighted toward the provision of
information. Recently a critic writing in the national
newspaper *Sovietskaya Kultura* (Soviet Culture)
dourly noted that "After studying TV programs for
the past few weeks and using fourth grade mathematics,
we calculated the percentage of entertainment value of
TV broadcasts at 6 to 7 percent."

Until very recently, about the only place you could
find a TV set in a Russian hotel was in the corridor.
There simply weren't enough sets to go around. All this
is changing, and the prospects are at least 50–50 that
you will have your own TV set in your room.

What to see on TV

There are four TV channels in Moscow. Channel 1 begins its broadcast schedule at 5 p.m. with children's shows. Channels 2 and 4 broadcast six hours each, from 6 p.m. to midnight. Channel 3 is a daytime channel devoted mainly to educational and teaching programs.

Watching what Russians call "the blue screen" is a good way to see at a glance what a serious society Communist Russia really is. A typical day's programming begins at 9 a.m. with a talk about health, followed by a music program, and then a talk by the First Secretary of the Moscow City Communist Party. Later in the day there may be a football match from Prague, a report on farming in Kazakhstan, a broadcast on "The Army in Our Lives," a recital of songs about Lenin, a program dealing with the latest Five Year Plan, or a panel show, "The Club of Cheer and Wit," in which viewers and a studio panel test each other's knowledge with such questions as "How deep is Lake Baikal?"

Programming ends at midnight with news and music. Crime news and films of violence are unknown on Soviet TV. The overall aim seems to be to present the viewer with the image of a calm and ordered society. Color TV has recently come to the USSR and there is one color channel in Moscow. But you are not likely to see color in your hotel; at the present time there are less than 2,000 color TV sets in the city.

where to go dancing

Muscovites primarily go to the recreation parks. No matter what age you are, or whether you are single, divorced, or married, you will enjoy yourself in the free-

and-easy atmosphere. In summer and winter people head for the dance pavilions in Gorki, Sokolniki, Izmailovo, or Hermitage Park (see pp. 172–4).

In autumn one of the most popular places is the Central Exhibition Hall in Manege Square, the home of the Golden Autumn Ball, which lasts two weeks.

There is also dancing aboard many of the river boats. The ship's masts are decked out with Japanese lanterns, the river breeze accompanies you, and the shore slips by as you dance. From May through September there are regular river boat dances. Check with the THEATRE desk in the Service Bureau for details.

sports

If you have the urge to jump in a pool, kick a football, row a boat, go fishing, or zip around on ice skates, you can do so, and for spectator sports fans, Moscow is a paradise. Someone once counted one hundred and twelve different sports events taking place on a single day. Not surprising: the Russians love outdoor exercise.

The gamut of spectator sports ranges from archery to wrestling to soccer to horse racing to ice hockey to you-name-it.

How to join in

For any spectator sport, just ask at the THEATRE desk in the Service Bureau for tickets. To find out what's currently going on, check either at that desk or in the English-language *Moscow News*, obtainable at any newsstand. If you want to participate in any activity yourself, inquire at the same desk; they'll be glad to make arrangements for you.

Sports stadiums

Lenin Central Stadium *(Luzhniki, Metro: Sportivnaya)*

Luzhniki, located a little more than 15 minutes by subway from Revolution Square, is eye-catching. Described as a "township of sports," it is all of that and more. It has more than 130 installations for summer and winter sports, and its various grandstands can seat 150,000. It is the biggest spectator sports complex in Europe: track, open-air swimming, volleyball, basketball, fencing—the list runs on and on.

Open to visitors year round.

Dynamo Stadium *(36, Leningradsky Prospekt)*

Some of the best soccer in Europe can be seen here at the home of the Moscow Dynamos. Stadium seats 60,000. Go prepared—all spectator seats are without cover.

Locomotive Stadium *(125a, Bolohaya Chorhiaovohaya Street)*

Amateur athletics, most notably soccer. Stadium seats 40,000, partly under cover.

Individual Sports—Watching or Playing

Boating

Boats are available at most of the city's 14 parks. Rates range from 20 to 40 kopecks an hour. Gorki Park (see page 172) has a collection of unsinkables guaranteed to tone up even the flabbiest muscles.

Chess

Dozens of chess clubs in the city. A partner is usually available at the *Central Chess Club, 14, Gogol Boulevard*. Kibitzers are welcome.

Cycling

For spectators only. *The Velodrome, 31, Leningradsky Prospekt.*

Fishing

Really serious or prolonged fishing expeditions should be arranged *before* you leave for the USSR. For simply a day out, there is plenty available. If you have left your fishing equipment at home, inexpensive rod and line can be purchased in the G.U.M. Department Store (see page 286). The Service Bureau's THEATRE desk can arrange a half-day or full-day outing for you. The city is surrounded with rivers, ponds, and reservoirs. Lots of action.

Horse Racing

This is a great evening out. At the *Hippodrome, 22, Begovaya Street.* Better arrange to have an Intourist guide along to help with translation. Also, the best way to go is by taxi (less than 2 roubles). It is certainly not chic, and you don't have to dress for the occasion. But there's plenty of action, and you can bet small amounts on the tote. There is a crowded restaurant, but your best bet will probably be the soft drink and hot-dog stands. Racing begins at 5 p.m. on Wednesdays and Saturdays. On Sunday, the fillies take off at 1 p.m.

Motorbike Racing

Russians are wild about it. Every weekend (except for the worst of winter) the hrmmphhhh and grrrrr of engines, the smell of oil, can be found in half a dozen locations around the city. Chiefly it is the heavy stuff—skidding down gullies, barrelling up hills. There are always hot-dog stands, and a good place to view the goings-on. You will need your Intourist guide for the half-day, and probably also the rental of a car. If the sport interests you, check with the THEATRE desk, who can call the Central Motor-cycle Committee.

Ice Skating

Between October and April at dozens of locations all around the city. There are rinks in every major park, and at various stadiums. It is one of Moscow's principal outdoor pastimes, and to the tune of "The Merry Widow" you can join in the nippy enjoyment of it all. In summertime there are several indoor ice-skating rinks (see page 174). *Tip*: bring your own boots and skates.

Skiing

This is a huge subject. Russians love the sport, and Moscow has every imaginable variety of skiing within a 100-mile radius of the city. If you've forgotten your skiing gear, don't worry. You can purchase equipment at a store such as G.U.M. or the Beriozka (see page 286). For cross-country and simple downhill skiing, Sokolniki Park is a great favourite of Muscovites (see page 173). For something comparable to Vermont or Salzburg, *Zvenigorod*, about 60 kilometres from Moscow, is the place. Moscow has about 150 days of snow a year.

Swimming

The biggest open-air swimming pool in the city (in all Europe, for that matter) is the *Moskva Swimming Pool*, 37, Kropotkinskaya Embankment. It's a great experience. With average daily attendance around 15,000, and with 2,000 in the pool at any one moment, you are not short of company.

The strictest sanitary measures are observed. The water is changed three times a day by means of a huge filtering station next to the pool.

This pool is heated in wintertime, so even when the mercury is below zero you can enjoy swimming here.

Some novel features include an ersatz beach surrounding the pool, and a full medical staff in case of emergencies. There is also a sundeck. If you want to meet Russians of either sex, this is THE place. A little suntan lotion goes a long way in Russia.

You must bring your own bathing suit. There are changing rooms, and attendants to take care of your personal property.

A single ticket costs 50 kopecks.

The Moskva Pool is open daily from 7 a.m. to 11 p.m. You reach it by any of several routes: the Metro to Kropotkinskaya Station; trolley-buses 11, 15, or 31; or bus 8.

A *day at the beach*

The nearest beaches are less than an hour away from the city center:

The Dynamo Bathing Beach (*Leningrad Highway, Khimki Reservoir*) can be reached by taking the Metro (Green Line) to the Rechnoi Vokzal stop, which is the end of the line. You can make the trip without a single transfer by getting aboard at Sverdlov Square. As you exit from the subway, you will see Friendship Park directly opposite. The beach lies within the park.

You can also drive there. The best plan is to hire a car and driver from Intourist for the day or half-day. You do not need a guide, but you might want to pack sandwiches and soft drinks for a picnic.

If you drive yourself, proceed up Gorki Street from the direction of Manege Square, crossing the Boulevard Ring—Tverskoy Boulevard with its monument to Pushkin to the left, and Strastnoi Boulevard to the right. At the intersection of Gorki and the Sadovoye Koltso

(Garden Ring) is Mayakovsky Square, with its monument to the poet Mayakovsky at its center. This square is the main crossroads of the city. Here begins the Leningrad Highway, which leads to the river port of Khimki. Driving along the highway, you pass by Sheremetyevo Airport, and beyond it the village of Pokrovskoye-Streshnevo, site of a beautiful park. As the highway continues northwards, more and more construction of modern apartment buildings appears. A new overpass has been built across the railroad line in Koptievo. At the end of the highway, beyond Moscow's city limits, the Khimki River Terminal comes into view. An alternative is **Seryebryany Bor** (Silver Grove) **Beach**, a popular recreation spot on the banks of the Moscow River, which has a pine forest, a boathouse, and well-kept sandy beaches.

Follow the same instructions as above. When you get to the River Terminal, you board a motor boat to Seryebryany Bor. If you aren't taking an Intourist guide along, have the Service Bureau write out clear instructions in Russian so that you can be sure of boarding the right boat at the terminal.

At both places admission is 50 kopecks per person for the day, and you should bring your own towels and bathing suits.

Both open from 7 a.m. to 11 p.m.

shopping

introduction

Let's be blunt: shopping in Moscow can be a test of nerves and stamina—for a Russian. For you, it can be both fun and an adventure. Fun, because you possess hard currency and with it you can enter a world of luxury shopping denied to ordinary Muscovites.

You can patronize the Beriozka (Birch Tree) shopping chain. These attractive shops are full of such tempting articles as Czech glassware, Lithuanian amber, Siberian diamonds, North Russian lace, cameras, watches, caviar.

For those who want to get off the well-beaten tourist path, there is plenty of excitement in shopping Russian-style. Moscow is full of curious and interesting shops. But you will need patience, you will need know-how (supplied below), and you will need an *avoska*.

An *avoska* is the shopping net that most Russian shoppers carry; translated literally, the word means "just in case." For local residents the *avoska* comes in handy "just in case" the food store has acquired a supply of hard-to-get oranges or the shoe store has in stock some imported footwear. You too should have your *avoska*, "just in case."

Let's begin

Important for newcomers to the city to know are the three or four major shopping areas in the heart of town. First, *Kalinin Prospekt*. Nowadays the most elegant quarter of the city. Kalinin has a chic, up-to-the-minute look with glittering shops, cafes, restaurants. The emphasis is on items of popular appeal: cosmetics, books, records, photographic equipment, gourmet foods. Second, *Arbat*, a colorful, old-fashioned shopping street that leads off from the spacious, rectilinear Kalinin Prospekt. The shops here sell second-hand books, antiques, Havana cigars, sheet music, and posters. Third, *Gorkovo*, the city's main artery, a street of theatres, large shops, restaurants and cafes: window-shopping is a pleasure here.

Hours

Moscow stores, in general, are open from 11 in the morning until 7 in the evening. Most stores close for lunch, usually between 2 and 3 p.m. each day. Many shops are open on Saturdays and all *food* stores (*gastronomy*) are open on Sunday. Speciality stores often close on Mondays.

Since the majority of Russian women work, you will find the shops crowded during the evening hours.

How to shop

Don't be put off by the congestion inside the average shop. A great deal of time is wasted because of the antiquated layout of many stores (although, to be sure, extensive modernization is going on all the time). One thing to grasp immediately is that you *pay in advance* for almost everything in Russia. In your hotel, for example, you pay for your telephone call when you book it, just as you pay for your tour before you take it. In a store, you begin by reaching a counter, pointing to the item requested, finding out the price— you can signal the clerk to write it down for you if you speak no Russian. You then go to the cashier's desk, or *kassa* (usually by the door), and get a receipt.

Finally, you go back to the counter, the clerk examines your receipt, and hands over your purchase.

where to shop

Department Stores

The biggest store in the country is the G.U.M., which faces the Kremlin. Quite an experience. You push inside, scramble up staircases (no Moscow store has an elevator or an escalator), shove your way to counters. Crowded at all times, G.U.M. was built in the 1880's and is more a covered market than a department store in the Western sense. The boutique idea has not yet arrived in Russia, but G.U.M. may prove to be its forerunner. Originally it was a "trading hall" where merchants rented space to sell their wares. Inside you will find yourself wandering through a complex of low arches under a glass-roofed arcade. There are dozens of shopping alcoves. Other "department stores" in Moscow are quite similar. In none of them will you find American Express, Diners' Club, BankAmericard, or any other credit services available to foreigners. Nor will you find gift-wrapping, shipping, or delivery to your hotel. What ·you purchase you pay for in cash (roubles) and carry out with you.

Speciality Shops

Don't mistake Russian speciality shops for the aristocratic/exclusive/expensive London prototype.

There is virtually no escape from mass production in the USSR. What you are *not* going to discover in Moscow is the kind of little shop that sells hand-made shoes or jewelled Easter eggs. What you *will* find—if

you look hard enough—are rare books at reasonable
prices, terrific posters at dirt-cheap prices, marvellous
postage stamps (North Vietnam, Cuba, USSR, etc.),
smashing fur hats, four star brandy from Armenia, and,
if you are lucky, old samovars.

For years, shopping in the Soviet Union was a glum
experience indeed. Until recently most shops possessed
no names at all, only numbers. Thus, Vegetable Store
No. 67 or Gastronom No. 32 of the Moscow Food
Trust was the way a store might typically be identified.
All this is now changing, and changing rapidly. The
Party leadership has poured millions of roubles into
improving goods and services. When Mrs. Ivanovich
asks for service in a store nowadays, she is no longer
treated like an enemy of the people.

New and attractive shops are going up all over
Moscow. Many of them have names, a real novelty in
Russia. A shop that sells amber, for instance, is called
Amber (ЯНТАРЬ). A glassware outlet is named Crystal
(ХРУСТАЛЬ), and a souvenir emporium, Gifts (ПОДАРКИ).
True, Moscow is, all in all, still a city of shortages. But
a word of optimism: for those who are enterprising
there are some surprisingly good buys available.

Beriozka (Birch Tree) "dollar" shops

Named after the birch tree, a symbol of Russia, the
Beriozka chain accepts only hard currency. Such stores
are useful for visitors who don't speak Russian, because
there are always plenty of English-speaking sales people
to assist you. You can pay in traveler's checks, or any
form of hard currency.

Beriozka stores range from counters in hotels to mini-
department stores. They carry a wide variety of goods—

many of which are scarce in ordinary shops. In your hotel, for instance, you can drop into the Beriozka for a package of American cigarettes (about 50 cents) or a bottle of duty-free vodka (about $4) or a helping of black caviar (85 cents an ounce), and you'll find the shop less crowded than most Moscow stores, so you can browse without being knocked off your feet. *Do remember to keep all receipts for hard-currency purchases.* You may need these at Customs later.

a word about prices

The Soviet Union is one of the toughest countries in the world in which to calculate the value of money. Some things are astonishingly cheap, some items seem fantastically overpriced.

What is alarming to you, however, is not necessarily upsetting to a Soviet citizen. Consider Natasha, your Intourist guide. Her monthly wage is roughly equal to a weekly wage in the United States for a comparable position. But Natasha's rent is only a small slice of her income—no more than 7 percent in a modern block, as little as 3 percent in an old building. A day nursery for her child will cost only 12 roubles a month. Health care is free, except for medicines. There is a paid vacation of at least 15 work-days a year, and income tax is negligible.

The overall average wage in the Soviet Union (1973) is 128.5 roubles a month ($177.92). Soviet citizens spend proportionately more on food, clothing, and luxury goods than we do in the West. On the other hand, your Russian friends would probably be aghast at the amount of income you spend on housing, health

care, and income tax. Here are some prices at random.
The rate of exchange is calculated at 1 rouble being
equal to $1.39.

	Roubles	Dollars
Man's narrow tie	1.45	2.02
Chocolate bar	0.78	1.00
Cheap cotton dress	24.00	33.61
Women's shoes (imported)	40.00	55.60
Man's black suit	127.00	176.53
12-inch LP record	1.10	1.53
Plastic briefcase	16.40	22.80
Zhiguli (Fiat) car	5,500.00	7,645.45

A simple calculation shows that if a Russian earns
128 roubles a month, it will cost him three years' wages
to buy a small car.

Keep in mind that in a state-controlled economy,
prices are used to control demand. The authorities
clearly encourage the wide sale of cultural items such
as records and books (which are inexpensive) and
discourage the sale of automobiles, liquor, and fur
coats (which are expensive). Another reason why many
prices are high is sales taxes—in other words, a Soviet
citizen pays his taxes every time he makes a purchase.

How you can benefit

For visitors, all personal services are cheap; getting
your hair cut, having a shampoo and set, sending your
shirts and blouses to the laundry. Bargain prices here.
All fares are cheap inside the Soviet Union—you can
fly from Moscow to Leningrad, a distance of over 400
miles, for less than 20 roubles. Taxis in Moscow, as another example, are amongst the cheapest in the world.

And anything of a cultural nature is cheap: tickets to the
opera, ballet, concerts, and LP records. Art books are
also available at unbelievably low prices.

Don't forget that the Beriozka stores, which accept
foreign currency only, in return offer large discounts on
everything from vodka (duty-free) to folk art.

what's where in moscow

From your midtown hotel you can walk to almost all
the stores listed below. Consult the map in the front
and those on pages 103, 109, 118, and 128. You can also
ask your Intourist guide to accompany you. Be forewarned: shopping, at least in the manner in which
foreigners often approach it, is considered a slight aber-
ration by Russians. For working mothers in Moscow,
shopping is more often than not a chore—something
that has to be crowded in after a hard day's work. The
idea of spending "free time"—as the Russians call it—
enjoying shopping would strike most Muscovites as
crazy. All the same, after a day or so spent studying the
socially significant, you might welcome a go at shopping.
Here is where you find what in the city.

Antiques & Junk

Try the "commission shops," often resorted to by
hard-up Russians who want to sell Grandma's samovar
or Grandpa's old marble ink-stand. The shops charge
the seller a commission (hence the name) and resell at
a price considered appropriate for the article. Prices
are erratic. You can find a scratched silver-plate fruit
bowl priced at 200 roubles and at the same time a

magnificent eighteenth-century ivory miniature priced
at 40 roubles.

Diplomats and permanent residents tend to beat
you out of the better bargains, so get there early in the
day. Stock turnover is rapid.

Gorkovo No. 46

A great favourite with the diplomatic corps. Items
on sale here range from ivory letter-openers to crystal
chandeliers. The store is crammed with African carvings,
Art Nouveau lamps, amber beads, and bronze statues.
It also specializes in china and porcelain. A great deal
of this is of the "junk" variety, but you can get nice
old-fashioned fish platters big enough to serve a 40-
pound sturgeon. None of these items is cheap, but
you will certainly get some amusement looking around
a commission shop and possibly find a treasure.

A *word of caution:* Because Soviet Customs are very
sticky about second-hand goods leaving Russia, be sure
to retain the price tag affixed to the commission shop
purchase. That tells them you purchased the goods
legitimately.

Quite clearly such objects as fish platters and turn-
of-the-century samovars do not fall into the category
of *objets d'art* or antiques (anything more than 100
years old). If something does, you ought to ask Intourist
for help *before* you make the purchase. To export works
of art (see under "Galleries," page 277) you need the
special permission of the Ministry of Culture in the
form of an "export certificate," and you will have to
pay duty amounting to 100 percent of the price
indicated in the permit.

Icons, in particular, arouse the suspicion of Soviet Customs officials, who happily confiscate them at the airport if you do not have the necessary documents. If your heart is set on that eighteenth-century chandelier, then allow plenty of time for your Service Bureau to get the paperwork in order (and don't forget that 100 percent duty charge).

Arbat No. 19

If you don't find what you want at Gorkovo No. 46, you can take a taxi (about ten minutes' ride) to Arbat Street. If you have a taste for Victorian landscapes, ruined castles, pastoral Russian scenes, all in heavy gilt frames, this is your kind of place. The paintings are stacked floor to ceiling. Prices are clearly marked in violet ink. Once again, keep in mind that if you purchase a painting, you will need a special export certificate, so discuss the matter first with Intourist.

Across the room from the paintings there is a crowded showcase filled with bibelots and cast-off heirlooms. You won't find Nicholas II's snuff-box here, but you will see elaborately carved walking stick handles, granny glasses, old seals, nineteenth-century jewellery, and enameled teaspoons.

Arbat No. 32

A few doors away is yet another commission shop, and it looks like the prop room for *The Forsyte Saga*— marble statuary, bronze horses, gilt candelabra. Behind the counters are shelves stuffed with ash-trays, Czech crystal vases, cut-glass fruit bowls, and lots of candle-holders. The candle-holders range in price from 10 to

20 roubles each. A clock made out of aluminum, shaped like a Sputnik and chiming the Kremlin bells, priced at 75 roubles, is a not untypical item.

Books, New & Second-hand

More books are published in the Soviet Union than in any other country. There are more than 200 publishing houses which issue books in 122 languages. There is no Soviet city without several good bookstores, and the public appetite for books is enormous. Most books are non-fiction, there are very few detective stories, and no "pulp" fiction at all. A great deal of care and attention is paid to children's books. Keep an eye out for them, they are often beautifully illustrated. There are plenty of bargains in English-language books available—a complete set of Lenin's writings (43 volumes), for example, priced at less than 2 roubles a volume. How do you get them home? Here's how: you take your purchase down to the International Post Office in the Hotel National on the corner of Gorkovo and Manege Square (see page 21). The clerk unwraps your books, examines them, then re-packs them (no charge) for you. You address them and pay a quite nominal amount of postage for shipping.

Kalinin Prospekt No. 26

The Moscow House of Books (Dom Knigi) is the city's largest (and newest) bookstore. It is especially rich in art and architecture, Russian literature, and textbooks. In other departments of the store you can buy postcards and posters.

Kuznetsky Most No. 18

Books in foreign languages, including English, French, and German.

Gorkovo No. 15

The Druzhba (Friendship) *Bookstore* offers books from Hungary, Czechoslovakia, Poland, East Germany, Rumania, North Vietnam, Cuba, and all other Communist-bloc countries. The prices are ridiculously low. For example, a remarkable book on Mongolian costumes with several hundred color plates was priced at 6 roubles; there are sumptuously printed art books from East Germany and Czechoslovakia that range in price from 3 to 7 roubles—comparable U.S. prices would be $15 to $45.

Gorkovo No. 8

Across the street from No. 15 are more books in foreign languages. There is a wide selection of technical and scientific books here. Subjects range from computer technology to oil pipeline transmission.

Kirov Street No. 13

There are plenty of second-hand bookstores, but this is the very best. If you go up the creaky staircase to the second floor, you can buy old prints for as little as 1 rouble apiece. They also have interesting used art books, and a remarkable collection of nineteenth-century postcards, both Russian and foreign. Definitely worth a visit.

Buttons & Badges

For military types there are Soviet Army brass buckles complete with hammer-and-sickle insignia, tank badges, air force wings, sharpshooter badges, and a wide variety of buttons to be found in the military de-

partment in G.U.M. These are also available in
Ts.U.M., the Central Department Store in *Petrov Street*.

Cameras & Photographic Equipment

The big Beriozka department store opposite the
Novo-Devichy Convent has by far the most comprehensive stock of camera equipment and film supplies. Most Beriozka shops and counters sell a range of
modestly priced 35 mm Russian cameras and exposure
meters. Prices range from 30 to 150 roubles.

Russian optical and camera equipment is considered
well made by most photographic experts. Though lacking the finish and super-perfection of Japanese and
West German wares, it is sturdily functional and made
for hard use.

The photographer interested in special equipment
might try the photo department in G.U.M. There one
can find such oddities as "the Photo Sniper," a
formidable super long lens camera complete with
gunstock mount and mahogany carrying case. Capable
of snapping a close-up of the star atop the Kremlin
towers from a distance of half a mile. Price: 300
roubles. Also available in G.U.M. is a unique panoramic
camera (35 mm) which takes in everything in view
without a millimetre of distortion. Price: around 80
roubles. For miniature enthusiasts there are 8 mm
Minox-like cameras available, about 15 roubles, complete with carrying case.

Carpets
G.U.M.
Beriozka *at Novo-Devichy*
Apartments in Moscow are small and crowded, so

Muscovites like their carpets rich and colorful. It is not unusual in a Russian home to find a carpet on the bedroom wall rather than the bedroom floor. Deep burgundy red with plenty of diamond or paisley in the pattern is the thing. Wall-to-wall carpeting is unknown in Russia, where linoleum is the usual floor covering with a rug or two added when salary allows.

G.U.M. has a wide selection, but the best display is at the major Beriozka store opposite Novo-Devichy. Rugs and carpets from Bokhara, Tadzhikistan, and the Soviet Far East, as well as recent imports from Poland and India, are on sale. Prices—not cheap—range from about 50 to several hundred roubles.

For the average visitor, probably not worth much more than a passing glance. For a carpet expert, well worth a look in case something really fabulous has slipped into Moscow.

Chessmen and Chess Sets
Kutuzovsky Prospekt No. 24
Beriozka *at the rear of the Hotel Rossiya*

In the Beriozka on *Kutuzovsky Prospekt* just past the Hotel Ukraine (on the left-hand side) can be found the best choice. A hand-carved set made out of wood with mother-of-pearl insets can set you back 200 roubles. The price varies with the quality, but a wide range can be found here. Also worth trying is the Beriozka store in the *Hotel Rossiya* near Red Square. Pocket chess sets for travellers are sold everywhere. A standard off-the-shelf item in G.U.M. and other department stores is a chess clock or timer. A pair mounted in a handsome stained-wood box will cost you around 14 roubles.

China and Glass
G.U.M.
Gorkovo No. 4
8/2, Kirov Street
Gorkovo No. 15

For the widest selection of china in modern or traditional Russian design, try the ground floor of G.U.M. Prices are very reasonable and you can ship home via the International Post Office (see page 21).

For glass, especially if your taste runs to cut glass, visit 15, *Gorkovo*, which has a large stock of everything you could put on a coffee table or window ledge—ash-trays, vases, fruit bowls, tea glasses, the works.

Clocks and Watches
All Beriozka Stores

One of the best bargains in Moscow is a watch. They come in a wide choice of styles, all inexpensive, ranging in price from 4 to 30 roubles. They are mostly named after highlights of the Soviet space program: Vostok, Sputnik, and so on. A 6 rouble watch bought by an acquaintance of ours is still running flawlessly after six years of hard wear.

They can be bought at any Beriozka outlet.

Coins, Old and New
Vneshtorgbank Gold Shop, *Pushkin Street* No. 9

If you are a coin collector, the Vneshtorgbank Gold Shop on *Pushkin Street* is well worth a visit. It is for foreigners only, and you can leisurely examine gold and silver coins from all over the world. The atmosphere is subdued and discreet. They also do a nice line in proof and mint sets of modern Russian coins; these make a nice 5 or 6 rouble gift. It is possible to buy the first revolutionary silver rouble here for a few dollars. You can also spend a thousand dollars or so on a rare gold piece from British Papua.

For the collector of American gold pieces, they have Indian heads, eagles, and Liberty's at prices that are lower than at home. A good present: Nicholas II 10 rouble gold pieces which you can make into cufflinks. Monday through Friday, from 10 a.m. to 4 p.m.; on Saturday, 10 a.m. to 2 p.m.

Craft Shops
All Beriozka Stores
9, Kutuzovsky Prospekt

For embroidered blouses, balalaikas, guitars, matryoshka dolls, lacquer ware, painted trays, hand-carved wooden toys, amber beads, and other folk art, you cannot do better than visit the Beriozka store at the rear of the Hotel Rossiya near Red Square. If you seek more variety (and would like to pay in roubles) visit 9, Kutuzovsky. You can spend anything from a few kopecks for a wooden toy to more than 100 roubles for an elaborately painted Palekh cigarette box. It's worth noting that the red, black, and gold lacquer kitchen bowls and utensils are washable in hot water, and can be used as everyday housewares. Guitars and balalaikas are a bargain, priced between 10 and 20 roubles.

Diamonds
Vneshtorgbank Gold Shop, *Pushkin Street No.* 9

You can buy Siberian diamonds at this store (see "Coins" above). The assistant in the demure black dress will sell you anything from a fraction of a carat to a bauble the size of the proverbial pigeon's egg. There are no bargains. Prices are comparable to those in London, Amsterdam, or New York, with this difference—you are assured by the Soviet government of the gems' authenticity.

Embroidery
Beriozka, *Hotel Rossiya*
G.U.M.

A table runner made in Estonia or a multicolored pillow from Azerbaijan is yours at Beriozka. Prices, however, are exceptionally steep. Apparently, if you want old-fashioned handicrafts rather than mass production, you simply have to pay the price. They also have a selection of tablecloths and napkins to match. G.U.M. has a small selection of the above and they can be purchased with roubles.

Flowers
Revolution Square Metro
Arbatskaya Square Metro
Manege Square
Gorkovo

For your room, for your Intourist guide, or for the kindly lady who guards your keys and takes your telephone messages. Can be bought at flower stands outside various Metro stations; in the underground walkway at Gorkovo and Manege Square; and in kiosks along Gorkovo.

Food
Kalinin Prospekt Shopping Centre
14, Gorkovo

For those who want to prepare their own lunch, Moscow is full of food stores. You can do fairly well by pointing to what you want. If you just wish to sample the atmosphere, and see how Muscovites do their shopping—they tend to be daily rather than weekly shoppers—you really ought to visit the big new supermarket (one of the few in Russia) on Kalinin. Notably missing are the "specials" so familiar to U.S. consumers. There are no mark-downs or clearance sales in Russia.

A startling contrast is a visit to Gastronom No. 1 at 14, *Gorkovo*; open 9 a.m. to 10 p.m. Before the Revolution it was known as *Yeliseyevsky's* and catered to the carriage trade. Anyone familiar with London will be reminded of Fortnum & Mason by its lavish, turn of the century, Art Nouveau decor.

Behind plate-glass windows is an interior where Muscovites shop under enormous crystal chandeliers. The tea counter is in mock Chinese style, all red and gold, and the shop fittings are virtually unchanged from the Nicholas and Alexandra era. The store sells everything from black bread to caviar. There are wines from Georgia, brandies from Armenia, salted herring from the Baltic, dried and smoked fish of all varieties. The staff wear white and scurry back and forth behind the high glassed-in counters. If you have a sweet tooth, take a look at the candy counter. Russian chocolates and candies are first-class and imaginatively packaged. A *word about caviar:* This is best purchased at the airport just before leaving the USSR. It can be found in the Beriozka store in the Departure Hall. The price fluctuates between 80 kopecks and 1 rouble per ounce. This is a great bargain compared to Western prices, which are often triple or quadruple the Soviet price. While dealers insist that color and grain size are not indications of quality, the usual rule of thumb is, the bigger and blacker the better. The finest varieties of caviar are Beluga and Sevruga. It is available in sizes of one ounce and up. A caviar "pound," by the way, is really 14 ounces.

There is one thing you should be aware of: fresh caviar is infinitely superior to the vacuum-sealed processed caviar which needs no refrigeration. The taste is altogether different. The processed caviar costs almost as much as the fresh but has a waxy, salty flavor. You are allowed to bring caviar into the United States and Britain. It should be kept in a cool place, and this does pose a problem if you are making a transatlantic crossing. However, I have carried fresh caviar in the plane's cabin on several Moscow–New York trips, and it has been none the worse for the journey.

Foreign Newspapers

Hard to find in Moscow. In theory, it is possible to buy the leading world newspapers—the London *Times,* *Le Monde,* the *Herald-Tribune,* the *Frankfurter Allgemeine*—at the newsstands in such leading hotels as the National, Rossiya, Intourist, and Ukraine. In practice, you have to ask, and even then will be rewarded only occasionally with an under-the-counter copy.

Always available is the English-language *Moscow News*, which provides a useful guide to what's going on in the city, but unfortunately no news.

Furs
Beriozka *at the Novo-Devichy Convent*
Vneshposyltorg, *Profsoyuznaya Street No. 16*
Furs are a major Soviet export, so it is not surprising to find them readily available for hard currency. Prices are reasonable by world standards. On the other hand, the styles look thirty years out of date. The best buys are the fur hats, which can be found at most Beriozka stores. For a selection of fur coats and hats, visit the main Beriozka store near the Novo-Devichy Convent. For the widest choice in Moscow furs, head directly for the Vneshposyltorg's Fur Salon.

Fashion Shows
G.U.M.
Dom Modele
There are daily fashion shows at G.U.M. What is shown there is available as a pattern for home sewing elsewhere in the store. If you wish to see the latest designs in men's and women's wear, then a visit to *Dom Modele*, the Ministry of Trade's House of Fashion, is a must on your trip. Here you will find the nearest thing to couture in Russia. Some of the new designers (like everybody else in Russia, they work for the government) are brilliantly imaginative. The Ninotchka era—if it ever existed—has gone forever. At the Dom Modele, attractive models parade up and down the runway showing this year's line to an audience that consists mainly of Muscovites, with a sprinkling

of foreigners like yourself. As each model displays a garment, the commentator describes its features and announces a pattern number. Downstairs, patterns corresponding to the garments shown are sold for approximately 50 kopecks a pattern. What your neighbor (if he or she is a Russian) does is to take the pattern home to cut and sew—or find the "little woman around the corner" to make up the pattern.

Galleries: Paintings & Prints
Kutuzovsky Prospekt No. 24
25th October Street No. 8/1
Petrov Street No. 12
Gorkovo No. 46-b

Somebody has counted more than 400 private art galleries in Paris; there are less than half a dozen contemporary art galleries in Moscow. These are run by the state, of course, and keep to the "Socialist realism" tradition. Many of the canvases will appeal to those who "like a good story" in their paintings. Here can be seen such classic themes as *Harvesting on a Collective Farm*, *Refineries in Baku*, *A Fishing Camp in Siberia*, *Tempering the Steel*, and so forth. Prices for oils range from 150 to more than 1,000 roubles. Remember: It is important to take an Intourist guide with you if you are serious about purchasing an oil painting. Soviet government forms have to be correctly filled out for the export of original works of art.

If you are interested in prints, then you are in luck. There's no red tape involved at all. You can buy them, take them back to your room, and leave the USSR with them with nothing more than the receipt for payment. Soviet graphic design is really impressive, and in this field artists appear to have been given a lot more freedom in their choice of themes. Nature, of course, predominates. There are marvellous landscapes available. Also, themes galore from the rich and fantastic world of traditional Russian folk tales. Best of all are the prices. Framed in starkly modern metal frames, they represent one of Moscow's best tourist buys, with prices running from a couple of roubles up to 15 or so. Most are priced around 5 roubles. The finest selection in the city is to be found at *46-b, Gorkovo* (a few doors from Moscow's best antique store).

This account would not be complete without a cautionary word about Soviet citizens who solicit you with an offer of icons or "modern"—meaning abstract—art. Both are illegal to purchase except under government auspices. The best advice if approached is, don't get involved. In a way it is very sad. There is a really fine school of "unofficial" or underground art—abstract and pop artists. You may see examples of their work if you are privileged to have Soviet friends and visit their apartments. All the same, as long as you are a guest in the Soviet Union it is simply not worth breaking Soviet laws to obtain such paintings.

Galleries: Posters
Arbat Street

The poster collector or the student of propaganda cannot do better than visit the poster shop on Arbat Street. You will find it a few doors down from the Praga Restaurant on the right-hand side walking away from Kalinin. As you enter, you can see at least 50 examples, each neatly numbered for reference on the walls behind the counters. There are posters celebrating Lenin, supporting the drinking of more milk, glorifying electric power, denouncing Yankee Imperialism, and so forth. The typography and graphic design are amongst the world's best, and so for 15 kopecks apiece you can paper your room with the latest agit-prop; also available here are picture postcards on every imaginable Soviet theme, at 2 kopecks apiece.

Guns

Beriozka *by Novo-Devichy Convent*

The ground floor of the city's largest Beriozka store is the place to visit if you are a dedicated hunter. The stock is not large, but the things that *are* displayed are beautifully hand-made and reasonably priced. If you intend to buy, ask one of the English-speaking assistants for the proper documentation so that you may take your purchase out of the USSR.

Hairdressers: Women

House of Beauty (Institut Krasoty), *Kalinin Prospekt*
Shopping Center
All Major Hotels

All the major hotels have beauty parlors, and there are several along Kalinin Prospekt, including the House of Beauty, not far from Manege Square. No appointments are necessary. Prima ballerinas and daughters of the top ranks of the Soviet hierarchy have long favored the salon in the *Hotel Ukraine* on Kutuzovsky Prospekt. The hairdressers at the *Hotel National* have an excellent reputation, and there is a manicurist available (clear lacquer only) at a cost of 75 kopecks. If you color your hair, bring your own coloring. (The most popular hair

280)

coloring in the USSR is henna red, followed by black.) A permanent wave costs about a rouble, a comb and set 75 kopecks. The art of hair-styling is comparatively new to the USSR, and the customer needs to have a certain sense of adventure.

Hairdressers: Men
All Major Hotels

Neat, brisk, clean. No rock music, no hair-styling, no hair nets. Price around 1 rouble.

Information
Street Kiosks
Intourist Offices

If you are looking for Uncle Vanya or Grandmother Natasha who lives "somewhere" in Moscow, you can *buy* information for two kopecks at any street kiosk. Telephone books are scarce, and never available in hotel rooms, but every kiosk has an up-to-the-minute telephone directory. For non-Russian-speaking visitors, Intourist is your refuge and solace. The head office is located at 16, *Karl Marx Prospekt*, next to the Hotel National, and the general-enquiry telephone number is 229-94-52.

Jewelry and Silverware
Beriozka, *24, Kutuzovsky*
Beriozka, *12, Gorkovo*
Beriozka, *rear of Hotel Rossiya*
Yantar (Amber), *13, Stoleshnikov Pereulok*

For a look at high-priced gold and precious stones, try the Beriozka shop at *24, Kutuzovsky Prospekt.* As in all jewelry stores in Russia, the choice and selection are very small. Prices are not bargains. Typical examples are a heavy, rippled-gold cigarette case at 1,200 roubles; a peanut-sized opal ring at 700 roubles; a garnet ring at 135 roubles (garnets are a favorite of Russian women). Presumably the representatives of the Fabergé tradition of fine craftsmanship have all been enlisted in the Soviet space program. In any event, Soviet jewelry is one giant step backward from Czarist craftsmanship. Other places to examine baubles are: *Beriozka, 12, Gorkovo*; and *Beriozka, rear of Hotel Rossiya*. There is a great deal of amber jewelry around, and if your taste runs to huge, gob-like amber necklaces, the first place to look is *Yantar, 13, Stoleshnikov Pereulok.*

The art of silverwork, however, has not dimmed in modern Russia—the craft tradition is very much alive, especially in filigree and inlay work. Excellent examples can be found in the various Beriozka stores.

Kitchen Equipment

G.U.M., *Red Square*
Ts.U.M., *Petrov Street*

If you enjoy the art of cooking, there is much to discover in the hardware departments of these big stores. You can find carved wooden salad servers, kitchen knives from Volgograd, soup bowls in all sizes, moulds for jellies and cakes. Well worth a look. Prices very reasonable.

Laundry

Personal laundry is usually done within the hotel (see page 62). One-day service is normal, as it is also for pressing. Dry cleaning is a different matter. There are

very few dry-cleaning establishments in Moscow, and
it is usually impossible for a visitor to obtain such a
service.

Messengers
Intourist
If you are a businessman in need of such services,
contact the Service Bureau in your hotel.

Music: *Phonograph Records & Sheet Music*
All Beriozka Stores
6/2, Arbat Street
2, Petrov Street
17, Kirov Street
House of Books,   *Kalinin Prospekt*
13, Herzen Street
15, Gorkovo
14, Neglinnaya Street
Russia is the world's best bargain spot for classical-
music lovers. It is possible to buy everything that Shostakovich ever recorded in the USSR—an oeuvre running
to more than half a hundred recordings—and actually
receive change from roubles! Record stores are crowded.
Russians are crazy about music, as everybody knows, and
the government helps keep up the enthusiasm with low-
priced recordings. An average price for a 33⅓ disc is a
rouble.

Recording standards, however, vary widely. A substantial number of records are made at live concerts,
and these come complete with foot shuffling and spo-
radic coughing. There are also many recordings from
Poland, Rumania, and other Eastern-bloc nations. It is
possible to buy rare records from Cuba in Moscow.

Ask for balalaika and folk music recordings and your choice will run into the hundreds. All Beriozka stores have a selection of records, although they tend to be of limited choice. The real music lover will visit the *House of Books* in the Kalinin Prospekt shopping area, or stores at 6/2, *Arbat Street*, 2, *Petrov Street*, or 17, *Kirov Street*. As with records, so with sheet music. There is plenty of choice, and prices are a give-away by Western standards.

Although Igor Stravinsky received no royalties in the USSR, his music is widely published in Russia, and can be bought at such sheet music stores as: 13, *Herzen Street* (the store is inside the Tchaikovsky Conservatoire); 14, *Neglinnaya*; and 15, *Gorkovo*.

Musical Instruments
Beriozka Stores

Guitars, balalaikas, harmonicas, and piano accordions at exceptionally reasonable prices can be found in many Beriozka outlets. For the widest choice, head for the *Beriozka near the Novo-Devichy Convent*.

Needlework
G.U.M., *Red Square*
Beriozka *rear of Hotel Rossiya*

If you are in need of supplies or looking for patterns you can find both in G.U.M. (See also "Embroidery.")

Optical Equipment
G.U.M., *Red Square*
Beriozka *near the Novo-Devichy Convent*

Binoculars, and telescopes terrestrial and astronomical, can be found on the second floor of G.U.M. There is also a varied selection at the main Beriozka store.

Perfume & Cosmetics

G.U.M., *Red Square*

7, Marx Prospekt

6, Gorkovo

12, Pushkin Street

10, Petrov Street

When Premier Khrushchev visited the White House, the gift he brought for Jacqueline Kennedy was an assortment of Soviet perfumes. Unused, they now rest with many other souvenirs of the Kennedy years in a Boston warehouse. Russian women love perfume, and there's lots of it around.

The industry is supplied with the floral richness of the Caucasus: jasmine, orange and lemon, lavender, acacia; from the Soviet Far East come the vital essences: cinnamon, ambergris, lemon grass, and ylang-ylang. Scent is a matter of taste. Packaging—a mighty factor in perfume buying—is an art in the Soviet Union, and your choice is wide and varied. Watch for *Kreml*, a heavy-scented yellow perfume which comes in a marvellous crystal bottle shaped like the towers of the Kremlin. There are also apple-shaped flacons, cannon-shaped bottles, and so on. Prices are low. Kreml, for example, costs less than 3 roubles a bottle. As for cosmetics, there is more variety available than ever before. Lipsticks, however, still run to variations on carmine red, and face powder is little more than perfumed baby powder. G.U.M. in Red Square has one of the city's finest selections. There are *Kosmetica* salons in every part of the city.

Photography

G.U.M., *Red Square*
Beriozka, *near Novo-Devichy Convent*
16, Kutuzovsky Prospekt

Film and camera supplies are plentiful at the addresses named. Film processing is, however, a problem for visitors. You can buy East German black-and-white and color film in most Beriozka shops. (See also under "Cameras & Photographic Equipment.")

Radio & Television Sets

Beriozka, *near Novo-Devichy Convent*
G.U.M., *Red Square*

All Beriozka stores carry a wide selection of Japanese and Soviet-made transistor radios. Prices are comparable to those in tax-free stores in other countries. Russian models are rugged and serviceable. In the Beriozka stores you get a price break for paying in hard currency —you pay roughly one-fourth of what a Soviet citizen would pay. A magnificently polished (it is reported that they do the polishing in labor camps) television set is priced at 97 roubles; but where could you use it? The Soviet TV system operates on different line frequencies to the USA and most European countries. If you run out of batteries for your own transistor, visit Beriozka.

Secretarial Services

Intourist

Ask the Service Bureau in your hotel. Intourist is usually glad to provide assistance to businessmen and scholars who need specialized services. Prices vary and are subject to some negotiation with Intourist.

Sports Equipment

G.U.M., *Red Square*
Ts.U.M., *2, Petrov Street*
Detsky Mir, *Marx Prospekt*
Beriozka, *Novo-Devichy*

All big department stores have excellent sports departments, where you are likely to find everything from footballs to skis, gym suits to fishing tackle. The state encourages *everyone* to be athletically active, and the factories do their bit by sending out a plentiful supply of equipment. Try, in this order, *G.U.M.*, *Ts.U.M.*, *Beriozka*, and—for young people—*Detsky Mir*.

Stamps

20, Kuznetsky Most
16, Dzerzhinsky Street
15, Gorkovo

Collectors will find what they want in the city's largest stamp shop, located at *20 Kuznetsky Most*. Also worth a visit is the stamp collector's shop (usually filled with small boys) at *16, Dzerzhinsky Street*. For stamps of all Socialist countries, including North Vietnam and North Korea (but excluding China), visit *15, Gorkovo*. Collecting is a major hobby in the Soviet Union, and stamps can be bought at almost every kiosk and newsstand. Also, they come in books by theme: space achievements, sports, ecology, military preparedness, social services, etc., etc. These make inexpensive and colorful presents to take home with you. There are literally hundreds of stamps devoted to Lenin and his works. They are picturesque, inexpensive, and wonderfully various.

Tobacco & Cigars

Havana, *Komsomolsky Prospekt*
Beriozka Stores

If you smoke menthol cigarettes, bring your own. Otherwise, most U.S. brands (and some British) are available at 40 cents a pack at any Beriozka store. If you would like to sample Soviet brands, they come in two main varieties. The older generation still prefer the *papirosy*, cardboard tubes loosely filled at one end with a strong-smelling tobacco known as Mazurka; these come in attractive presentation boxes containing up to 200 cigarettes, and make an off-beat gift. The other variety is quite similar in appearance to the standard Western cigarette. Russians generally prefer Bulgarian cigarettes to their own, but most visitors claim neither variety is a taste treat.

Cigars are another matter. Russians, as a people, are not cigar smokers. Presumably the vast quantities of Cuban cigars on the Soviet market are the *quid pro quo* in trade for Soviet aid. Until very recently, most Cuban cigars available in Moscow were hardly worth the 65 kopecks to 1.50 roubles each that they commanded. Wrapped in cellophane, they had been poorly handled and had not been kept in a humidor. This is now changing, at least at the *Havana*, on Komsomolsky Prospekt, if nowhere else. There a cigar aficionado can see an eye-popping display of all the great names—Upmann, Hoya de Monterey, Punch, Ramon Allones. Also available are gift-packaged containers.

A magnificent crock made of glazed earthenware, from the famed *Vuelta Abaco* region of Cuba, with fifty Partegas, complete with a tobacco harvesting scene, costs 25 roubles. There are other cigar stores in Moscow, but none to compare with the *Havana.* Here—and here alone—the cigars are firm, plump, and aromatic. For the casual smoker or the individual who wants only to take two or three cigars home, all Beriozka stores sell Cuban cigars. *A word of warning:* Cuban cigars are not allowed into the United States.

Toys & Games
Detsky Mir *(Children's World)*   2, *Marx Prospekt*
Igrushky, *Kutuzovsky Prospekt*

"Yes, we have a privileged class in Russia," a Russian writer once told a visitor, "—our children." Children have plenty of choice when it comes to toys. You will therefore find much to amuse and enchant you in the toy shops. Prices are reasonable. Russian soft toys are superb, and dolls come in at least two dozen varieties (wetting, crying, glamorous, folk-costumed, with or without real hair, etc., etc.). Bicycles, toy cars, and mechanical toys that work are in plentiful supply. The two best spots in Moscow are *Detsky Mir*, and *Igrushky*, a stone's throw from the Hotel Ukraine. Both open 11 a.m.–7 p.m. Monday through Saturday. Closed Sunday.

Turkish Baths
Near Hotel Metropole

Decidedly not on the beaten path, the baths are next door to the Hotel Metropole, and you have to make reservations. Three hours is about the usual time. Massage is available from an ancient attendant who, for a couple of roubles, will knead your skin back to glowing health. What you get for your money is private use of the steam room (all marble and green-tiled) and the baths. Russians usually bring a few bottles of beer with them to drink after the sauna. You can also throw some of the beer on the hot stones to provide a more pungent steam. No mixed sexes. Bring your own towels. You can book this treat through Russian friends or ask Intourist to make the arrangements.

Wines & Spirits
(See pages 207–11, page 274.)

In addition to Soviet wines and spirits, you can buy, at about one-third the usual price, French, British, and some U.S. wines and spirits at the supermarket in the Kalinin shopping plaza. Most Beriozka outlets in hotels also sell vodka for hard currency.

moscow's best buys: two lists

If you have 50 roubles for gifts:

Page ref.		Price range	
272	Nest of *Matryoshka* dolls	2–10	roubles
271	Soviet watch (man's or lady's)	5–15	"
289	Bottle of Soviet champagne	3–4	"
278	Collection of posters	2	"
277	Several framed modern prints	10–15	"
270	Chess clock	10–15	"
287	Box of (200) *papirosy* cigarettes	8	"
284	Bottle of Kreml perfume	3	"
267, 282	LP records & books	the balance	

If you have 100 roubles for gifts:

business

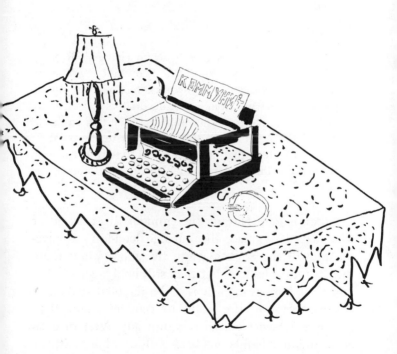

The view from your hotel is fine, but you are here to do business. You have something to offer. Now, how to find your opposite number in the USSR? Here we list a few ways through the vast rabbit warren of Soviet officialdom. It is not going to be easy. You are forewarned.

introduction

The mind which is ever ready to change will be subjected to endless argument and constant attack by the Soviet colleague who is quick to sense the opportunity. Pressure from Soviet negotiators will be redoubled and may result in complete exhaustion on the part of the American so that he comes to the point at which he feels that he never wants to see a Russian again and is thoroughly miserable in the performance of his job.

Professor John Hazard, the eminent Russian scholar who helped negotiate the wartime lend-lease arrangements with the Soviets, wrote the above words more than two decades ago, but they still hold true. For the impatient businessman, it is to be doubted if there is a worse place in the world to transact affairs than Moscow. A Soviet official can turn any Western businessman into a blubbering baby within 24 hours. Still, if you need the business, you will have to learn to trade Soviet-style.

To begin with, you will quickly find that you do not

deal company-to-company in the USSR. Instead, you *must* deal with one of the twenty-five or so trading corporations, each of which is responsible for one sector of the planned Soviet economy. *Techmashimport,* for instance, is the place to go if you want to sell the Russians a polyethylene plant or other chemical equipment. *Sudoimport* is in charge of buying ships, *Medexport* is the organization you deal with when you wish to buy Soviet drugs, and so forth. Before you leave for the Soviet Union, you can get expert advice as to which trading corporation you need from the U.S. Department of Commerce if you're an American, and from the Board of Trade if you're British.

You will learn to cope with such minor irritations as the question of punctuality. When a Soviet official invites you to a meeting at 10 a.m. sharp, *you* will be there at 10 a.m. on the dot. Your Soviet host may appear half an hour later, without apology. A conference with Soviet officials may find the principal among them excusing himself half-way through your discussions: he has to attend yet another meeting down the corridor. Or, again, the scheduled conference with Sergei Andreyevich will not be possible, you are informed, because Sergei Andreyevich has "suddenly been called out of Moscow." In sum, patience and endurance are required in doing business with the Soviets. Six months of negotiating time is standard procedure where a major contract is involved.

There is, nonetheless, a positive side to the coin: Russians tend to develop firm product loyalty, and once a solid trading relationship has been established you will have a strong advantage over any competition hoping to enter this market.

Pasteur's well-known adage "Chance favors the prepared mind," is particularly appropriate to remember when you do business in the Soviet Union. A story floating around Moscow not long ago concerned a woman who ran into her neighbor in the local grocery store. "Guess what?" she said to the neighbor. "I was shopping down the street and I found what I've been looking for for years. My dream came true." The neighbor asked, "What did you buy?" "A mink stole." "Oh," the neighbor said in a disappointed tone, "I thought maybe you had found a tea kettle."

Well, a Los Angeles businessman heard this story. He had a small factory specializing in moulding bomb cases for the Defense Department, and that particular contract was being phased out. He thought, Why not tea kettles?

After a visit to Moscow he landed a substantial order with a Soviet agency. So, somewhere in Los Angeles, they are making tea kettle moulds for the USSR. The point of the story (if it needs to be spelled out) is the importance of knowing beforehand what the Soviet Union wants. The Soviets operate according to a one year and a five year plan. If the plan does not provide for purchases of the kind of item you are selling, you will be wasting your time in Moscow.

A typical deal

The Soviet negotiators will call for the Western firm to supply a prototype model, component parts, and technical assistance for the Russians to develop, design, and produce the given item under a long-term licensing arrangement. Generally speaking, Soviet agencies do not buy finished consumer or industrial goods. They buy "know-how" in the form of licensing arrangements.

We once asked a man who had spent the better part of his life negotiating business deals with the Russians what he had learned. His answer: "Follow through on your end of the transaction; the Soviets will always deliver what *they* promise." It seems to be a general consensus amongst experienced traders that the Soviets are meticulous in keeping to the letter of any business agreement, and they expect you to be equally meticulous. When you promise delivery dates, they must be kept. Everything in modern-day Russia is part of the Five Year Plan. Once you conclude a deal, you too become part of the Soviet national economic plan.

how the plan works

Two dozen men—the presidium of Gosplan, the Soviet planning agency—are responsible for planning twenty years ahead the future welfare of 241,748,000 people. They propose no legislation, issue no "cease and desist" orders, prosecute no industries; but the Central Committee of the Communist Party will rarely act on economic affairs without first checking with Gosplan.

As you read this, Gosplan is watching closely over the Soviet Union's ninth Five Year Plan, covering the period 1971–75. This plan is intended to give light industry and consumer goods a slight edge over heavy industry. At the same time, Gosplan is putting the finishing touches to the 1976–81 plan, and is working out on computers the general economic thrust that will guide the country up to the year 2000.

We have nothing like Gosplan in the West.

Certain large corporations such as du Pont, General Motors, and Unilever may attempt to project production in terms of demand. In the Soviet Union, however, the Gosplan economists compute supply and demand for the whole economic structure. As a Soviet tract observes: "Thanks to a single state plan, it is possible to provide for correct proportions between manufacture and consumption, between supply and demand."

Inside Gosplan's offices, within a stone's throw of the Kremlin, there are more than a thousand individuals working under the presidium's supervision. Feeding information into Gosplan is a nationwide network of computers. Each of the Soviet Union's 15 republics has a regional planning board. Every factory, every collective farm, every district, feeds economic news into the Moscow-bound information stream.

All this is terribly relevant to your hopes of selling goods and services in the USSR. It is important to realize that you will be trading in a collective society. Decisions are made on the basis of Gosplan's economic blueprint—*never* on an individual basis. Thus, in bringing a business proposition to Russia, try to learn from your Soviet colleagues where what you have to offer might fit into that blueprint.

In recent years the IBM World Trade Corporation has sold the Soviet Ministry of Chemical Industry a large computer, and a Chicago company has sold a 16-lane bowling alley to the Ministry of Culture. The Pepsi-Cola people have worked out an ingenious joint venture: to sell Pepsi to the vast Russian soft-drink market, and to merchandize Stolichnaya-brand vodka in the USA. There are many other examples.

The huge Kama River project alone could bring $1 billion worth of tool and construction equipment orders to the West. Natural gas and oil developments could generate another $3 billion worth of orders. The Soviet Union has a gross national product of around $570 billion, with a purchasing power second only to the trillion-dollar U.S. market.

The potential for trade is clearly there.

making contact

A businessman we know with a long record of success in dealing with the Soviets always brings a typewriter with him. As soon as he checks into his hotel, he writes a brief note to the Soviet agency where he is doing business. Downstairs, in his hotel, he gets the Intourist Service Bureau to write out the address on the envelope in Russian, and then he takes a taxi and leaves his letter at the Soviet trade agency along with his visiting card. They call him the same day. He swears it works every time.

You may well have written before your trip and not received a reply. Chances are they were translating your letter, then translating their own reply.

The telephone is another potential hazard. As an instrument it is still viewed with the deepest suspicion in Russia. Of course it does not work very well. The crackling, burbling, and static make it resemble a samovar rather than the object Mr. Bell invented. Letter-writing seems to work better.

Soviet trading organizations are established along conservative lines and are extremely status-conscious. It is important that you establish at what level you are dealing. Of course, it is best to start at the top—Soviet executives are disinclined to delegate authority.

If you can arrange it before you leave home, try to have a Commerce Department or Board of Trade representative (as the case may be) get in touch with his counterpart in Moscow. Your Embassy, U.S. or British, can be very helpful in arranging contacts—though they do like advance notice of your arrival, and some information on the kind of business you intend to transact.

British businessmen should also get in touch with the USSR section of the London Chamber of Commerce, which is the largest of its kind in the world: USSR Section, London Chamber of Commerce, 69 Cannon Street, London. Telephone 01–248 4444 Extension 38.

An invitation to lunch on your part will usually be received with pleasure by your Soviet colleagues. The best advice is not to stint on the entertainment of your guests: choose the most expensive restaurant within your budget (see pp. 213 ff.). While business should not be the main topic of conversation, it is wise to conclude the occasion by getting a firm commitment for a future meeting.

Finally, if a woman is present at the lunch or dinner, bring along a bouquet of flowers, a small gesture that is always good manners in the USSR.

negotiating

As any regular reader of the Soviet press will tell you, Soviet managers—from foremen to members of the government—are adept at passing the buck. In recent years Moscow bookstores have been selling a Russian translation of *Executive Leadership Course*, a primer of business principles first published in the United States.

Nevertheless, when you come face to face with Soviet officials it is necessary to bear in mind that they think very differently from you. In a collective society, decision-making is a collective process. So when you attend a serious meeting, come prepared with a *written outline* of your proposal, preferably written in Russian. This makes things easier all around.

If you are dealing with middle-level management, every decision will require a conference with a superior. He in turn may have to seek authority from a still higher level. You may assume from the start that the people you are dealing with know their business. Trading corporations that deal with foreign firms are staffed with able men who are familiar with what you have to offer. They will argue forcefully on contract details when the time comes.

Patience is the most important quality you can bring with you to the Soviet Union. In business discussions it must be remembered that the Soviet representative sitting opposite is not really a "negotiator" in the full sense of that term. Before any deal can be concluded, he will have to talk with many other people who rank above him. Essentially he functions as a kind of transmission belt—from you to his superiors, and from them to you in terms of various factors and considerations stemming from Gosplan's economic blueprint. The final decision, you can be sure, will be made outside the conference room you are sitting in.

Wearing the opponent down is an old Russian negotiating tactic. Diplomats call it the "head-against-the-stone-wall" technique. In a complicated transaction there may be as many as fifty or sixty points of disagreement. In these circumstances, a Soviet negotiator might try for an "Agreement in Principle." The bottom line on such an agreement usually finds you holding the "principle" while the actual practice works to the Soviets' benefit.

Endurance is another Russian trait; so is stubbornness in pursuit of a goal. On the other hand, the word "compromise" is not of Russian origin; it is seldom used in the Soviet Union except as an expression of disgust.

Of course, all the above is only to get you started—the rest is up to you. Be patient.

making the deal

Whether you are selling paper cups, vending machines, or a foundry for the Kama River truck complex, there are certain Soviet trade practices that you should be aware of before you put pen to paper. Look the contract over line by line. Pay special attention to (a) the terms of payment; (b) quality-control and inspection clauses; (c) arbitration requirements; (d) patent and trademark protection.

Terms of Payment

Flexibility is the key to this clause. You may be asked to consider barter in lieu of dollars or other hard currency. Occidental Petroleum, a long-time trader with the USSR, took several thousand tons of nickel in exchange for goods in one deal. In Vienna, there are businessmen who specialize in "switch" trading. Entrepreneurs like Dr. Armand Hammer of Occidental Petroleum and Berthold Beitz of Krupp have pioneered such bilateral and trilateral trading arrangements. Negotiations determine the commodities involved, payment involved, and where the goods can be marketed. An American farm-implement manufacturer might be offered 200,000 tons of Siberian crude in return for his goods. This may, or may not, turn out to be a good deal. The point is to be prepared for compensatory trading before you leave for Moscow.

Estimates of Soviet gold reserves range from $3 billion to $18 billion. But it is not likely that you will be paid in that substance. What are you going to do when they offer you four million raincoats in return for your computers? When the Russians do pay in hard cash, it is usually within thirty days of receipt of goods.

A *word of caution:* it is usually impossible to write escalator clauses into Soviet contracts. If your cost of manufacture soars because of inflation, that's too bad. Remember this before you sign.

Quality Control & Inspection

Soviet contracts usually include a clause that allows inspection of goods or equipment before shipment. Expect to be host to various groups of Russian experts in your home town during the life of the contract. High-quality packing is another stipulation. Handling in Russia is anything but gentle and the customer expects the goods to arrive in one piece. Better figure extra expenses for the crating.

Arbitration

Be careful here. Your Soviet friends will suggest that disputes be arbitrated by the Foreign Trade Arbitration Commission of the USSR. Only Soviet nationals are on the commission, however, so you're not likely to get much of a break in the event of a dispute.

There is, however, plenty of precedent for third-country arbitration. In such cases, disputes can be settled in Stockholm, Helsinki, or Zurich. Obviously you don't expect disputes in *your* contract, but it is wise to consider what could happen if misfortune arises. In the crunch, where you arbitrate will be a matter of how solid your bargaining position is.

Patent and Trademark Protection

This is a sticky area. To be sure, the USSR is a member of the Paris Union—the International Convention for the Protection of Industrial Property.

Nevertheless, unless your product is patented under Soviet law, the fact that you possess a U.S. or West European patent will not prevent its being copied in the Soviet Union. Unless you are careful, your industrial equipment may be copied without any payment beyond the original sale price. The proper procedure is to arrange patent protection in the USSR, and other Eastern-bloc countries, by filing in Moscow—in fact, this is the only way to enforce contractual commitments during the life of the business deal.

summing up

A businessman in Moscow told us his particular technique for winning fat contracts. "To tell you the truth," he said, "I wasn't having much luck until the Japanese traders arrived in the early nineteen-fifties.

"As you know," he continued, "between 1957 and 1968 Soviet-Japanese trade increased more than thirty times, which is absolutely sensational. So I decided to study their work habits. One day, over at the Ministry of Light Industry on Kirov Street I had been sitting for about four hours next to a man from Mitsubishi. As it turned out, we were both there trying to arrange a barter deal—mine was to swap some Siberian lumber for some gas turbines from Holland. Well, after four hours of waiting I quit and went back to the hotel. All that week I made my morning call at the Ministry, and every time I showed up, my friend from Mitsubishi was there reading his Japanese newspaper. Finally I asked him what kept him going. He told me it was a matter of 'giri'—the word means 'duty,' 'honor,' 'face,' 'respectability.' I mean, he was *obsessive* about winning an order.

"The next day, I went out and bought myself an inflatable cushion. From that day on, I learned to practice 'giri' in Moscow."

Of course, there is a footnote to this little story: Nowadays Japan is one of the Soviet Union's leading trading partners in the non-Communist world.

All the same, Soviet trade with the West is growing at a whopping annual rate of 10 percent, and the prospects are for more trade in future years.

So if you don't want to bring an inflatable cushion, remember that the man from Mitsubishi is likely to be down the hallway. To beat him, you will need endurance, patience, and a touch of *giri*.

some useful addresses and phone numbers

Information and advice on trade are handled by the Ministry of Foreign Trade (Vneshtorg), Smolenskaya Square, No. 32/34. You may telephone your enquiries till 5 p.m. Monday–Friday, to the following number: 244–19–47. During evening hours, try 244–24–09.

Soviet Trading Companies

The majority are located in the Ministry of Foreign Trade Building on Smolenskaya Square. The exceptions are specifically noted.

Aviaexport 244 26 86
Avtoexport 244 28 48
Avtopromimport 244 45 13

Energomashexport
   Mosfilmovskaya St. No. 35 . . . . 139 53 36
Exportkhleb 244 47 01

Exportles 241 60 44
Exportljon
  Arkh. Vlasova St. No. 33 .... 128 07 86

Litsenzintorg
Kakhovka St. No. 31 .... 122 02 54

Mashinoexport
Mezhdunarodnaya Kniga 244 10 22
Mashinoimport 244 33 09
Mashpriborintorg 244 27 75
Medexport
  Kakhovka St. No. 31 .... 121 01 54
Mezhdunarodnaya Kniga 244-10 22

Neftekhimpromexport
  Ovchinnikovskaya Nab. 18/1 .... 220 11 09
Novoexport
  Bashilovskaya St. No. 19 .... 285 66 90

Prodintorg 244 26 29
Prommashexport
  Ovchinnikovskaya Nab. 18/1 .... 220 15 05
Prommashimport 244 431 57
Promsyrioimport
  Arkh. Vlasova St. No. 33 .... 128 07 75

Ranoimport 244 37 61
Raxnoexport 251 48 97

Selkhozpromexport
  Ovchinnikovskaya Nab. 18/1   220 16 92
Skotoimport
  Makarensko St. No. 6 .... 297 22 32

Vneshtorgreklama
  Kakhovka St. No. 31 Korpus 2 . . . . 121 04 34
Vostokintorg 244 20 34

Zapchastexport
  2nd Skotoprogonnaya St. No. 35 . . . . . . 278 63 05

The Moscow Chamber of Commerce is
  located at Kuibysheva St. No. 6.
  Telephone: 221 08 11

Head Customs Office
  Telephone: 228 70 06

Foreign Business Representatives
Société Nationale de Siderurgie Algerienne (*Sr.*
  Pereyaslavskaya 14, Apt. 45 Telephone: 81–88–82)
Tracosa (Belgium) (*Tryokhprudny Per. 11/13*
  Telephone: 99–91–69)
Finnish-Soviet Chamber of Commerce
  (*Pokrovsky Boulevard 4/17 Telephone: 27–37–24*)
Franco-Soviet Chamber of Commerce
  (*Pokrovsky Boulevard 4/17, Apt. 3 Telephone: 97–*
  90–92 & 97–48–35 & 27–32–45)
Goldschmidt S.A. (France) (*Hotel Ukraine,*
  Room 559 Telephone: 43–25–59)
Régie Nationale des Usines Renault
  (France) (*Hotel Pekin, Room 1001 Telephone: 53–*
  83–86 & 53–84–78)
Rhone-Poulenc S.A. (France) (*Hotel Ukraine,*
  Room 428 Telephone: 43–24–28)
Satra Corp. (USA) (*Hotel Metropole, Room 425*
  Telephone: 25–64–25 & 25–66–49)

308)

Sofracop (Banque de Paris et des Pays-Bas (France)
(*Hotel Pekin, Room 802 Telephone:*
53–81–72 & 53–81–52 & 53–92–22)

Speichim-Ensa (France) (*Hotel Berlin, Rooms*
316, 319 Telephone: 23–12–80, 25–68–66, & 25–
68–61)

Anton Ohlert (West Germany) (*Hotel Metropole,*
Room 372 Telephone: 25–63–72)

Braun & Co. (West Germany) (*Bolshaya Pereyaslav-*
skaya 13, Apt. 33 Telephone: 84–44–49)

Compagnía Generale Interscambi-Cogis
(Italy) (*Hotel Ukraine, Room 2615 Telephone:*
43–20–95)

Ente Nazionale Idrocarburi (ENI) (Italy)
(*Hotel Ukraine, Room 415 Telephone: 43–24–15*)

Fiat (Italy) (*Tryokhprudny Per. 11/13 Telephone:*
99–09–32 & 99–09–36)

Finmeccànica (Italy) (*Hotel Ukraine, Room*
944 Telephone: 43–29–44)

Grace Italiana S.P.A. (Italy) (*Hotel Ukraine,*
Room 839 Telephone: 43–28–39 & 43–09–50)

Montecatini Edison (Italy) (*Pokrovsky Boule-*
vard 4/17, Apt. 16 Telephone: 27–37–43 & 97–47–57)

Novasider (Italy) (*Tryokhprudny Per. 11/13 Tele-*
phone: 99–09–32 & 99–09–36)

Olivetti (Italy) (*Hotel Metropole, Room 405 Tele-*
phone: 25–64–05 & 25–60–13)

Rest-Ital (Italy) (*Hotel Ukraine, Room 986 Tele-*
phone: 43–29–86)

Ataka Sangyo (Japan) (*Tryokhprudny Per. 11/13*
Telephone: 99–82–85)

Chori (Japan) (*Hotel Ukraine, Room 915 Tele-*
phone: 43–29–15)

Dokai Boeki (Japan) *(Hotel Ukraine, Room 1710 Telephone: 43-31-70)*

International Trading Co. Ltd. (Japan) *(Hotel Metropole, Room 505 Telephone: 25-65-05 & 25-66-16)*

Eskra Sangyo (Japan) *(2nd Poklonnaya Ul. 8, Apt. 93 Telephone: 148-12-02)*

C. Itoh & Co. Ltd. (Japan) *(Tryokhprudny Per. 11/13 Telephone: 99-25-31 & 99-23-29)*

Japan Sea Trading Co. Ltd. (Japan) *(Hotel Ukraine, Room 501 Telephone: 43-25-01)*

Kanematsu Gosho (Japan) *(Hotel Ukraine, Room 915 Telephone: 43-03-12 & 43-20-91)*

Kawakami Boeki (Japan) *(Hotel Ukraine, Room 915 Telephone: 43-29-15 & 43-04-54)*

Marubeni Iida Co. Ltd. (Japan) *(Pokrovsky Boulevard 4/17, Apt. 29 Telephone: 97-29-27 & 97-32-93)*

Mitsubishi Shoji Kaisha Ltd. (Japan) *(Pokrovsky Boulevard 4/17, Apt. 17 Telephone: 97-55-99 & 97-67-69)*

Mitsui Bussan (Japan) *(Tryokhprudny Per. 11/13 Telephone: 99-42-23)*

Nichimen Jitsugyo (Japan) *(Hotel Leningrad-skaya, Room 641 Telephone: 25-56-41)*

Nissho-Iwai Co. Ltd. (Japan) *(Hotel Ukraine, Room 801-802 Telephone: 43-28-01 & 43-28 -02)*

Progress Trading Co. Ltd. (Japan) *(Tryokhprudny Per. 11/13 Telephone: 99-65-43)*

Sogo Boeki (Japan) *(Hotel Leningradskaya, Room 301 Telephone: 25-53-01)*

Simitomo Shoji Kaisha Ltd. (Japan) *(Hotel Leningradskaya, Room 601 Telephone: 25–56–01)*

Tokyo Boeki (Japan) *(Pokrovsky Boulevard 4/17, Apt. 30 Telephone: 98–34–80 & 98–50–63)*

Toyo Menka Kaisha Ltd. (Japan) *(Hotel Ukraine, Room 815 Telephone: 43–28–15 & 43–34–46)*

Toyo Rayon (Japan) *(Hotel Ukraine, Room 2214 Telephone: 43–22–14)*

Wako Koeki (Japan) *(Hotel Ukraine, Room 659 Telephone: 43–26–59)*

Stemmler-Imex N.V. (Netherlands) *(Hotel Yuzhnaya, Room 58 Telephone: 34–96–24)*

Ciba-Geigy (Switzerland) *(Hotel Leningradskaya, Room 201 Telephone: 25–56–77)*

General Products Corporation (Switzerland) *(c/o K–600 International Post Office Moscow)*

Indreba (Switzerland) *(Hotel Ukraine, Room 528 Telephone: 43–25–28)*

Industrial Trading Trust S.A. (Switzerland) *(Hotel National, Rooms 215 & 426 Telephone: 03–70–28 & 03–61–61)*

ICL Ltd. (U.K.) *(Ul. Vavilova 83, Rooms 4–5 Telephone: 134–95–49)*

M. Golodetz Ltd. (U.K.) *(Tryokhprudny Per. 11/13 Telephone: 99–28–83)*

Chase Manhattan Bank N.A. (U.S.) *(Hotel Metropole, Room 227 Telephone: 25–62–27)*

Occidental Petroleum Corp. (U.S.) *(Hotel National, Room 450 Telephone: 02–46–16)*

Satra Corp. (U.S.) *(Hotel Metropole, Room 425 Telephone: 25–64–25)*

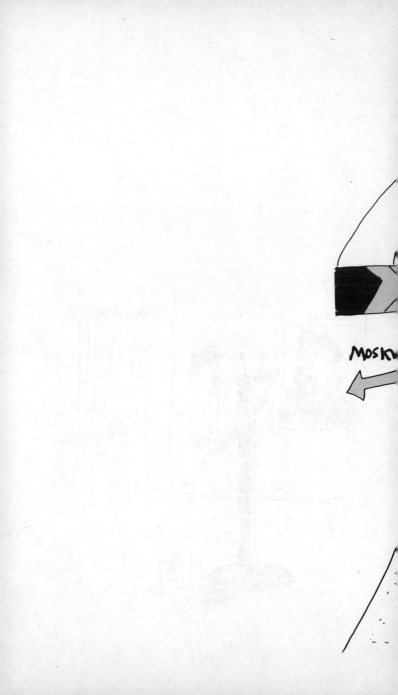

MOSKV

getting home

If you are with a tour group, there is little to concern yourself about; if you are travelling independently, the main thing is to make arrangements at least two days before departure. Confirm your airline reservation (see below) well ahead of time. Advise Intourist that you will be leaving on a specific day and that you will require transportation to the airport.

Before you leave for the airport, make sure that you have no food coupons left over. These are supposed to be refundable, but few people have ever had the privilege of collecting. So blow the wad on your last dinner. As for your Russian money, this is easily exchanged at the airport. It is very important that you allow plenty of time for this, however, as there is nearly always a line at the bank window.

Another point to remember: don't cash in your roubles until your excess baggage has been weighed. Unlike some airlines, Aeroflot is scrupulous about overweight and will charge you for it. This means going to yet another window before you are allowed to proceed to Customs. Here you pay the excess baggage charge and receive a receipt which is then affixed to your ticket. Only then should you exchange the balance of your roubles. For this operation you will need to present your Customs Declaration form, the one you filled in when you entered the Soviet Union.

If Russian friends have come to the airport to see you off, this is where you will say farewell. Then you pass through the green-hatted border police, up the stairs, and enter the departure lounge. If you have some time to spare, there is one last Beriozka store located here. It is rather a good one, filled with records, mandolins, balalaikas, cameras, fur hats, and of course vodka and caviar. You pay in hard currency.

Moscow is now behind you. As the Russians say, *Dasvidanya!*

Airlines

Afghan *Hotel Metropole, Room 433 Telephone:*
   25–64–33
Air Algérie *Kutuzovsky Prospekt 7/4. Korpus 6,*
   Apt. 20 Telephone: 43–94–53
Air Canada *Hotel Metropole, Room 383 Telephone: 25–63–83 & 25–60–83 & 25–69–26*
Air France *Hotel Metropole, Room 305 Telephone:*
   25–63–05 & 25–62–28 & 25–65–07 & 21–10–97
Air India *Hotel Metropole, Room 413 Telephone:*
   25–61–00 & 25–64–13
Alitalia *Hotel Metropole, Room 205 Telephone:*
   25–62–05 & 25–60–27 & 25–66–95
Austrian *Hotel National, Room 442 Telephone:*
   92–53–63
Balkan *Hotel Metropole, Room 2045 Telephone:*
   25–60–11
British Airways *Hotel National, Rooms 375–376*
   Telephone: 03–94–63 & 03–55–87
Cubana *Pomerantsev Per. 8 Telephone: 46–21–00*
Czechair *2-ya Brestskaya 21/27 Telephone: 50–02–40 & 50–45–71*
Egyptair *Hotel Ukraine, Room 744 Telephone:*
   43–27–44

Finnair *Hotel Ukraine, Room* 844 *Telephone:* 43–
24–44 & 43–38–08

Interflug *Hotel Ukraine, Room* 543 *Telephone:*
43–25–43

Iranair *Hotel Ukraine, Room* 486 *Telephone:* 43–
24–86

JAL *Hotel Ukraine, Room* 843 *Telephone:* 43–20–98 &
43–28–43

KLM *Hotel Tsentralnaya, Rooms* 215–216 *Telephone:*
29–02–85 & 29–07–29 & 29–25–39

Lot (Poland) *Smolenskaya Pl.* 13/21 *Apt.* 161 *Telephone:* 41–56–00

Lufthansa *Hotel Metropole Rooms* 313 & 315
Telephone: 25–63–13 & 25–63–15

Malev (Hungary) *Proyezd Khudozhestvennovo
Teatra* 6 *Telephone:* 92–04–34

Pan Am *Hotel Metropole, Room* 239 *Telephone:*
23–51–83 & 25–64–06

Sabena *Hotel Metropole, Room* 386 *Telephone:*
25–63–86 & 25–64–28

SAS *Hotel National, Room* 206 *Telephone:* 92–66–61;
night: 92–00–34

Swissair *Hotel National, Room* 226 *Telephone:*
03–68–63 & 03–74–58

Yugoslav *Hotel Ukraine, Room* 401 *Telephone:*
43–24–01

Travel Agencies
American Express *Hotel Metropole, Room* 384
Telephone: 25–63–84

Balkantourist *Hotel Metropole, Room* 2045 *Telephone:*
21–85–75

Orbis (Poland) *Hotel National, Room 104 Telephone:*
  03-74-39
Reisenbüro DDR *Hotel Berlin, Room 230 Tele-*
  phone: 25-60-30 & 94-88-93

appendixes

emergency

FIRST AID, AMBULANCE	Dial 03
POLICE	Dial 02
FIRE	Dial 01
TRACING PEOPLE IN HOSPITAL	Dial 94–31–52

If you are in distress

The Soviet health care system can claim to be among the best in the world. The USSR has more hospital beds, nurses, and doctors than any other country. Medical service is free of charge. It is available in any city or town throughout the country.

Doctor's visits and first aid treatments are free of charge. However, visitors are required to pay for any medication or hospital treatment required.

Expenses for hospital treatment must be paid in foreign currency or roubles at the rate of $13.50 per day for each day of hospitalization. They may be covered by unused days of services purchased.

All Moscow hotels have access to a doctor, and many of the larger hotels have a resident medical staff. Call the desk or tell the *dezhurnaya* in case of sickness. If you use special medication, it is advisable to bring it with you to the Soviet Union. If you need a pharmacy, Intourist will guide you to the nearest one. There are no 24-hour drug stores in Moscow, so plan ahead.

For visitors in need of medical attention of the first aid variety, contact Intourist. You will probably be sent to the **Tourist's Clinic, 12, Herzen Street** (telephone: 29–73–23 or 29–03–82).

Both the British and the U.S. Embassy have an M.D. on their staff for their own requirements. In a grave emergency, they can be called for advice (see below). In most instances, they will refer you to local medical care.

Claims and refunds

If you have to cut your trip short, you can only get a refund inside the USSR in roubles. To get your money back in the currency you paid in, you will have to see your travel agency. It is very important that you ask Intourist in Moscow for a credit memo, known as a *spravka*, before leaving the city. You will also be subject to a cancellation fee which is calculated at 20 percent during "Season" and "High Season" and 10 percent during "Off Season."

Refunds are only issued for full unused days of service. Separate or partial services are not refundable.

more useful addresses

Embassies

United States (*Ul. Chaikovskovo 19/23, Telephone: 52-00-11/19; Office hours Mon–Fri: 9 a.m.–1 p.m.; 2 p.m.–6 p.m.*)

United Kingdom (*Naberezhnaya Morisa Toreza 14, Telephone: 31-95-55/6/7; Office hours Mon–Fri: 9 a.m.–12.30 p.m.; 2.30 p.m.–6 p.m. Consular Section Mon–Fri: 9:30 a.m.–12 noon; 2:30 p.m.–5 p.m.*

Commercial & Cultural Offices *Kutuzovsky Pr. 7/4* 41-10-33

Argentina (*Ul. Lunarcharskovo 8, Telephone: 41–66–81; Office hours Mon–Fri: 10 a.m.–1 p.m.; 3 p.m.–6 p.m.*)

Australia (*Kropotkinsky Per. 13, Telephone: 41–20–35 or 41–20–36; Office hours Mon–Fri: 9:30 a.m.–1 p.m., 2:30 p.m.–6 p.m.*)

Austria (*Starokonyushenny Per. 1, Telephone: 02–19–41 or 02–20–39; Office hours Mon–Fri: 10 a.m.–1 p.m., 3 p.m.–5 p.m.*)

Bangladesh (*Zemledelchesky Per. 6 46–79–00*)

Belgium (*Khlebny Per. 15, Telephone: 90–22–37 or 90–10–06; Office hours Mon–Fri: 9:30 a.m.–1 p.m., 2:30 p.m.–5:30 p.m.*)

Bolivia (*Lopukhinsky Per. 5, Telephone: 02–25–09 or 02–25–14; Office hours Mon–Fri: 9:30 a.m.–1 p.m., 3 p.m.–6 p.m.*)

Brazil (*Ul. Gertsena 54, Telephone: 90–40–22 also 90–40–23/4/5/6; Office hours Mon–Fri: 10 a.m.–1 p.m.; 3 p.m.–5 p.m.*)

Bulgaria (*Leningradsky Prospekt 20, Telephone: 51–57–60 or 50–06–83; Office hours Mon–Fri: 9 a.m.–1 p.m.; 2 p.m.–5:30 p.m. Sat: 9 a.m.–2 p.m.*)

Burma (*Ul. Gertsena 41, Telephone: 91–05–34; Office hours Mon–Fri: 9:30 a.m.–1 p.m., 1:30 p.m.–5:30 p.m.*

Burundi (*Uspensky Per. 7, Telephone: 99–72–00 or 99–48–58; Office hours Mon–Fri: 9 a.m.–1 p.m., 2 p.m.–5 p.m.*)

Cambodia (Khmer Republic) (*Leninsky Pr. 45, Room 414 Telephone: 135–13–94; Office hours Mon–Fri: 9 a.m.–1 p.m.; 2 p.m.–5 p.m.*)

Cameroon (*Ul. Vorovskovo 40, Telephone: 90–65–49; Office hours Mon–Fri: 9 a.m.–12 noon; 1:30–5:30 p.m.*)

Canada *(Starokonyushenny Per. 23, Telephone: 41–90–34, 41–50–70, 41–91–55, Night: 41–90–34; Office hours Mon–Fri: 9:30 a.m.–1 p.m., 2 p.m.–6 p.m.)*

Ceylon *(Ul. Shepkina 24, Telephone: 81–96–26; Office hours Mon–Thur: 9:30 a.m.–5:15 p.m., Fri: 9:30 a.m.–5:30 p.m.)*

Chad *(Ul. Elizarovoy 10, Telephone: 27 88 50; Office hours Mon–Fri: 9 a.m.–1 p.m.; 2 p.m.–5 p.m., Sat. 10 a.m.–2 p.m.)*

Chile *(Ul. Sadovo Triumfalnaya 4/10, Telephone: 99–75–74; Office hours Mon–Fri: 9 a.m.–1 p.m.; 3 p.m.–6 p.m.)*

China *(Leninskiye Gory, Ul. Druzhby 6, Telephone: 43–15–40; Office hours Mon–Fri: 9 a.m.–12 noon, 3 p.m.–6 p.m.)*

Colombia *(Ul. Burdenko 20, Telephone: 46–64–31; Office hours Mon–Fri: 9 a.m.–1 p.m.; 3 p.m.– 6 p.m.)*

Congo *(Kropotkinsky Per. 12, & Pomgrantsev Per. 11, Telephone: 46–00–76/7; Office hours Mon–Fri: 9 a.m.–5 p.m., Sat. (skeleton staff) 10 a.m.–2 p.m.)*

Cuba *(Mosfilmovskaya Ul. 40, Telephone: 47–45–55, 47–45–70; Office hours Mon–Fri: 9 a.m.–1 p.m., 3 p.m.–5 p.m., Sat: 9 a.m.–3 p.m.)*

Cyprus *(Ul. Gertsena 51, Telephone: 90–21–54; Office hours Mon–Fri: 9 a.m.–1 p.m.; 2 p.m.–6 p.m.)*

Czechoslovakia *(Ul. Yuliusa Fuchika 12/14, Telephone: 53–75–07; Office hours Mon–Fri: 8:30 a.m.–5 p.m.)*

Denmark *(Per. Ostrovskovo 9, Telephone: 02–78–66; Office hours Mon–Fri: 10 a.m.–12 noon)*

Egypt *(Ul. Gertsena 56, Telephone: 91–32–09; Office hours Mon–Fri: 9 a.m.–3 p.m., Sat: 10 a.m.–1:30 p.m.)*

Ethiopia *(Kropotkinskaya Nab. 35, Telephone: 03–11–65; Office hours Mon–Fri: 9 a.m.–1 p.m.; 3 p.m.–6 p.m., Sat: 9 a.m.–1 p.m.)*

Finland *(Kropotkinsky Per. 15/17, Telephone: 46–45–40; Office hours Mon–Fri: 8:30 a.m.–12:30 p.m., 2 p.m.–5:15 p.m.)*

France *(Ul. Dimitrova 43, Telephone: 31–85–06 & 31–85–08; Office hours Mon–Fri: 9:30 a.m.–1 p.m.; 3:15 p.m.–6:45 p.m., Sat: 9:30 a.m.–1 p.m.)*

Germany, East *(Ul. Stanislaskovo 10, Telephone: 94–00–25; Office hours Mon–Fri: 8 a.m.–5:15 p.m.)*

Germany, West *(Ul. Bolshaya Gruzinskaya 17, Telephone: 55–00–13; Office hours Mon–Fri: 8:30 a.m.–1 p.m.; 3 p.m.–6 p.m.)*

Ghana *(Skaterny Per. 14, Telephone: 02–18–70/1; Office hours Mon–Fri: 9 a.m.–1 p.m.; 2:30 p.m.–5 p.m.)*

Greece *(Ul. Stanislavskovo 4, Telephone: 90–22–74; Office hours Mon–Fri: 9:30 a.m.–1 p.m.; 3:15 p.m.–6 p.m., Sat: 10 a.m.–2 p.m.)*

Guinea *(Pomerantsev Per. 6, Telephone: 02–46–52; Office hours Mon–Fri: 9:30 a.m.–4 p.m.)*

Hungary *(Mosfilmovskaya Ul. 62, Telephone: 143–86–11/15; Office hours Mon–Fri: 8:30 a.m.–5:30 p.m.)*

Iceland *(Khlebny Per. 28, Telephone: 90–47–42; Office hours Mon–Fri: 9 a.m.–5 p.m.)*

India *(Ul. Obukha "6/8", Telephone: 97–08–20; Office hours Mon–Fri: 10:30 a.m.–12:30 p.m.; 2:30 p.m.–4 p.m.)*

Indonesia *(Ul. Novokuznetskaya 12, Telephone: 31–95–49; Office hours unavailable)*

Iran *(Pokrovsky Boulevard 7, Telephone: 97–46–19; Office hours Mon–Fri: 9 a.m.–3 p.m., Sat: 9 a.m.– 2 p.m.)*

Iraq *(Pogodinskaya Ul. 12, Telephone: 46–37–20; Office hours Mon–Fri: 9 a.m.–4 p.m.)*

Italy *(Ul. Vesnina 5, Telephone: 41–15–34/35/36; Office hours Mon–Fri: 9:30 a.m.–1:30 p.m., 4:30 p.m.– 7:30 p.m., Sat: 9:30 a.m.–1:30 p.m.)*

Japan *(Kalashny Per. 12, Telephone: 91–85–00/01; Office hours Mon–Fri: 9:30 a.m.–1:30 p.m., 2:30 p.m.–6 p.m.)*

Jordan *(Sadovskikh Per. 3, Telephone: 99 34–30; Office hours Mon–Fri: 9:30 a.m.–2 p.m.; 3 p.m.– 5:30 p.m.)*

Kenya *(Ul. Bolshaya Ordynka 70, Telephone: 33–86–65; Office hours Mon–Fri: 9 a.m.–12:30 p.m.; 2 p.m.– 5 p.m.)*

North Korea *(Ul. Stanislavskovo 9, Telephone: 90–60– 13; Office hours Mon–Fri: 9 a.m.–1 p.m.; 3 p.m.– 7 p.m.)*

Kuwait *(3rd Neopalimovsky Per. 13/5, Telephone: 45–08–25; Office hours Mon–Fri: 9:30 a.m.–5:30 p.m.)*

Laos *(Ul. Kachalova 18, Telephone: 90–12–81; Office hours Mon–Fri: 9 a.m.–1 p.m.; 3 p.m.–5:30 p.m.)*

Lebanon *(Ul. Sadovo-Samotechnaya 14, Telephone: 95–20–83; Office hours Mon–Fri: 9 a.m.–1 p.m.; 2 p.m.–5 p.m.)*

Libya *(Merzlyakovsky Per. 20, Telephone: 91–11–75/76; Office hours Mon–Fri: 9 a.m.–3 p.m.)*

Luxembourg *(Khrushchevsky Per. 3, Telephone: 02–21–71; Office hours Mon–Fri: 9:30 a.m.–1 p.m.; 2:30 p.m.–6 p.m.)*

Malaysia *(Mosfilmovskaya Ul. 50, Telephone: 47–15–14;*
Office hours 9 a.m.–1 p.m.; 2 p.m.–5 p.m.)

Mali *(Novokuznetskaya Ul. 11, Telephone: 31–22–60;*
Office hours Mon–Fri: 9 a.m.–4 p.m.)

Mexico *(Ul. Shchukina 4, Telephone: 02–13–56;*
Office hours Mon–Fri: 9 a.m.–1 p.m.; 2:30 p.m.–
5 p.m.)

Mongolia *(Ul. Pisemskovo 11, Telephone: 90–30–*
61 & 90–67–92; Office hours Mon–Fri: 9 a.m.–1 p.m.,
2 p.m.–6 p.m.)

Morocco *(Per. Ostrovskovo 8, Telephone: 02–01–95,*
02–33–50; Office hours Mon–Fri: 9 a.m.–6 p.m.,
Sat: 9 a.m.–1 p.m.)

Nepal *(2nd Neopalimovsky Per. 14/7, Telephone:*
41–94–34; Office hours Mon–Fri: 9 a.m.–1 p.m.;
2 p.m.–5 p.m.)

Netherlands *(Kalashny Per. 6, Telephone: 91–29–99;*
Office hours Mon–Fri: 9:30 a.m.–1 p.m.; 2:30 p.m.–
6 p.m.)

Nigeria *(Ul. Kachalova 13, Telephone: 90–37–83/*
5/7/8; Office hours Mon–Fri: 9 a.m.–5:30 p.m.,
Sat: 10 a.m.–2 p.m.

Norway *(Ul. Vorovskovo 7, Telephone: 90–38–72;*
Office hours Mon–Fri: 9 a.m.–1 p.m.; 3 p.m.–5 p.m.)

Pakistan *(Ul. Sadovo-Kudrinskaya 17, Telephone:*
50–39–91; Office hours Mon–Fri: 9 a.m.–5 p.m.)

Peru *(Smolensky Boulevard 22/14, Apt. 12, Telephone:*
46–68–36; Office hours Mon–Fri: 9 a.m.–1 p.m.;
3 p.m.–6 p.m.)

Poland *(Ul. A. Mitskevicha 1, Telephone: 290–49–*
11/15; Office hours Mon–Fri: 9 a.m.–5:30 p.m.)

Rumania *(Ul. Mosfilmovskaya 64, Telephone: 143–04–*
20; Office hours Mon–Fri: 8:30 a.m.–1:30 p.m.,

2:30 p.m.–5:30 p.m., Sat: 8:30 a.m.–1:30 p.m.)

Senegal (Ul. Donskaya 12, Telephone: 36–20–40;
Office hours Mon–Fri: 9 a.m.–1 p.m.; 3 p.m.–6 p.m.)

Sudan (Ul. Vorovskovo 9, Telephone: 90–39–93;
Office hours Mon–Fri: 9:30 a.m.–1 p.m.;
2 p.m.–5 p.m.)

Sweden (Ul. Mosfilmovskaya 60, Telephone: 47–90–09;
Telex 7408, 7536; Office hours Mon–Fri: 9 a.m.–
1 p.m., 2:45 p.m.–6 p.m.)

Switzerland (Stopani Per. 2/5, Telephone: 95–53–22;
Office hours 9 a.m.–1 p.m.; 2:30 p.m.–6 p.m.)

Syria (Mansurovsky Per. 4, Telephone: 03–15–21;
Office hours Mon–Fri: 9 a.m.–2:30 p.m.)

Tanzania (Pyatnitskaya Ul. 33, Telephone: 31–81–46;
Office hours Mon–Fri: 9 a.m.–1 p.m.; 2 p.m.–5 p.m.)

Thailand (Eropkinsky Per. 3, Telephone: 02–48–74;
Office hours Mon–Fri: 10 a.m.–1 p.m.; 3 p.m.–5 p.m.)

Tunisia (Ul. Kachalova 28/1, Telephone: 91–63–78;
Office hours Mon–Fri: 9 a.m.–3 p.m., Sat: 9 a.m.–
1 p.m.)

Turkey (Ul. Gertsena 43-a, Telephone: 90–46–06;
Office hours Mon–Fri: 9:30 a.m.–1 p.m.;
3 p.m.–6 p.m., Sat: 10 a.m.–1 p.m.)

Uganda (Per. Sadovskikh 5, Telephone: 53–05–74/76;
Office hours Mon–Fri: 9:30 a.m.–1 p.m.; 2 p.m.–
5 p.m.)

Uruguay (Ul. Zholtovskovo 28, Telephone: 99–53–04;
Office hours Mon–Fri: 10 a.m.–1:30 p.m.; 2:30 p.m.–
5 p.m.)

Vietnam, North (Ul. Bolshaya Pirogovskaya 13,
Telephone: 45–10–92 (night), 46–68–07; Office hours
Mon–Fri: 9 a.m.–12:30 p.m., 1:30 p.m.–5 p.m., Sat:
9 a.m.–12:30 p.m.)

Yugoslavia *(Mosfilmovskaya Ul. 46, Telephone: 47–42–21; Office hours Mon–Fri: 9 a.m.–5:30 p.m.)*

Zambia *(Pr. Mira 52a, Telephone: 81–05–66/7/8; Office hours Mon–Fri: 9 a.m.–1 p.m.; 2 p.m.–5 p.m.)*

Government

Except for the signing of nonproliferation arms agreement and peace treaties, and the negotiation of favorable trade deals, the men who pound the Soviet Union's corridors of power are inaccessible to visitors from the West. In vain, Top Journalists, Captains of Industry, Political Big-Wigs seek audience with the people who really "run Russia." Alas, all doors are closed. Still, for those who would try, here are the addresses and phone numbers. Yours is the next move.

Presidium of the Supreme Soviet *(House of Government, The Kremlin, Telephone: 24–05–55)*

Council of Ministers *(The Kremlin, Telephone: 95–90–51)*

Central Committee of the Communist Party, *(Staraya Pl. 4, Telephone: 95–15–11)*

Komsomol Headquarters *(Ul. Bogdana Khmelnitskovo 3/13, Telephone: 26–35–01/2/3/4/)*

Executive Committee Moscow City Council, *(Ul. Gorkovo 13, Telephone: 94–09–90)*

State Committee for Cultural Relations with Foreign Countries *(Pr. Kalinina 9, Telephone: 41–93–61)*

Ministry of Foreign Affairs *(Smolenskaya-Sennaya 32/34, Telephone: 44–16–06; Press Department Telephone: 44–15–81)*

Ministry of Health *(Rakhmanovsky Per. 3,*
  Telephone: 28–44–78)
Ministry of Higher Education *(Ul. Zhdanova 11,*
  Telephone: 90–04–40 ext. 209)
Ministry of Culture *(Ul. Kuibysheva, Telephone*
  (Foreign Dept): 21–48–44)

Social and educational organizations

There are many organizations that welcome foreign
visitors and students in Moscow. However, it is wise to
contact them before you leave home. If you are going to
the Soviet Union as part of a delegation, then almost
certainly one or another of the following organizations
will be sponsoring your visit inside the USSR.

Soviet Peace Committee *(Ul. Kropotkinskaya*
  10, Telephone: 46–94–36)
Soviet Committee of Afro-Asian Solidarity *(Ul.*
  Kropotkinskaya 10, Telephone: 46–07–28)
USSR Red Cross and Red Crescent *(Kuznetsky*
  Most 18/7, Telephone: 28–20–22)
Union of Societies of Friendship with Peoples of
  Foreign Countries *(Headquarters Kalinin Prospekt*
  14, Telephone: 94–99–32)
House of Friendship *(Kalinin Prospekt 16,*
  Telephone: 44–40–87)
Institute of Soviet-American Relations *(Telephone:*
  28–60–85)
USSR Academy of Sciences *(Leninsky Prospekt 14,*
  Telephone: 33–25–53)
Moscow State University *(Leninskiye Gory,*
  Telephone: 139–10–00) (switchboard)

Lumumba University *(5th Donskoy Proyezd 7, Telephone: 34–00–11 ext. 7)*

Maurice Thorez Language Institute *(Ul. Metrostroyevskaya 38, Telephone: 46–83–66)*

suggestions for reading

This list is bound to be eclectic. The books that follow are ones that I have read (in some instances, many times over) and enjoyed. It is not meant as a scholarly guide to what's in print on the enormous subject of Russia. But the reader should find all of them useful, informative, and enjoyable.

General

Wright Miller, *Russians as People* (Dutton, 1960). Far and away the best single book on the character, customs, and traditions of Russia, past and present. A standard work in many American universities.

John Gunther, *Inside Russia Today* (Harper, 1957). This book has been revised through the early sixties. It is a little out of date as to politics and living conditions, but the descriptions of the country are vivid and remain useful.

Nagel Travel Guide USSR (McGraw-Hill, 1965). Contains much information that a close reader will find in Baedeker's superb *Russia* (1914). It contains numerous errors, but remains a highly useful guidebook.

Information Moscow, Victor Louis Associates. Extremely hard to find. Published in Moscow annually.

Mervyn Jones, *The Antagonists* (Clarkson Potter, 1962). A highly readable journalist's portrait and comparison of America and the USSR. Well worth hunting down in the library.

Irving R. Levine, *Main Street, U.S.S.R.* (Doubleday, 1959). A delightful series of essays on the day-to-day life of ordinary Russians.

Klaus Mehnert, *Soviet Man and His World* (Praeger, 1962). An absorbing look at Soviet society and how it has developed since 1917.

History

John Reed, *Ten Days That Shook the World* (Vintage Books, Knopf, 1960). An enthralling eyewitness account of the Bolshevik Revolution by a young American reporter who today lies buried within the Kremlin Wall. A standard work for anyone interested in Communism and how Lenin seized power in Russia.

Anatole G. Mazour, *Russia Past and Present* (Van Nostrand, 1957). A readable account of the influences that have moulded modern Russia.

Alan Moorehead, *The Russian Revolution* (Harper, 1958). A popular journalist's account.

E. H. Carr, *The Bolshevik Revolution* 1917–23 (Penguin Books). Easily the most detailed and reliable history of the early years of Soviet power yet published.

Michael Florinsky, *The End of the Russian Empire* (Collier, 1960). Written four decades ago, Professor Florinsky's book remains the standard work on the end of Tsarism and the advent of Soviet power.

Bernard Pares, *A History of Russia* (Vintage Books, Knopf, 1965). If you want to read only a single book

on this subject, then Sir Bernard Pares's classic ought
to be it.

Politics

Leonard Schapiro, *The Communist Party of the Soviet
Union* (Random House, 1960). The outstanding
work on both the organization and the history of the
party.

Merle Fainsod, *How Russia Is Ruled* (Harvard U. P.,
1963). A highly readable account of the major institutions of Soviet society and how they work.

J. Hazard, *The Soviet System of Government* (Chicago
U.P., 1960). A useful book to read alongside
Fainsod's *How Russia Is Ruled*. The emphasis in
Professor Hazard's work is on the interrelationship
between Soviet institutions and the ideology of
Marxism, the social structure, and the various pres-
sure groups in Soviet society.

Bertram Wolfe, *Khrushchev and Stalin's Ghost*
(Atlantic, 1956). A well-written account of "de-
Stalinization," along with the full text of Mr.
Khrushchev's famous "secret speech" denouncing
Stalin.

Isaac Deutscher, *Stalin* (Oxford U.P., 1949). The
standard work on the subject.

Education, Business, Arts, and Science

U. Bronfenbrenner, *Two Worlds of Childhood: U.S.
and USSR* (Russell Sage Foundation, 1970). A report
based on nine visits to the USSR on the differences
between child-rearing in the two countries.

U.S. Department of Health, *Education in the USSR,*

(Government Printing Office, 1957). A somewhat dated but still excellent introduction.

David Granick, *The Red Executive* (Doubleday, 1960). Quite the best book on the role of the managerial group in Russia. The Soviet executive is analyzed with reference to his American counterpart.

Joseph Berliner, *Factory and Manager in the USSR* (Harvard U.P., 1957).

Jay Leyda, *Kino, A History of the Russian and Soviet Film* (Allen and Unwin, 1960). A major work by a lifelong student of Soviet cinema.

Tamara Talbot-Rice, *A Concise History of Russian Art* (Abrams, 1963). The best popular introduction to the subject of icon art that I know, and a lively account of the main trends in the development of art in Russia.

J. H. Billington, *The Icon and the Axe* (Knopf, 1968). An analytical history of Russian culture.

G. Hamilton, *The Art and Architecture of Russia* (Penguin, 1954). A standard work.

Mark W. Hopkins, *Mass Media in the Soviet Union* (Pegasus, 1970). Far and away the best introduction to how the state-owned conglomerate of newspapers, TV, radio, and periodicals is managed by the Communist Party.

Literature & Fiction

Nothing beats reading a good Russian novel if you wish to get a feeling for the Russian people. Among the classic Russian novels, Tolstoy's *War and Peace* and *Anna Karenina*, the short stories of Gogol and Chekhov. Amongst writings of the Soviet era:

Nadezhda Mandelstam, *Hope Against Hope* (Atheneum, 1970). A sensitive and searing account, in diary form, of the horrors of life under Stalin.

Thomas Whitney, *The New Writing in Russia* (U. of Michigan Press, 1964). One of the most outstanding anthologies of recent years, chosen to illustrate the pains and pleasures of Soviet life.

Boris Pasternak, *Dr. Zhivago* (Signet, 1958). A vividly written portrait of Russian country life, but ignores the genuine enthusiasm that helped build modern industrial Russia.

Ilya Ehrenburg, *Memoirs: 1921–1941, The War: 1941–1945, Post-War Years: 1945–54* (World). Immensely readable story of a fascinating life by the Soviet Union's leading journalist; a powerful political testament.

Alexander Solzhenitsyn, *One Day in the Life of Ivan Denisovich* (Penguin). Life in Stalin's political camps, and a constant theme of discussion amongst dissidents in modern Russia.

Olga Carlisle, *Poets on Street Corners* (Random House, 1968). A sampling of the best Russian poets of the century, assembled by a remarkable woman who has long-established credentials as an interpreter of the current Russian scene.

Y. Yevtushenko, *A Precocious Autobiography* (Dutton, 1964). Nowadays a pillar of the Soviet literary establishment, the author gives full expression in this mildly rebellious book to his love for the Russian land and his love of literature.

Herbert Marshall, *Voznesensky: Selected Poems* (Hill & Wang, 1967). Excellent introduction to one of the Soviet Union's most outspoken poets.

Andrew Field, *Pages from Tarusa* (Little, Brown, 1964).
A sampler of the "new writing" that emerged after
Stalin's death.

George Feifer, *The Girl from Petrovka* (Viking, 1971).
A novel of contemporary Russian life, rich in satire,
by a young American who spent several years in
Moscow.

index

ДОСВИДАНИЯ

A Note About the Author

Desmond Smith is a British-born journalist who acquired his intimate knowledge of Moscow while working on assignment for ABC, one of three major U.S. networks for which he has been a producer. He has contributed articles to *The Nation*, *The New York Times Magazine*, and *Harper's*. He is presently the director of television in Montreal for the Canadian Broadcasting Corporation, and is just completing his second guidebook, *Smith's Montreal*.

A Note on the Type

The text of this book is set in Electra, a typeface designed by W. A. Dwiggins for the Mergenthaler Linotype Company and first made available in 1935. Electra cannot be classified as either "modern" or "old style." It is not based on any historical model, and hence does not echo any particular period or style of type design. It avoids the extreme contrast between "thick" and "thin" elements that marks most modern faces, and is without eccentricities which catch the eye and interfere with reading. In general, Electra is a simple, readable typeface which attempts to give a feeling of fluidity, power, and speed.

The book was composed by The Haddon Craftsmen, Inc., Scranton, Pa. The book was printed and bound by Halliday Lithograph Corp., West Hanover, Mass.

Typography and binding design by Carole Lowenstein.